BODYLINE UMPIRE

Also by R. S. Whitington
John Reid's Kiwis
Bradman, Benaud and Goddard's Cinderellas
The Quiet Australian — the Lindsay Hassett Story
Simpson's Safari
Time of the Tiger — the Bill O'Reilly Story
Sir Frank — the Frank Packer Story
Fours Galore
Pictorial History of Australian Cricket
Captains Outrageous? — Cricket in the Seventies
Great Moments of Australian Sport

With Keith Miller
Cricket Caravan
Catch
Straight Hit
Bumper
Gods or Flannelled Fools?
Cricket Typhoon
Keith Miller Cricket Companion

With John Waite
Perchance to Bowl

With Victor Richardson
The Vic Richardson Story

BODYLINE UMPIRE

R. S. WHITINGTON

GEORGE HELE

RIGBY

RIGBY LIMITED • ADELAIDE • SYDNEY
MELBOURNE • BRISBANE • PERTH

First published 1974
Copyright © 1974 by R. S. Whitington and G. A. Hele
Library of Congress Catalog Card
Number 73-81612
National Library of Australia Card
Number and ISBN 0 85179 820 9

Wholly designed and set up in Australia
Printed in Hong Kong

To Matilda and Betty

CONTENTS

ACKNOWLEDGMENTS

The illustrations are reproduced from photographs which appeared in *The Turn of the Wheel* by P. G. Fender (Faber, London, 1929); *The Fight for the Ashes* by M. A. Noble (George G. Harrap, London, 1929); *In Quest of the Ashes* by D. R. Jardine (Hutchinson, London, 1933); *Cricket Crisis* by J. H. Fingleton (Cassell, London, 1946); and *The Fight for the Ashes* by J. B. Hobbs (George G. Harrap, London, 1933). Of these photographs, that of the Slips Catch by Hammond is copyright to Central Press Photos Limited, London, and those of Woodfull and Jardine, Bradman bowled by Bowes, and Woodfull struck by Larwood are copyright to Sport and General Press Agency Limited, London. Attempts to contact the present owners of copyright in other photographs have been unsuccessful, either because the original publishers had no record of sources or because no addresses could be found. Present owners of copyright are invited to contact the publisher.

LIST OF ILLUSTRATIONS

FOREWORD

To say that I was surprised when asked by Dick Whitington to write a foreword to this, his twentieth book, was indeed an understatement. As a bowler who has had the nightmare experience of bowling thirteen "no-balls" in that fateful first over at Worcester in 1938, and after having reached the doubtful honour of bowling 100 "no-balls" before May, perhaps one could be forgiven for never speaking to an umpire again, let alone writing a foreword to the story of his life.

I suppose Dick realised that George and myself have been very good friends for many years, and have spent many happy hours in each other's company and shared many a laugh.

George has taken us through the most exciting era of cricket in the telling of his wonderful experiences. Naturally he was in a perfect position to see and hear many things, but, typical of the man, he has refrained from telling all and has, as always, thought of the spirit of this great game of ours unlike, sad to say, some of the recent authors of cricket books.

Perhaps the friendship between George and myself was not as strong as that between Dick Hassett (Lindsay's brother) and a local Geelong umpire in the person of one Bill Rashley who, by all accounts, was not only a real character, but a law unto himself.

So much so, that he smoked his pipe incessantly throughout an entire game.

I believe that to see Bill give a decision through hands cupped around his pipe and with index finger raised, was indeed a sight to behold. One could only imagine the offending batsman awaiting his impending doom through a heavy smoke haze! However, Dick returned to Geelong after a very successful career in interstate and club cricket as a good slow bowler. He had a colossal wrong-un.

Occasionally, Dick decided to have a game with the Geelong locals and on one such Saturday morning, old Bill sighted him on the other side of the busy main street. With a welcome cry he made it to the other side through the screech of braking tyres—"Welcome back, Dick. I am glad you are going to have another go." Then, rubbing his cupped hands together, he said "Will we get any bloody wickets now!" That is what I call real friendship.

I well remember when George first stood in a District game in Melbourne. The match was between University (my old Captain, Les Keating, always referred to them as the fountains of knowledge) and my old Club, Richmond. We were trying out a young bowler, who was strong, fast, and very keen. He had to open the bowling to an international all-rounder so, naturally, he was very keyed up. When George took the colt's sweater he wished him good luck. After a few fast, wild deliveries, the young bowler found a good line and beat the batsman with three beautiful outswingers. As he passed the umpire George whispered "now bowl him an inswinger," which he did. The ball crashed into the batsman's pads and then uprooted the middle stump. The young buck, with youthful exuberance, turned in mid-air and with outstretched hands was making for George's end to express his gratitude. However, George's quick thinking saved a very embarrassing situation. He quickly made for square-leg, called "over," and turned his back on the approaching colt. "For goodness' sake, go away!" he whispered. I don't think George will ever forget that delightful incident.

Cricketers who played under George from 1918 to 1936 in Club, Shield, and International Test matches in Australia, regard him as either the greatest or one of the three greatest umpires of all time. The other two in this category would be Frank Chester of England and Bob Crockett of Australia. There has always been great conjecture whether Australian or English umpires are the best. Perhaps it is true to say that most of the English umpires have had first-class playing experience, but it has also been said that most of them have played until their eyesight has failed and then taken on umpiring!

George Hele was blessed with wonderful eyesight as becomes one with blue-grey eyes. I believe most of the famous Bisley riflemen were of the same eye characteristics. George, too, was also a straight shooter and would not stand for anything that was not in the true spirit of cricket. Perhaps his eyesight was not as sharp as that of our old friend Bill Rashley who, after giving a leg-before decision as "not out," explained to the enquiring bowler that it was a "half ball." "A 'half ball'?" asked the puzzled bowler. "Yes," said Bill, "half would have hit the wicket and the other half wouldn't, so I gave the batsman the benefit of the doubt."

The pleasure I have had penning these few lines has been in keeping with our friendship and so, George, let's hope that you may be spared to enjoy many more years "in the shade" watching yet another era pass pleasantly by.

E. L. McCORMICK

Time Long Past

SAINT PETER AND SATAN SPENT A RECENT SUNNY SUNDAY AFTERNOON on the fringe of Paradise chatting about cricket.

News had leaked to Saint Peter via his fourth-form monitors, Lord Harris and Sir Pelham Warner, that we earth-bound undergraduates consider cricket to be the noblest game. Saint Peter was keen to give it a "G" certificate in Heaven.

"I could pick a team to beat your best, 'Mepho,' beat 'em by an innings—at home or away," he said, as modestly as possible.

"Ridiculous, Pete."

"Why, I've got Grace, your namesake 'Demon' Spofforth, Vic Trumper, McCabe, Hendren, Mailey—even Doug Jardine for a start. You wouldn't have a hope in Hell."

Satan seemed unconcerned, unimpressed.

"I'll have to check on the 'Demon' and Doug," he replied. "I fancied they were down with me. Anyway, you wouldn't stand an earthly, Pete. *I've got all the umpires.*"

This is Bodyline Umpire George Hele's favourite cricket tale. He feels it might amuse his umpiring friends—especially those who have officiated in Melbourne footy finals.

On 23 November 1932, the November of the Bodyline summer,

1

Douglas Raymond Jardine, that austere, ascetic, and uncompromising England captain with the salmon-pink harlequin cap, dictated a letter to Australian cricket official Bill Kelly from a suite at Melbourne's graceful old Windsor Hotel.

It read:

Dear Mr Kelly,

It was so good of you to have a word with me about the umpires for the Tests today. As you know, we in England bracket Hele and Chester as the two best umpires in the world . . ."

In his book *Farewell to Cricket,* published after his retirement in 1949, Sir Donald Bradman wrote: "Next to Chester I would rank the Australian George Hele. I think the Englishmen who played under Hele would agree that he was the best Australian umpire between the two wars. They had every confidence in him."

One of the Englishmen who agreed was perhaps the greatest of all English batsmen, Sir Jack Hobbs, the "Surrey Master." In his Christmas mail in 1936 Hele received a book entitled *My Life Story,* the autobiography of Hobbs. It is inscribed "To my old friend Geo. Hele. In memory of the many happy hours we have spent together on 'The Middle.' Jack Hobbs. Xmas 1936."

George Hele was the first umpire to officiate in all five Tests of a series between England and Australia on debut. That was during the Percy Chapman and Jack Ryder series of 1928–29, the series that saw the Test debuts also of Don Bradman and Walter Hammond.

During the summer, Jack Hobbs' opening partner, Herbert Sutcliffe, came to George and said: "You are a better umpire than Bob Crockett ever was." George, fundamentally a very humble man, replied: "You never saw Crockett at his best."

Indeed, when the Australian authorities approached Hele in the middle of the 1924–25 series between England and Australia, asking him to officiate in the third Test, he asked which umpire, Crockett or Dave Elder, he would be replacing. When told the umpire who would be discarded was Crockett, George declined the invitation. "It would break Bob's heart," he said.

Crockett, who retired at the end of that series, stood in thirty-three Tests from 1901 to 1925. George stood in only sixteen Tests from 1928 to 1933—ten between England and Australia, five between

South Africa and Australia, and one between West Indies and Australia. That he should generally be classed as at least the equal of Crockett is a tremendous tribute.

Those who have watched Hele and have studied Colin Egar (who stood in twenty-nine Tests from 1960 to 1969), and Queensland Police Drug Squad detective Lou Rowan (who has officiated in twenty-six Tests since 1963), still regard George as the most outstanding Australian umpire they have ever seen.

It was in December 1971 that George crossed to my table during lunch at a Sheffield Shield game at the Melbourne Cricket Ground, prodded my chest with those formerly fateful fingers of his right hand, and signalled me into a quiet corner of the V.C.A. Delegates' room.

"I've read about fifteen or twenty books on the Bodyline series," he said, "and they all make me wonder whether I was there watching what happened from a distance of about twenty-five yards. I have not read one account of that rubber from a man who didn't have a personal or patriotic axe to grind and they all certainly ground them.

"I've been asked many times to write my life story and particularly my account of that battle between Jardine, Larwood, and Voce and Don Bradman, Bill Woodfull, Stan McCabe, and Bill Ponsford. I'd greatly appreciate it, if you'd help me. I'm an old man now, Dick, can't have long to go. I would like to reveal the truth as I saw it before the Greatest of all Umpires gives me out."

George and I were both born in South Australia, he in Brompton in the West Torrens territory and I in Unley Park, which is part of Joe Darling and Vic Richardson's old territory, Sturt. West Torrens and Sturt have been traditional enemies in club cricket, as Thebarton's best-remembered barracker, "Yorkie," would have confirmed. For years West Torrens and Sturt were to Adelaide club cricket what Norwood and Port, the Redlegs and the Magpies, are, or were, to its club football.

I warned George about this and thought fit to add: "Don't you remember giving a young Adelaide University batsman out leg before wicket to Freddie Brown in the M.C.C.–South Australia game at Adelaide Oval in November 1932?"

"I remember it well," replied George. "And you were plumb. The ball would have taken your leg bail if it hadn't hit your pad flap. I still want you to do my biography."

So now it's my turn, and you can regard anything I include in

3

George's favour as being utterly unbiased. I'd just hit a four to be 5 not out. That was my first big match. The ball, of course, would have missed the leg stump by a mile. And that's not all. In the second innings George ruled me run out for 0 at the bowler's end when wicketkeeper Les Ames threw the wicket down from square-leg without even removing his glove.

George, you're a brave old man. And, after discovering you have an even better and longer memory for cricket incident and anecdote than the late Victor Richardson, I'm a happy one.

George Alfred Hele was born at Brompton, not one of the blue-ribbon suburbs of Adelaide, on 16 July 1891, at the beginning of what is remembered as cricket's Golden Age. His father, Andrew William Hele, and mother, Elizabeth Ann Hele, named him (though he did not know it until he was eighty-one) after Adelaide's greatest all-round cricketer of that or any other time, George Giffen. George Hele learned the reason for the choice of his first name from his Aunt Daisy (Mrs Daisy Snook) in 1972 and wishes he had been let into the secret eighty or so years earlier. The knowledge could have proved useful at school.

In January 1891 his namesake had excelled himself by scoring 271 of 562 and taking sixteen for 166, surely the greatest all-round performance in all first-class cricket, while South Australia was defeating Victoria, of all States, by an innings and 164.

Andrew William Hele, according to his son, was "sports mad," especially about cricket and Australian Rules football. The effect his father's fanaticism had upon George's life story can be imagined as we proceed. Without it he would almost certainly have remained an unknown member of Adelaide suburbia. Thanks to it he came to be part of a world star cricketing fellowship, which included men of the calibre and status of the Duke of Norfolk, Sir Robert Menzies, Sir Pelham Warner, Sir Frederick Toone, and the cricketing gods of England, Australia, the West Indies, and South Africa.

Andrew Hele played on the mat for the Bowden Cricket Club in the Adelaide and Suburban Cricket Association and, in the eyes of his son, was "an excellent wicketkeeper." While Andrew was keeping wickets, his wife Elizabeth kept house, equally efficiently. It was important that she should, for George had three brothers—Roy, Gordon, and Frank—and two sisters—Ida and Mavis.

Like the man after whom he was christened, the boy George Hele began his cricket in the Adelaide parklands using a gum tree, a rusty old nail can, or a kerosene tin for a wicket; a piece of roughly-planed paling for a bat, and just about anything that would bounce for a ball. On a summer Saturday, behind his father, he trailed the two miles up and down the hill from Brompton to the Bowden Cricket Club ground near the old Bonython family home on Montefiore Hill and the present site of the statue known as "Light's Vision." Before play began he shared the somewhat dubious "honour" of wheeling the rolls of matting from the boundary of the sparsely-grassed and pebbly ground to the asphalt wicket.

George still believes matting provides the best surface on which boys can learn to bat and bowl. This is because it gives consistency of bounce and turn and is fair to both batsman and bowler. There were two types of matting then—coir (coconut) and string. Coir matting resembled the average front-door mat, except that it was of finer texture; string was a lighter woven mat, smoother and with a sheen on it.

Maybe those who provide playing conditions for youngsters in Australia's cities today might consider reverting to matting practice and match pitches. Sir Donald Bradman, Charles Macartney, and Stan McCabe learned to bat on matting at Bowral, Maitland, and Grenfell respectively, and Bill O'Reilly developed his leg-breaks and wrong-uns on it at Murringo near Young, at Wingello, and Goulburn. The kids of those days had become shaped in technique and style before they were introduced to turf wickets in their mid and late teens.

Every child has his most vivid early memories. George Hele's are of an Adelaide in which horse trams provided the only public transport; of when these horses, none of them exactly Carbines, Phar Laps, or Gunsynds, but with conical straw hats and fly nets over their heads and nostrils, drew the trams from the South Road and up the hill from the Port Road railway bridge to the Newmarket Hotel, on the corner of North and West terraces. He remembers how they harnessed another Clydesdale on to the shaft at the railway bridge to make certain the other two horses didn't drop dead.

George and his brothers did not own a pushbike between them. They developed gravel rash on their knees and shins, while dragging out of sight behind the rear of the horse trams when the conductors came to collect the pennies for their tickets. In those days a penny

5

would buy an ice cream, a *Popular, Magnet,* or *Gem* boys' magazine, or a bottle of stone ginger beer. Wagging it from suspiciously considerate conductors was vital.

A penny would also gain you admittance to the Adelaide City Baths, which were situated on the corner below Parliament House and across from Government House, where the Festival Theatre complex now stands.

The manager of the Adelaide City Baths at that time was Charlie Bastard. Understandably, he always pronounced his name "Bazztard," George recalls. As each youngster learned to swim the width of the main pool Charlie would give him a biscuit as a token, or emblem, of achievement.

Another of the young Hele's favourite haunts was Stan Leak's grocery shop in Pulteney Street, in the south-eastern corner of the city square mile bounded by the north, east, west, and south parklands.

One of his favourite early pastimes was watching a youngster pinging peas from his shanghai at the man who delivered the peas to Stan's shop. While the deliverer was chaining the wheel of his cart to a verandah post, he and his dog became the target of a volley of peas. Every time he looked up to ascertain the source of the missiles, the boy would be standing with folded arms and a most innocent expression on his face. The pea merchant eventually stationed a sentry in the shop and caught the culprit red handed, with his shanghai poised.

Most memorable of all George's early experiences, however, was the day in 1900 when his father first took him to watch a Sheffield Shield game at the Adelaide Oval between South Australia and New South Wales. He was only eight and sat in a front seat of the outer ground with his chin jammed between the tops of two of the pickets and his eyes glued on the play.

In that match Clem Hill scored 365 not out in a South Australian total of 576 and Victor Trumper 32 and 53 for New South Wales. George's father had said he was taking him to see the two greatest batsmen in the world. Looking back, even today, George retains great respect for his father's judgement.

His introduction to first-class cricket proved a particularly happy one. South Australia won by an innings and 36 against a team led by Montague Alfred ("Monty" or "Alf") Noble and containing, besides Trumper, such players as Reggie Duff, Syd Gregory, Frank

Iredale, Jim Kelly, Bill Howell, Harry Donnan, and Bert Hopkins.

Duff, as George extricated from his incredible memory while recounting this experience, was one of only two Australian batsmen who scored centuries on their first and last appearances against England—Duff 104 at Melbourne in 1902 and 146 at the Oval in 1905, and Bill Ponsford 110 at Sydney in 1924 and 266 at the Oval in 1934.

Another member of the visiting side in that match at Adelaide Oval in December 1900 was New South Wales' Aboriginal fast bowler, Jack Marsh. On his way to Adelaide with the New South Wales side on his first train journey, Marsh carried all his belongings for the two-week trip in one small paper bag. He had the bag in his hand when he collided with Syd Gregory in the carriage corridor, somewhere near Ararat, Victoria.

Gregory, who played in fifty-eight Tests for Australia, was taking a stroll in his pyjamas before turning in. Startled by the spectacular pyjamas, Marsh asked: "Where did you get those, Mr Gregory?"

"They were under my pillow, Jack."

Marsh had never owned pyjamas. He rushed to his sleeping compartment, looked under his own pillow, returned to Gregory in dejection and said, "There aren't any under *my* pillow Mr Gregory, I'm afraid." So New South Wales' fastest and most dangerous bowler spent the night, like all his earlier nights, either nude or in his underclothes.

There were narrow sightboards at the Adelaide Oval in 1900 and Andrew Hele always chose seats in line with the wicket at the northern end, the one nearest Brompton. George believes this is how, and why, he developed his early interest in umpiring. An inquisitive kid (he still is inquisitive), George asked his father, a man of monumental patience, just about every question a youngster can ask. Despite this, Hele Senior also took his son to football matches (always to watch West Torrens) from the time he was only five years old and too tiny to see the play. George invariably wanted to be taken home during the first quarter but was told, "Wait until the bell goes, son."

They had bells, as well as "lemons," at football in those days, instead of sirens and ear-bashing coaches. "I waited for a lot of bells to ring—not all of them school bells," George recalls. "I left school at thirteen and went to work in a cool-drink factory, belonging to Charlie Bastard's nephew."

The most puzzling problem George faced as a kid, however, was discovering how cricket umpires could tell whether a batsman was l.b.w. or not. Wickets were pitched eight inches wide then, not nine inches as they are today, and twenty-seven inches high, not twenty-eight. At first George thought every ball that hit a batsman on a pad meant he was out. A number of bowlers in the intervening seventy years seem to have held this view also. The law concerning l.b.w.s was less complicated then. Andrew Hele managed to explain its implications to his son.

The net result was that George did a bit of umpiring himself, "on the sly," in Adelaide Church Association games. He kept his activities secret from his parents, because he knew they wanted him to become a cricketer and that he'd earn a "kick in the backside" if they found out he was wasting precious time.

Even at the age of thirteen, George had realised that somebody has to umpire or there wouldn't be any sport. Millions of Australians, judging from comments at football, cricket, tennis, and boxing encounters have failed to recognise this fact at a considerably more mature age. And not only millions of Australians. During my now forty years in Melbourne and the environs I have attended 600 and more league football games, mostly in the Members' reserve. Having been reared in Adelaide and owing allegiance to no particular Melbourne club, I have been amazed and amused at the extremely biased attitude the average spectator adopts towards the unfortunate umpire. Umpires who, to me, have appeared utterly impartial, are castigated Saturday after Saturday for being "cheats," "mongrels," "monsters," and "nongs." Being unprejudiced has other advantages. You see and enjoy all, instead of only half, the play—an important consideration at a dollar for standing accommodation.

George found it necessary, however, to provide evidence that he was still engaging actively as a player in cricket. He concentrated on keeping wicket, because his father was a wicketkeeper for the Bowden Cricket Club in the Adelaide and Suburban Association and because, after climbing the fence of the Hindmarsh Oval one day, he discovered his dad standing "behind the dollies" for the West Torrens senior side. George learned later that Andrew had been conscripted into this role when the regular keeper failed to arrive, a not-unusual occurrence in those days of erratic public transport.

8

George was even more astonished and delighted when his father dismissed a couple of Sturt batsmen in a manner that would not have shamed even that aristocrat of the gloves, William Albert Oldfield.

George became wicketkeeper for the Brompton Methodists and took pride from the fact that he was serving the same religious denomination as Victor Trumper. He gained permission to practise on turf at the Hindmarsh Oval, thanks to his father's recently won prestige and influence there, and eventually won the position of regular wicketkeeper for West Torrens "Firsts."

Towards the end of his second season George suffered a groin injury. Naturally concerned about the risk of having both her husband and son injured in this manner, Elizabeth Ann Hele put her foot down. "If you really want to become an umpire and not a player, George, you become an umpire," she said. George sent his application to the South Australian Cricket Association to become a club umpire before his father's disgust could gain ground.

He believes he should have taken up football umpiring as well as cricket umpiring. This is because the first Christmas present he remembers receiving was a tin whistle. He became so proficient at blowing it that his father and mother gravely regretted ever having given it to him. "That whistling of mine came to be what is now known as noise pollution," George contends.

He had been acting as a cricket umpire off and on since the 1905–06 season, and decided to make it his main sporting mission at the end of the first World War. His experience as a wicketkeeper, standing behind the line of the ball, had helped him, unwittingly, to fit himself for his eventual role.

Prior to this, Elizabeth Hele had had the final say with regard to her husband's own sporting activities. Andrew William gave up the unequal struggle about the time the *Titanic* was colliding with that iceberg in the Atlantic, and became the original first-class cricket umpire in the Hele family. Following the second World War, his grandson Ray became the third of three successive generations of Hele umpires.

I have gathered from George that the husbands in the Hele families did their adjudicating on the sports field; their wives fulfilled that function in the home.

Though New South Wales won the Sheffield Shield six times in succession between 1901–02 and 1906–07 and Victoria won it in

1900–01 and 1907–08, there were some splendid cricketers for youngsters to watch in South Australia in the years immediately preceding the first World War. Prince Alfred College contributed two national captains in farmer-politician Joe Darling and race handicapper Clem Hill, both of them superb, hard-hitting, left-handed batsmen. Though "Australia's Dr Grace," George Giffen, and the barrel-chested fast bowler who bumped that ball through Grace's beard, Ernie Jones, were in the evening of their unforgettable careers, Edgar Mayne, Charlie Dolling, Claude Jennings, Algie Gehrs, Bill Whitty, and Joe Travers were in their prime. The South Australian Cricket Association had shown initiative and sound commonsense by importing John Neville Crawford from Surrey, and establishing a precedent for the importation later of Don Bradman, Clarrie Grimmett, Jackie Badcock, Les Favell, Ashley Mallett, Terry Jenner, Gary Sobers, and Barry Richards.

Crawford, according to the Adelaide-born and reared A. G. "Johnnie" Moyes (author of *Australian Cricket, A History*) was the finest all-round cricketer he ever saw. He retained this opinion of Crawford, even after watching Walter Hammond, Keith Miller, Jack Gregory, and Gary Sobers.

Crawford was in his early twenties when he moved to Adelaide, following a disagreement with the Surrey County Cricket Club committee.

Before transferring to Otago, New Zealand, just prior to the first World War, he scored 1,512 runs at 40·86 and took 120 wickets at 23·86 in forty-one first-class games for South Australia. He was a magnificent fieldsman, too.

Crawford played his full part in helping South Australia to win the Sheffield Shield in 1909–10 and to regain it in 1912–13.

According to Hele, Crawford was close to Maurice Tate's pace as a new-ball bowler, slightly slower than John Snow. He was the kind of cricketer "Australia could do with today."

When one remembers the part Capetonian, Basil D'Oliveira and Tony Greig (from East London, South Africa) played in retaining the Ashes for England in 1972, it says much for Australia's integrity that it refrained from including Crawford in its Test sides from 1907 to 1912. At that time a migrant resident could represent his adopted country against any other, even against his country of origin with that country's permission.

10

Australia lost five Tests against England from 1910 to 1912 and won only two without calling upon Crawford. This in spite of the fact that William Lloyd Murdoch, born in New South Wales, represented England against South Africa at Cape Town in 1892, and Jack Ferris, also born in New South Wales, took thirteen wickets for 91 runs for England, also at Cape Town, against the Springboks in that same Test before losing his life fighting for Queen Victoria's England in the Boer War.

In case Jim Swanton reads this, it should perhaps be stated that Charles and Alec Bannerman and William Midwinter, all three of whom represented Australia in the 1870s and early 1880s, were all natives of England; and wicketkeeper Hanson Carter and that "Rupert Brooke" of Australian batsmanship, Archie Jackson, were born in Yorkshire and Scotland respectively.

Before moving his domicile to New Zealand, Crawford scored 354, with 14 sixes and 45 fours, for the 1914 Australian side against South Canterbury at Christchurch. He and Victor Trumper added 298 for the eighth wicket in sixty-nine minutes. Yes, 298 in sixty-nine minutes! At another stage Crawford and Monty Noble hit 50 runs in nine minutes.

When they built the present scoreboard at Adelaide Oval in 1911, a prize was offered to the batsman who made the first century and to the first bowler to take five wickets in an innings after its installation. Crawford won both prizes. We could do with more "Pommie" migrants like him. He was, for a time, a master at St Peter's College, Adelaide. One of Adelaide's cricket-loving lawyers called him the "Paris Nesbitt of cricket," after that brilliant, ill-fated, and ephemeral Adelaide barrister, who always refused to pay for admission to the Adelaide Oval, insisting that it was public land.

George insists I also inform you that Ernie Jones was not, as is classically believed, the only bowler to deliver a bumper through the brindle of W. G. Grace's beaver. George is adamant that Jack Crawford was another perpetrator of this atrocity. Nor did he say, "Sorry, Doctor, she slipped."

Another great and superbly graceful cricketer to watch, whom George remembers as being one of the delights of his childhood, was that one-time steam-engine stoker and later successful South Australian sheepfarmer, Bill Whitty. Bill died early in 1974, aged eighty-six, in Mount Gambier.

11

Whitty, in George's opinion, had the most beautiful bowling action of any left-hander, and used the bowling creases more effectively than any other bowler of his type—medium fast left-hand swing—whom he has watched. He delivered from over and around the stumps during the same over. When delivering from close to the stumps, he released the ball virtually from in line with the middle stump. From around the wicket this ball surprisingly would become an outswinger to a right-handed batsman; from over the wicket it could become either an inswinger or an outswinger, so perfect was his body action.

Whitty could become temperamental at times. When his new-ball partner in a Shield match was struck hard against the pickets for 4 at the Adelaide Oval, he went as red in the face as those fires he used to stoke on the engines of the South Australian Railways. New balls never stayed red very long on the drier Adelaide Oval of those times.

With batsmen such as Trumper and Duff, Darling and Hill, and new-ball bowlers like Jones, Crawford, and Whitty to watch, it is not surprising that the teenage Hele often ran the whole way from work down King William Road and over Adelaide's River Torrens bridge, anxious not to miss the first ball of any first-class match at the Oval.

He *did* miss the first ball of one such game—New South Wales versus South Australia on 20 December 1912. It was a bad ball to miss for, with it, Bill Whitty bowled Victor Trumper.

George hasn't quite forgiven Whitty for this.

The previous summer he had watched Vic score 214 not out, with twenty-five boundaries in 240 minutes, against South Africa.

George took his lunch hour, a very elastic hour, from about noon to one o'clock then. He did so because the first deliveries of matches, even of Sheffield Shield matches, created the kind of suspense that is nowadays most unusual. In those times, indeed right up until the 1950s, opening bowlers did their utmost to make the first ball they delivered their best of the day, while the opposing batsmen were at war with their nerves and unused to the light and the state of the wicket.

Though he took that elastic lunch hour on big match days, George has no cause to feel conscience-stricken about the amount of work he performed as a youth and young man in return for his poor wages.

That modern cricket-lover, Bob Hawke, might be concerned to know that this young "scab," as he might now be regarded, worked sixty hours a week for the sum of five shillings, beginning at 6 a.m. each Monday and ending at 4 p.m. on Saturday. In addition, he willingly undertook the chores around the family home that youngsters then had to perform as a matter of course—chopping wood, mowing lawns without the aid of power mowers, raking paths, and helping his mother with the washing up.

Much of his leisure time was spent in travelling to and from work on the horse trams. To travel the two miles from the Bastard drink factory, just off the Grange Road near the Hindmarsh Oval, to the city took half an hour. To walk from his home in Brompton to the factory, a distance of two miles, and back again each day, occupied more than an hour.

But life to a youngster seemed good then. There was so much to do, that *had* to be done, that kids rarely suffered from the psychological dilemmas that beset so many of them today.

George's association with the West Torrens cricket and football clubs gained him good friends, many of whom have remained loyal throughout his long life, others of whom have passed on.

Of them George remembers and cherishes the company and companionship of West Torrens and State batsman Andy Smith, who transferred from East Torrens to West Torrens. He will also never forget the friendship of such fine men as Hughie Bridgman, State batsman and selector and West Torrens captain; Dick Tompkins, West Torrens Club secretary; Roy Brown, that club's football captain; Roly Ridings, father of Sid, Ken, and Phil; Gordon Inkster, the most enormous wicketkeeper he has ever seen (but a great help to Port Adelaide's wrist-spinner, dentist Norman Williams); Joe Travers, the only Australian, other than Charles Bannerman, who played and umpired in a Test match; and Albert Ambler, the only wicketkeeper George remembers who wore his cap back to front.

This preference of Albert's, George says, originated after Ambler appealed for a stumping with the batsman yards from his ground, only to be denied the wicket because, in the opinion of the umpire, the peak of his cap had protruded in front of the bails.

Years later, when Ambler was keeping wickets for South Australia against the M.C.C., Jack Hobbs crossed to George and said, "He's very quiet, George."

13

"Yes, he's naturally quiet, Jack," replied Hele. He deduced that the "Surrey Master" appreciated having a silent "Aunt Sally" behind him. It must have been a pleasant change from "Mr Owzat," George Duckworth, for instance—or, for that matter, most of our modern wicketkeepers.

The greatest batsmen have always placed great importance on undivided and constant concentration. This probably explains their tremendous consistency.

George Hele is a meticulous person. He likes to have everything just so, from the gleam of his leather shoes to the fall of his tie and the set of what remains of his hair. Regarding his hair, he reminds me of the conductor of the Palestine Symphony Orchestra whom I watched taking his team through Beethoven's *Pastoral Symphony* and Ravel's *Bolero* in the Mograbi Hall, Tel Aviv, the night Hitler invaded Russia. This old gentleman, Ben Haim, had only two white hairs. He combed one of them towards his left and the other towards his right ear and was equally meticulous about his conducting.

You need to be meticulous, I guess, to become a great conductor, a great umpire—a great anything.

George Hele was twenty-seven when he stood in his first Grade game as an umpire at the Adelaide Oval in 1918. During the first over of the day a confident appeal came for a catch at the wicket. George gave a very disgruntled batsman "out." This being his first match as a grade umpire, he worried about the decision for the remainder of the afternoon.

He dined that evening at his parents' home and confided his concern to his father.

"Do you believe the batsman was 'out,' George?" Andrew Hele asked.

"Yes, Dad."

"That's all that matters, then."

The following Saturday the batsman concerned came to George and apologised for showing his feelings.

"I was mad at you because I wanted to make some runs." he said.

George says the incident taught him a lesson which he carried throughout his career as an umpire. The lesson was that when he was acting with a new umpire he always took the first over to allow his colleague to settle down.

The incident also reminded George of one that occurred in a game

14

in England. The pavilion at this ground was straight behind the wicket. When appealed to, the umpire at the pavilion end gave a batsman "out." As the batsman passed him, he growled, "I wasn't out."

Said the umpire, "You have a look in tomorrow morning's paper and you'll see whether you were out or not."

"Have a look yourself," replied the batsman. "I'm the editor."

George the Giant Killer

W HEN J. W. H. T. DOUGLAS BROUGHT THE NINETEENTH ENGLISH side to Australia in October 1920, George Hele took leave from his job to watch the New Year Test in Melbourne and the heat wave Ashes-decider in mid-January in Adelaide.

In Melbourne, George saw his pal "Nip" Pellew score the first of his two Test centuries and Jack Gregory the second of his two. While Charles Kelleway was earning the name "Rock of Gibraltar" by creeping to 147 in seven hours at Adelaide, George kept his blue eyes glued on Test umpires Bob Crockett and Dave Elder.

But Kelleway's snail-like progress (which prompted the comment from England's Cecil Parkin that The Rock "might be a mighty player in the next world, where time won't matter") did not divert Hele from his ambition. "Just fancy being out there umpiring for those giants," he kept thinking, as "Nip" worked towards his second century in two Tests.

While Australia was taking the series five-nil at Sydney on 1 March, George umpired a club game at the University Oval, Adelaide. Joe Travers, who took 115 wickets for South Australia before serving the Adelaide Club and his State as an official, came to him at the tea interval on the first Saturday of the match.

"Had a letter from the S.A.C.A., George?" he asked.

16

"No, Mr Travers. What's it about?"

"You'll find out in due course."

The following Saturday Travers put the same question and received the same reply. The final game of the M.C.C. tour, the match against South Australia at Adelaide, was due to begin the following Friday.

It was on the Monday of that week that Mrs Hele rang her husband at his work to tell him that a letter had arrived for him in an S.A.C.A. envelope. "Open it, dear, and tell me the worst," George said.

He thought Joe had arranged to dismiss him from his position as a club umpire.

"You've been appointed for the game against the M.C.C. on Friday, George," Mrs Hele said.

George said nothing about the letter at work until the next morning. Then he took it to his boss, Murray Fowler.

"Want the time off, George?" Fowler asked.

"Yes. I've only been a first-grade umpire for about two years. I think it's a great honour."

"It certainly is, George. Congratulations and good luck," said Fowler.

Hele could hardly believe that within a few days he would be associating with such world-famous cricketers as Jack Hobbs, Wilfred Rhodes, Frank Woolley, Cecil Parkin, Johnny Douglas, and A. C. Jack Russell. He had heard about the English judge who returned home one night and proudly told his wife he had touched the hem of Johnny Tyldesley's coat on St Pancras Station.

He saw more than enough of Rhodes and Russell in that game on the Ides of March 1921 at Adelaide Oval. While England was replying to South Australia's first innings 195 with 627, Rhodes scored 210 and Russell 201. J. W. H. T. ("Johnny Won't Hit Today") Douglas got 106 not out and South Australia's four spin bowlers, Norman Williams, Ernie Loveridge, Andy Smith, and Arthur Richardson, had 108, 102, 119, and 110 respectively, in their bowling slots on the informative, often all too informative, Adelaide Oval scoreboard.

To George's, if not the bowlers', disappointment, Hobbs scored only 18 before being caught by substitute Don McKenzie off Williams. But he stayed long enough for the immaculate young umpire behind the bowler's wicket to decide he was technically the most

17

correct batsman he had watched. George has not changed that opinion he formed on his first close sight of John Berry Hobbs.

"Jack's footwork, the placement of his feet, reminded me of the world's finest pugilists," he says. "And, during conversations, he revealed his deep knowledge of the game and of the art of batsmanship. When I asked him why he took guard 'middle and leg,' he replied, 'English and Australian pitches differ. The Australian ones are faster and for a time present a problem for touring English batsmen. I'm a great believer in covering my wicket. If I'm struck on my pads in front of the stumps 100 times, only on about eighty of them am I given out. The other twenty times could bring me twenty centuries, instead of being bowled.'"

It is advice worth considering. In all first-class matches Hobbs scored a record 61,221 runs including 197 centuries, also a record. He also still holds the record for having made two separate hundreds in a match on six occasions. In all classes of cricket he scored 244 centuries—sixteen of these in one English first-class season.

That first meeting with Hobbs remains one of the delights of Hele's life. He was to umpire five Tests in which Hobbs participated and watched him in Australia in 1907–08, 1911–12, 1920–21, and 1924–25 as well.

Of Hobbs, Hele says: "He was a very quiet man, the epitome of the reserved Englishman I have read so much about. When the M.C.C. or England took the field he never failed to bid me 'good morning.' He greeted me by my Christian name, not my surname, as so many other Englishmen always did.

"Occasionally during one of his innings he would pass some pertinent remark or other. Often, when his partner was dismissed he would say, 'What a foolish stroke to make.' His mind was always set upon what he was doing and his quietness was the result of his intense concentration. He gave to his batting the degree of concentration chess players give to their chess. Even during the unpleasant 'Kippax Incident' at Sydney in 1928–29, all he ever said to me was 'How's that, George?' It seems he said a bit more than that to Alan, though."

Hele also found "mystery" bowler Cecil Parkin different from the average Englishman. "He was a cricketing comedian similar to Arthur Mailey, Patsy Hendren, and George Headley, that great West Indian batsman," George says. "He was the first cricketer to

Copy of a letter in which Douglas Jardine expresses his high regard for George Hele as an umpire

HOTEL   WINDSOR

23rd November '32.

Dear Mr. Kelly,

      It was so good of you to have a word with me about the umpires for the Tests yesterday.   As you know, we in England bracket Hele & Chester as the two best umpires in the world.   To my mind, the second best umpire we have seen to date stood with Hele at Adelaide, but I understood that he is very new to the highest Cricket, and further, that at Sydney we shall see the umpire who stood in all 5 Tests v S. Africa.   So before I say any more I would like to see him; Woodfull, I think, approves of him.

      Again many thanks,

        Yours sincerely,

          (Sgd.)   DOUGLAS R. JARDINE.

flick the ball up with the sole of his boot to avoid having to bend. He did this to perfection and benefited all his fellow bowlers. The first Australian to copy him was fast bowler Jack Gregory. Jack was deeply grateful to Cecil, who was virtually an off-spin bowler. Occasionally, Parkin delivered a normal leg-break at fast medium pace. This, I gathered, was his 'mystery' ball. If he had another, it failed to leave its hiding place when I was watching him. There *were* no other mysteries about his bowling. Maybe that 'mystery' ball was just another piece of British propaganda."

Parkin was not the success in the 1920–21 Tests which his form for Lancashire suggested he would be. But he contributed greatly, as a character and funny man, to the summer's cricket and came to be the favourite butt for Arthur Mailey's sense of humour in the strip cartoons Mailey produced for the publishers of cricket booklets and for the Press, while his Test colleagues were either sleeping or celebrating. Parkin and Mailey became soul-mates that summer.

Parkin's most outstanding performance came in the earlier game between the M.C.C. and South Australia on the Englishman's road to the Tests. In South Australia's first innings of that November match he took eight for 55, bowling six of his victims. In South Australia's second innings he took none for 41. Whatever "mysteries" he presented appear to have been solved by those South Australian cricketing sleuths, Pellew, Percy Rundell, and Arthur Richardson.

All ten South Australian batsmen were "clean bowled" in their second innings, a remarkable occurrence. Has anyone, incidentally, ever seen a batsman "uncleanly" bowled?

The March M.C.C. versus South Australia game marked the final appearance in Australia of Wilfred Rhodes who, five years later at Kennington Oval, returned to Tests to help the twenty-one-year-old Harold Larwood regain the Ashes for England. In August 1926 Rhodes was forty-nine. On 29 October 1972, he turned ninety-five, the oldest Test cricketer of all time. Rhodes began Test cricket as England's Number 11 batsman in 1899. In the Fifth Test of 1903–04 at Melbourne he opened the England innings with Tom Hayward. England were all out for 61 (Rhodes 3) and Rhodes took a swift dive to Number 8. His 66 in the Fifth Test at the Oval in 1909, as a Number 3 batsman, brought him back to Number 2 in the second innings of that game and this time he made 54. He was Jack Hobbs' opening partner in the Second Test of 1911–12 at Melbourne and

A. P. F. Chapman, captain of the M.C.C. touring side of 1928–29 in the Fourth Test of that series shared with Hobbs in the still-record Test opening stand of 323, to which he contributed 179. He scored 59, 92, and 49 as an opener in the Triangular Series of 1912 against Australia, and opened with Hobbs in four of the five Tests in 1920–21. In his only other Test against Australia, that one at the Oval in 1926, he scored 28 and 14 at Number 7.

Rhodes also retains a share in the highest tenth-wicket Test stand, one of 130 for England. He was 40 not out at Sydney in 1903–04 when R. E. Foster was caught by Monty Noble for 287. The same courage he displayed as a cricketer helped him during decades of blindness in his old age.

It is cricketers like Hobbs and Rhodes and the gaining of their friendship that brings a glow to George's blue eyes now that he is an octogenarian himself. He believes that sport, and cricket in particular, is an even better medium for making friendships than freemasonry.

It is because of this belief that he has never forsaken his association with the West Torrens cricket and football clubs. One of his most treasured friendships today is that of Roy Brown, who led West Torrens to its South Australian football premiership in 1924. Every time he returns to Adelaide he stays with Brown.

"Roy's got the same kind of approach to life as Wilfred Rhodes and Vic Richardson had," George says. "Why, when Roy was seventy-two he bought an organ and he and his wife learnt to play it in their home. There were a few unharmonious months while they were learning, but today it's a pleasure to listen to them. They have recorded tapes of their music so they can listen to it when they're too old to play, and be able to pass them on to their two sons."

George would like those of his West Torrens club friends who are living to know just what "pillars of strength" they have proved.

George feels that, next to cricket, Australian Rules football has been the sporting "love of his life" and he followed it just as keenly when he moved his home to Melbourne as he had in his fortieth year.

He believes that his forty years in Adelaide and just more than forty in Melbourne place him in a unique position to judge the comparative standards of football in Australia's two "Queen Cities of the South."

As there are still football fanatics among my own oldest friends in Adelaide, notably John Davey, Graham Williams, Ray Barber, Keith Butler, and Russell Longmire, perhaps I had better dissociate

20

myself from what George has to say on the relative merits of V.F.L. and S.A.N.F.L. football.

"Even today when I go to Adelaide and down to the Adelaide Oval I never get to first base in persuading my pals that the greatest footballers Australia has owned have come from Victoria. I believe that Victoria's footballers and football teams have for the most part been in a class way above South Australia's, making full allowance for the fact that North Adelaide beat Carlton by a point in 1972.

"As a youngster I was just as starry-eyed a South Australian as most of my old friends who stayed in Adelaide are now. I noticed the difference in style and standard of Victorian football, however, during the first game I watched in Melbourne, one between Carlton and Melbourne at Princes Park.

"Football in Melbourne, as I saw immediately, was played in a much harder, more determined, and more desperate fashion than in Adelaide. It still is. At the end of that game between Carlton and Melbourne at Princes Park I was foolish enough to ask my host, 'How many players will be reported?' 'What for?' he asked. 'If the players who took part in about a dozen or more incidents today came before the S.A.N.F.L. Commissioner, they'd be out for the season,' I said.

"Reportable offences *did*, of course, occur in Adelaide. One which I was told of came when a player threw the ball in the umpire's face and manhandled him into the bargain. The Commissioner suspended the player for several years. 'It might as well be life,' called the player. 'Well, life,' responded the Commissioner, amending his sentence.

"Years later the Commissioner saw the player in an audience he was addressing. He was sitting alongside the very umpire he had assaulted. Noticing how friendly they seemed the Commissioner paused in his address and said, 'I'll bet your neighbour is sorry today he threw that ball at the umpire who's sitting beside him.' 'Yes, Mr President,' called the player, 'I wish it had been a brick.'

"The second game I saw in Melbourne was dominated by that three times Brownlow and three times Sandover medal winner, Haydn Bunton. The difference between the standard of Adelaide and Melbourne football was even more indelibly imprinted on my mind, and my lingering South Australian loyalties were not sustained the next week when I watched a duel between Laurie Nash and Reg Hickey in a game between South Melbourne and Geelong.

21

"Those loyalties vanished completely when I went to the M.C.G. to watch Victoria play South Australia. Victoria's goalsneak Billy Mohr was injured during the first quarter. Moved to replace him, Nash kicked eighteen goals in the last three quarters. About forty years later I met Laurie at the M.C.G. and told him I'd seen him kick those eighteen goals. 'I'd have kicked a lot more,' he growled, 'if those blighters had passed the ball to me occasionally.'

"Between 1933 and 1973 I've seen some truly great footballers in Victoria—Ivor Warne Smith, Bert Chadwick, Jack Regan, Ron Durham, Jack Dyer, John Coleman, Ron Todd, Dick Reynolds, Haydn Bunton, Bill Morris, Reg Hickey, Gordon Coventry, Bob Pratt, Ted Whitten, Bob Rose, Ron Barassi, 'Polly' Farmer, Ian Stewart, Bob Skilton, Alex Jesaulenko, Geoff Southby, Fred Gilby, and John Nicholls among them. I think most of them would have got a guernsey for South Australia. I know some of them came to Melbourne from other States but, in my opinion, it was their participation in Melbourne football that took them to the heights they attained.

"I know Western Australia beat Victoria by nine points in the Carnival in Brisbane in 1961. In consequence the Victorians decided to choose another eighteen and pit them against their Carnival side. At the M.C.G. on Anzac Day 1962 the Second Eighteen gave the Carnival team what Lou Richards described as a 'donkey walloping.'

"That same year the V.F.L. decided to give their selectors a free hand in choosing the State side to play Western Australia. No restriction as to the number of players from each club was imposed. Victoria won by 102 points—by 26·9 to 9·9. For most of the forty years I've lived in Melbourne the State selectors have been permitted to pick no more than three players from any one club. Despite this handicap, the 'Big V' has maintained a marked superiority over all other States in Carnival and home-and-away matches.

"Even now, when I go to watch a football game in Adelaide, I can find very few South Australians willing to admit that Victorian football is of a higher standard than Adelaide's. One of the exceptions is South Australian and Australian Services team pace bowler Graham Williams, who lived for years in Melbourne. Another, and I insist that he admits it, is my current biographer, who now follows Carlton but as a boy idolised Sturt, and still does.

"Adelaideans choose to stay oblivious to the fact that South

Australia assembles its teams for training runs weeks before games against Victoria, whereas Victoria only names its teams on the eve of the event and gives them only one practice together.

"I'm not saying all this because I'm a turncoat. I'd like to see South Australia and Western Australia defeat Victoria far more often, and I'd like to see the standard of club football in Adelaide and Perth approach nearer to the Melbourne standard. It won't, in my opinion, until South Australians and Western Australians admit the truth. Having admitted it, there are a number of constructive moves they could make.

"One of those moves, in this age of television, is for Adelaide's and Perth's club coaches and the men appointed to coach State sides to show their charges films of Melbourne club games and of inter-state games in which Victoria takes part, pointing out to them the way in which the Victorians excel, how they always back up and have a man running past to help the player in trouble or to start a chain of passes which takes the ball right down the ground.

"Some people are going to tell me to stick to cricket and ask me what I know about football. Well, I *did* play three winters of football for West Torrens in the Patriotic League during the first World War and, in case anyone starts sending me white feathers, I *did* try to join the First A.I.F. in 1916 but was rejected."

Two friends of George's and mine who *did* receive white feathers, while walking along Grenfell Street during the second World War, are former State cricketer John Davey and his pal, that infallible watcher of big cricket at Adelaide Oval, Bey Campbell. John lost his sight before that war began and Bey one of his legs.

When the character planted a feather in each of their lapels, Bey Campbell fairly frothed at the mouth. "What's bothering you, Bey?" John asked. Bey explained and then added, "What's making me furious is that I can see him, but can't catch him, and you could catch him, but can't see him."

George Hele freely admits South Australia has produced some footballers who were great in any company. Among them he instances that Hercules among ruckmen Tom Leahy, the Jesaulenko of the 1920s, "Snowy" Hamilton, Frank Golding, who proved himself a champion up forward and then at full back, Vic Richardson, Harold Oliver, Horace Riley, Jack Daly, Dan Moriarty, Jack Tredrea, Vic Cumberland, "Shine" Hosking, Bruce McGregor, Frank Magor,

23

Wally Allen, "Nip" Geddes, Frank Hansen, Jack Owens, Ken Farmer, "Wacka" Scott and his brother Basil, Alick Lill, Alec Bent, Tommy and Bobby Quinn, Percy Lewis, "Diver" Dunne, Phil Matson, Ian McKay, Alby Bahr, "Shrimp" Dowling, Bert Congear, Alec Conlin, Dick Head, Bobby Barnes, Bruce Townsend, and Hurtle Willsmore.

One of the greatest individual performances he watched was that of "Snowy" Hamilton in the Victoria–South Australia game at the M.C.G. in 1926, the day when Hamilton "almost controlled the second half of that match from the half back right position."

But he gives it as his final and considered judgement that the greatest footballers he has seen were Victorians—either Victorian born or imported—*and* that Victoria has produced, and is still producing, a far higher proportion of champions than any other State.

Having said all this, George, who came second in a long-distance kick competition with a drop-kick of seventy yards at the Hindmarsh Oval about fifty years ago, is happy to return to cricket. You'll find him behind an outsize pair of dark glasses next time he arrives at Adelaide Oval for a footy match between Victoria and South Australia—with "Captain Blood" Jack Dyer and "Big John" Nicholls at his side as bodyguards.

Bradman Goes Bung

GEORGE HELE HAD A DEMANDING BIG-MATCH DEBUT IN THAT GAME between the M.C.C. and South Australia at Adelaide Oval in 1921. Three batsmen were run out, three dismissed l.b.w., three caught at the wicket, and three stumped. He was called upon to give more than his share of the twelve decisions.

He had learned, however, that umpiring in all classes of cricket brings its problems and perplexities, that it demands diplomacy, exact knowledge of the laws of the game, and the ability to be impartial and definite in the interpretation and application of them. Umpires are luckier than judges, as Victorian Supreme Court Judge Nelson once emphasised. The decisions of cricket umpires are not subject to appeal.

The cricketer who helped Hele most along the road was Victor Richardson. George remembers Vic as the "fairest and most fearless sportsman" he knew, as a man always ready to play his full part in a crisis—to defend what he believed to be right and change what he believed to be wrong. Vic was one of the panel who appointed umpires for district games in Adelaide. He knew he was less popular in Port Adelaide than in his sporting kingdom, Sturt. He grew to have great respect for George as an umpire. When Sturt played Port Adelaide at Alberton, Vic often saw to it that George went along.

Much of Vic's unpopularity at Port Adelaide derived from his position as commander of a squad of strike-breakers which operated on the Port River and Outer Harbor docks during the first World War. Soon after the Kaiser went into exile Vic took his team to Alberton with George as one of the umpires. Vic was usually at his best when the going was tough. He scored a century on the second Saturday to win the game for Sturt. As he was leading the players from the field he saw some of his wartime wharfie enemies preparing the kind of reception scorers of centuries have reason not to expect.

Richardson was particularly proficient with his fists, having trained himself to be so with professional boxers at "Red" Mitchell's Adelaide gymnasium. As he neared the boundary gate he turned to Hele and said, "Take my bat, George. I want my hands free."

Just as George began to believe he might have to involve himself in a pretty unpleasant free-for-all, help came from an unexpected quarter. Standing inside the gate was that giant dock-worker "Sheaney" Magor. Magor threw his shoulders back and pushed out his barrel of a chest. Turning to the potential assailants, he said, "If any of you attack Vic Richardson you'll have to fight me, too."

There ended the crisis.

In another match George gave Vic Richardson "out" when Vic clearly believed he was not. He glared at George as he passed him on the way to the pavilion. Later that day he came to George and said, "Sorry, George, I shouldn't have behaved like that."

During the match between Archie MacLaren's 1922 M.C.C. side and South Australia at the Adelaide Oval, Hele faced quite a different dilemma. MacLaren, the ultimate in English aristocrats, was fifty-one years old when he brought the young Percy Chapman, Chapman's brother-in-law-to-be, Tom Lowry, of New Zealand, W. W. Hill-Wood, the Hon. F. S. G. Calthorpe, and some supporting professionals to Australia. Archie's luxuriant hair was white as snow.

Arthur Richardson, 150, and Victor, 118, hit off with a huge stand in South Australia's first innings 442. In the Englishmen's first innings MacLaren could manage only 18 of 205 before being caught and bowled by ferocious left-handed hitter and right-handed pace bowler, Bruce Townsend. When MacLaren batted again in the follow-on, Port Adelaide spinner Norman Williams took pity on him. "How can I bowl this poor old codger out, George?" he asked Hele before beginning one of his overs.

George kept his own counsel.

MacLaren scored 41 before Williams had him stumped and during the following month notched a double century in New Zealand. It was MacLaren who, while batting on the swift, smooth green carpet of the Sydney Cricket Ground, said, "You only have to poke your tongue out here and it's four."

In that game George faced a problem similar to the one Warwick Armstrong created by delivering two consecutive overs from the same end at Old Trafford in the Fourth Test of 1921. George managed to save MacLaren from committing the same embarrassing error. Vic and Arthur Richardson were both in their eighties on the first day when time came for the last over before lunch. MacLaren gave the ball to Hill-Wood, who was what used to be known as a "Christmas Day" slow bowler, a "Father Christmas"—by any standards.

Arthur Richardson had the strike and he drove the first three deliveries of the eight-ball over for four. "Turn it up, Arthur, get a single for God's sake," Vic called. "I'll handle this fellow," Arthur answered and swept past his century with 23 runs from the over while Vic was at the far end.

After lunch MacLaren began setting the field for the same end as Hill-Wood had bowled from before the interval.

"The other end, Mr MacLaren," George called from square-leg.

"No, we finished from that end."

"No, Mr MacLaren, we finished from *this* end."

While the M.C.C. captain was still disputing Hele's ruling, Hill-Wood advanced upon him. "The umpire's right, Archie," he said. "Don't you remember that maiden of mine before lunch?"

As we have seen, George Hele declined the opportunity of umpiring in the third, fourth, and fifth Tests of the Arthur Gilligan–Herbie Collins series of 1924–25. The circumstances of the invitation were these. George had been in poor health for most of that summer and had umpired in very few matches when his employer, Murray Fowler, summoned him to his office almost immediately after the New Year's Test, which ended on 8 January in Melbourne.

He was astonished to see Clem Hill sitting across the table from Fowler. "Mr Hill wants to have a word with you, George," Fowler said.

"I know you've been sick, George," Hill said, "but we want you

27

to stand on the first afternoon of a district game this weekend. If you come through that all right, you'll be certain to get the last three Tests."

"I'll give you leave, George," Fowler said.

It was in the face of this situation that Hele inquired which umpire he would be replacing, was told Bob Crockett, and then declined the opportunity he had been seeking for so long, on the grounds that the replacement of Crockett during the series would "break his heart."

Crockett was an old man in 1924–25. He had been umpiring Tests since 1901–02—thirty of them in all. He made mistakes in those last three Tests of 1924–25 and was not appointed again for Test matches, though he stood, by M.C.C. captain Harold Gilligan's special request, during a limited tour in 1929–30. When asking for Crockett Gilligan, who brought Duleepsinhji on his one playing tour of Australia, informed the Australian authorities that, when Crockett was umpiring, neither he nor any of his men would appeal unless they were absolutely certain a batsman was out. The Englishmen, Gilligan said, "wanted to have the honour of playing under such a grand old umpire."

It was during the November 1929 game between Gilligan's men and South Australia that the tall and elegant left-hander Frank Woolley, the "Pride of Kent," came to George Hele early in his second innings.

"Who's the keeper, George?" Woolley asked.

He should have known. That keeper, the late Charlie Walker, had stumped him for a duck in his first innings, off Clarrie Grimmett.

"Charlie Walker," George replied.

"Tell him not to put his gloves so close to the stumps when he's taking the ball or he'll get hurt."

Woolley was a glorious late-cutter of the ball, with emphasis on the word "late." George was fond of Charlie Walker. He told him of Woolley's warning. Charlie took no heed. The next time Woolley late-cut Grimmett he took the right glove right off Walker's hand, causing him to dance like a dervish in pain while the ball sped to the fence. Woolley scored 146.

George stepped on to the Anglo-Australian Test-match stage simultaneously with the twenty-year-old Don Bradman, the twenty-five-year-old Walter Hammond, and the twenty-eight-year-old

28

Douglas Jardine in that "Summer of the Masters," 1928–29. He still doubts whether England has sent a stronger batting line to Australia than Hobbs, Sutcliffe, Hammond, Jardine, Hendren, Chapman, and the choice of Maurice Leyland, Ernest Tyldesley, or Phil Mead. For Australia, Bradman batted Number 5, 6, or 7.

Hele was thirty-seven and had been umpiring for ten seasons in Adelaide club cricket and for seven in first-class games when he was named as Dave Elder's partner for the one and only cricket Test ever played at Brisbane's Exhibition Ground. He had been through all but what he calls "the big hoop," had his laws of cricket off pat and, thanks mainly to his family upbringing, was a man of his own mind.

He knew most of the Australian team well and was no stranger to Hobbs, Sutcliffe, Chapman, Hendren, and Tate. He felt equipped for the function he had to perform, confident of his ability to handle what might come. This was just as well, with the "Kippax Incident" less than a month ahead.

"To me," George says, "one cricket match, be it district, Shield, or Test, was much of a muchness so far as the actual umpiring was concerned. I was thrilled, naturally, at the prospect of umpiring for such great English batsmen as Hobbs, Sutcliffe, Hammond, Jardine, Hendren, Chapman, and Mead and such great bowlers as Larwood, Tate, and White, in addition to the Australians, in the same game; of watching them perform from the best positions in the world—the batsmen from the far end of the pitch, the bowlers from behind their backs.

"The 1928–29 series was a far happier one than the 1932–33 series was to be. During it I developed friendships with the English players that provide some of my happiest memories of cricket. My friendship with Harold Larwood survived even the Bodyline series and persists to this day. I saw Harold at the Sydney Test in 1971–72 and asked him what he thought of John Snow. 'A good medium-pacer,' Harold replied. Doug Walters kindly note.

"My associations with Maurice Tate, Patsy Hendren, Percy Chapman, Ernie Tyldesley, Maurice Leyland, and George Duckworth were a delight. These men were characters in their own right as well as great cricketers. All of them had superb senses of humour. I even got on well with Douglas Jardine.

"Maurice Tate had the broadest and most persistent smile of all

29

the cricketers I've known. He liked to chat to you all the time, before and after just about every ball of every over he bowled. He didn't seem to be able to bowl at his best if you wouldn't talk to him, thinking he had offended you. He was that good-hearted.

"For good humour Patsy Hendren was also outstanding. As we were taking the field he would often say, 'Come on George, I'll race you to the wicket.' During one Test of 1924–25, I remember, he picked up an apple near the boundary instead of the ball and returned it on the half-volley to Herbert Strudwick. The apple split in half and spattered all over the man who was to become Patsy's lifelong friend. In the gloaming of their years they sat alongside one another in the Press boxes of England, scoring for Middlesex and Surrey.

"Patsy Hendren, Don Bradman, Leo O'Brien, and Neil Harvey had the most accurate long-distance returns to the stumps I've seen. Bradman was perhaps the most phenomenal of the three. After lunch one day during the Adelaide Test of that summer I was about to straighten the stumps so that play could resume. 'Leave them as they are a second, George,' Don called. He was standing at square-leg with the ball in his hand. With three successive throws he hit the one stump visible to him three times then ran off to the boundary chuckling to himself. Throwing, by and large, is better now, however.

"I don't believe Percy Chapman could ever have had an enemy in the world. During the second innings of the Brisbane Test, when he was 27 not out, he took a swipe to leg at a ball from Grimmett. He just touched the ball with the edge of his bat, overbalanced, and was still out of his crease when Bert Oldfield whipped off the bails. Recovering himself Percy then stumbled and fell on to the stumps. He was squatting uncomfortably on one of them, grinning towards me at square-leg when he called, 'How was I out, George?' I pointed to Dave Elder at the bowler's end. Dave was standing like the Statue of Liberty. 'Caught, I gather,' called Chapman, and walked off with a beam all over his pink and freckly face.

"At one stage of the Fifth Test at Melbourne the crowd was unusually quiet. This didn't suit the volatile, excitable George Duckworth. He came to me and said, 'The crowd's very quiet, George. Let's rouse them a bit. I'll appeal for a catch to one wide of the stumps but, for goodness sake, don't give it out.' When the right ball came George gave his wild Red Indian warwhoop. So did the crowd. 'That's better, George, now they're enjoying themselves.' Duckworth was a good fellow. A brave one, too. He took a terrible pounding on his wrists that summer from Maurice Tate. He was the first wicketkeeper to have gloves made with extra bars on them for wrist protection."

England held the Ashes when the 1928–29 series began. She was led by the man who had regained them for her, Percy Chapman. Australia had a new captain, thirty-nine-year-old Jack Ryder, who had toured England in 1921 and 1926 under Armstrong and Collins. Of the 1926 side Collins, Bardsley, Macartney, Mailey, Arthur Richardson, and Johnny Taylor had retired.

George Hele does not agree with the criticism Ryder received for his leadership in 1928–29. He stresses: "Ryder's task against so great an English side was mammoth. The problems he faced have not been adequately assessed by his many critics. During the Brisbane Test Jack Gregory and Charles Kelleway broke down and took no further part in the series. Australia had lost her two new-ball bowlers.

"Australia lost the First Test by 675 runs, the second by eight wickets, the third by three wickets, the fourth by 12 runs, and won the fifth by five wickets. Clear evidence this that Australia improved under the captaincy of the man who at eighty-four is still the 'King of Collingwood.'

"Had the Australian selectors chosen Bert Ironmonger for the Third Test at Melbourne, Hobbs and Sutcliffe could not have staged that phenomenal stand on the sticky wicket in England's second innings. Australia would have won that game and, with the confidence gained from victory, most probably would have evened the series in the Fourth Test at Adelaide, the Test we lost by 12 runs.

"A captain can only lead the teams he is given. After Gregory and Kelleway broke down he had to choose between 'Stork' Hendry, Otto Nothling, Ted A'Beckett, and Grimmett as his new-ball bowlers. He tried Nothling and Grimmett in Sydney, A'Beckett and Hendry in Melbourne and Adelaide. Australia can have had no weaker opening attacks until Stan McCabe and Mervyn Waite performed this role at the Oval in 1938 and Hobbs and Sutcliffe were as fine a pair of opening batsmen as England ever owned.

"When Tim Wall replaced A'Beckett for the Fifth Test the Australian attack became worthy of the name."

George had umpired in the Sheffield Shield game between New

31

South Wales and South Australia in which Don Bradman began his first-class career with a century. Of the young Bradman, he says: "He was only a teenager then, just a bright, happy, smiling boy with a world to conquer. I could tell, that day in Adelaide, that New South Wales had discovered yet another champion to follow the long line of Charles Bannerman, William Murdoch, Victor Trumper, Charles Macartney, Reggie Duff, and Alan Kippax.

"Don was a cordial kid who seemed to love batting more than anything in life—even more than fielding along the boundary, in which he took great joy. The quality which impressed me most was his confidence in himself, even in the company of Alan Kippax, the New South Wales captain, Tommy Andrews, Arthur Mailey, Bert Oldfield, and other established players. His fielding impressed me even more than his batting in that game at Adelaide Oval. His throw was so fast and so accurate, its speed quite astounding from one so small.

"Don had scored centuries in his first club and Sheffield Shield games, and in his first international game, against the M.C.C. I was anxious to discover how he would fare against England in his first Test match.

"The confidence of the youngster was revealed early in England's first innings of 521. One of Don's returns grazed Bert Sutcliffe's handsome dark head as he was scampering for his crease. Sutcliffe turned to him and said, 'I think you tried to hit me.' Don replied, 'I thought you knew my throw better than that. If I'd wanted to hit you, I would have.' "

Jack Gregory, who was thirty-one years of age, was bowling to his English counterpart Harold Larwood when he broke down on the second day of the Brisbane Test. He got a good-length ball to rise abnormally. It hit the shoulder of Larwood's bat and broke a piece from it. The ball cocked up in front of Larwood's face. Gregory turned and doubled back from his follow-through, dashed along the pitch and sprang to his right in a desperate attempt to make the catch. He fell prone on the pitch (see picture opposite page 34) and twisted his knee.

He had bowled forty-one overs to take three for 142. That night, when the Australian team doctor told him he would never play cricket again, Gregory cried in the dressingroom, such was his passionate love of the game.

In twenty-four Tests Gregory had scored 1,146 runs, including two centuries (the first 100 of his 119 against South Africa at Johannesburg in 1921–22 was reached in seventy minutes, still the record time for a century in any Test match) and seven fifties. He took eighty-five Test wickets at 31·15, and held thirty-seven catches.

George, who saw Gregory for the most part only in Shield and Test games in Adelaide from 1920 to 1927, considers him the most spectacular cricketer he watched and certainly the most spectacular slips fieldsman.

"I saw him walk behind Oldfield from the off side to the leg while a ball from Arthur Mailey was in flight. He had picked the wrong-un (off-break with leg-break action) by watching Mailey's fingers at the instant of release and he held the catch comfortably with two hands well to the leg side of the wicket.

"During the Adelaide Test of 1924–25 Gregory caught Hobbs literally beneath his bat and stroke, off Mailey. He could also leap high in the air to bring down one-handed catches as if he had climbed some invisible ladder. He demonstrated it by catching the unfortunate Hobbs—left-handed at first slip off fast bowler Jack Scott on the S.C.G. The now unfortunately extinct *Sydney Mail* got the picture for what, some 100 years from today, may be an astonished posterity."

Of Gregory the batsman, Hele says: "He was a natural left-handed hitter with a terrific reach. He had all the strokes but was especially strong on the off side. His cover-drive was his best stroke. To give him a rest before bowling, Herbie Collins used to bat Gregory high up the list on occasion. He opened with him at Durban against South Africa in November 1921 and was rewarded with a score of 51. Gregory batted second wicket to score that whirlwind 100 in seventy minutes at the Wanderers Ground in the Second Test of that summer. His previous Test hundred, under Warwick Armstrong at Melbourne on New Year's Day of 1921, was scored from Number 9. Promoted to Number 7 and Number 5, he scored 10, 78 not out, 77, 76 not out, and 93 in his remaining innings of the series."

Collins used him at Number 3 or Number 9 in 1924–25, depending upon the state of the game.

Of Gregory the bowler, Hele says: "His bowling approach was like an elephant stampede, and it was the most frightening spectacle I can imagine for a batsman. His last stride or leap was begun eleven feet back from the bowling crease, yet he bowled far less no-balls than Kelleway. In his prime he ranked for pace after Larwood, Ted McDonald, Wes Hall, and Frank Tyson, and level with Lindwall and Miller. Because of his great height, however, he could, in his prime, get the ball up higher from a fuller length than any of them. He resembled Ken Farnes in this respect, but was less accurate and, therefore, more frightening and dangerous, physically.

"I've not been on the field with a cricketer who loved playing cricket more than Gregory and it was a delight to watch him taking the ball when either Hanson Carter or Oldfield returned it to him. This procedure developed into a ceremony which the crowd enjoyed immensely. Gregory would begin his walk to his mark with his back to the keeper. Both Carter and Oldfield could lob the ball so Gregory could extend either his right or left hand behind him and catch it without turning his head—wrist reversed and hand underneath. This ritual also saved time. The consistency with which Carter and Oldfield lobbed the ball into the required spot was amazing and so much more attractive than the ponderous relaying of the ball around the inner fielding cordons that is repeated with such monotony today.

"Bowlers never rubbed the ball on the fronts of their trousers and shirts in those days. They used their hands and the sleeves of their shirts. They were most anxious to have their flannels as immaculate as possible, carrying themselves with a dignity and grace, some with an air of nobility that helped cricket to become known as the 'noblest of all games.' I have only to point to Vic Richardson, whom Sir Neville Cardus called 'The Guardsman,' to Gregory, Hammond, Kippax, Duleepsinhji, Sutcliffe, Woolley, Jardine, O'Reilly, and Oldfield to confirm my case.

"Now, even though the televising of cricket makes appearance even more important, fewer players appear to care. Old-time players walked to their fielding positions like soldiers on guard. The mutual congratulation, the 'kissing in the ring' that modern players indulge in at the fall of wickets, would have disgusted the champions of the first forty years of this century, and still disgusts those of them who have survived to watch it. The sleeves of the players of my time were rolled below the elbow or buttoned at the wrist. They looked like so many Jack Crawfords, that most immaculate of all tennis players—the late Queen Mary's favourite."

On their way to the First Test of 1928–29 at Brisbane the English-

Top: Gregory falls heavily in an attempt to catch Larwood off his own bowling during the First Test in Brisbane, 1928. The injury ended his Test career. *Bottom:* Duckworth often had to move wide to the leg side during the Second Test in Sydney, 1928

men totalled 406 (Jardine 109) against Western Australia, 528 (Hammond and Chapman each 145) and four for 341 (Leyland 114) against South Australia, 486 (Jardine 104, Hendren 100) against Victoria, seven for 734 declared (Hammond 225, Hendren 167, and Jardine 140) against New South Wales, 357 and two for 118 against an Australian XI, and 293 (Leyland 114) against Queensland.

With England seven for 442 in the First Test it was a fine time for Gregory and Kelleway to break down. The only four Australian batsmen to score centuries against Larwood, Tate, White, Freeman, and Geary had been Victor Richardson (231) and Dave Pritchard (119) for South Australia, Kippax (136 not out), and Bradman (132 not out—following a first innings 87) for New South Wales.

The England team selectors decided they could get by without their rather mechanical and moustachioed little wrist-spinner "Tich" Freeman in the Brisbane Test, though he had taken the record number of 304 wickets at 18·05 in England during the winter and captured seventeen wickets to "Farmer" White's fifteen, Larwood's twelve, Tate's nine, and Geary's eight on the present tour.

They went into the First Test with four bowlers and four proved to be what my then eighty-seven-year-old grandfather, Peter Whitington, used to call "an ample sufficiency."

Three of them—Larwood eight for 62, Tate five for 76, and White four for 7—took all the wickets. Gregory was "absent hurt" twice and Kelleway "absent ill" once to make up the twenty. For Australia that giant of a little man, Clarrie Grimmett, took nine for 298 from 84·1 overs, a matter of 673 balls. While England scored 863 runs in this Test Bert Oldfield allowed no byes.

England's topscorer, Patsy Hendren, followed his 100 against Victoria and 167 against New South Wales with 169 and 45. If the South Australian Cricket Association had had their way, Hendren would not have been playing. Patsy had signed a contract to be South Australian State cricket coach for three summers—1927–28, 1928–29, and 1929–30. When chosen for the 1928–29 M.C.C. tour of Australia he sought suspension of the contract, asking that it be extended to 1930–31 to compensate for his absence in 1928–29. The S.A.C.A. refused and Patsy cancelled the agreement.

The effect of Hendren's coaching of young South Australians in 1927–28 had been notable. Young batsmen who had been scoring between 200 and 300 a season for their schools found themselves

D. R. Jardine, whose stern approach to cricket made him increasingly unpopular with Australian crowds during 1932–33 with aggregates of over 1,000 that summer. Hendren had concentrated on teaching youngsters how to play strokes—how to drive, hook, pull, and cut—and kept them enthusiastic and happy between coaching seasons with his playful patter-humour that would have won him an engagement in any English music hall.

He had not believed that he would ever be chosen to play for England again. Patsy loved playing for England more than anything in life, which is why he first sought a year's release from and eventually cancelled his contract. To him representing his country at cricket was the ultimate honour.

In the net result, the S.A.C.A. embarked upon an overdone policy of importation in the mid-1930s that caused a considerable number of South Australian fathers to advise their sons to forget cricket and concentrate upon professional careers upon leaving school.

Over the decades South Australia had imported Bill Whitty from New South Wales, Jack Crawford from Surrey, and Clarrie Grimmett from Victoria. After the second World War it was to bring Les Favell, Colin Pinch, and Graeme Hole from New South Wales, Ashley Mallett and Terry Jenner from Western Australia, Gary Sobers from the West Indies, Barry Richards from South Africa, and Younis Ahmed from Pakistan.

These importations have helped the game in Adelaide. In 1935–36, however, the S.A.C.A. went to extremes. They brought Don Bradman, Ray Robinson, and Frank Ward from Sydney, and Jackie Badcock from Tasmania all in one year.

South Australia won the Shield in 1935–36 and again in 1938–39 but an undercurrent of bitterness, that took time to dispel, was created in Adelaide and in other States.

Good can come from mistakes, however. South Australia *did* get Don Bradman and he proved an ideal migrant in his loyalty to his new State in every field of his activities. Thanks to South Australia, Don became Australia's cricket captain, later an outstanding cricket administrator, and indeed the most powerful figure Australian cricket has known. Don has had his critics, and I have been one of the severest of them at times, but nobody could fairly claim he hasn't returned full value, prodigious value, in return for the opportunities given him.

Like Patsy Hendren, Don loved, and still loves, cricket.

Cricket in South Australia, thanks to Chappell (Australia) Incorporated (now disintegrated) and the S.A.C.A. policy of importing champions, is very much alive. So is it in Western Australia, which has, over the years, imported Bobby Simpson, Tony Lock, Ken Meuleman, Norman O'Neill, Peter Loader, Colin Milford, and Graeme Watson.

The cream of Australian cricket, as recent results in the Sheffield Shield competition have shown, took a trip on the Indian-Pacific from its old haven along the eastern seaboard.

Hendren was "a pretty nervous character," according to Hele, "but he gave no sign of it that 30 and 31 November at Brisbane during an innings which began when England was four for 161.

"Hammond began what was to be his most successful Test series in a disappointing manner. He failed to gain confidence, either in his first innings 44 or second innings 28. After England had begun with 85 from him and Hobbs, Herbert Sutcliffe fell to the Jack Gregory–Bill Ponsford trap, hooking at a rising ball and being caught towards deep fine-leg. It was the same trap that failed when Ponsford dropped a 'sitter' in 1924–25, the same trap which Sutcliffe had declared would never again be sprung on him successfully.

"The tremendous strength of England's batting resources was shown when Larwood produced a hectic innings of 70 (one six, one five, and seven fours) from Number 8 and Chapman hit lustily for 50 on the road to 521.

"Kelleway, one of the finest users of the wearing ball among new-ball bowlers I have known, had lost the hostility he had shown while taking fifteen English wickets at 21·00 in 1920–21 and fourteen at 29·50 in 1924–25. His thirty-four overs in that 521 of England's brought no reward for 77 runs.

"I could tell, as that innings rolled on at an average of three runs an over, that Australia had reached the end of an era of champions, whereas England had found a new cricketing 'Establishment.' The one young Australian champion making his bid was Bradman and our selectors decided to drop him for the Sydney Test. This, surely, was the most colossal error of judgement by any selectors in the entire history of the game. They contemplated changing their names by deed poll during the Australian winter of 1930.

"During the 1932–33 series one of those selectors came to me and complained at the selection of several of Australia's players. 'How can *you* criticise?' I asked. 'You dropped Don Bradman in 1928.'

37

"When Australia began its chase of 521, Larwood, then twenty-four, looked a completely different proposition from the thirty-three-year-old Gregory. Though he was eight inches shorter than Gregory, he began to make the ball lift higher from a good length and was several yards faster through the air.

"A ball of Larwood's first over moved slightly away to the off. Bill Woodfull followed it and the snick flew towards Chapman—to his left side at about shoulder height. The England captain flung out his hand and held the catch with his thumb and index finger. This was the finest freak catch I've seen. Indeed, Woodfull came to me later and asked 'Have you ever seen a more miraculous catch?' 'No, Bill,' I replied and that answer stands.

"Australia was one for 0 and, when the broadest bat in cricket, that of Bill Ponsford, failed to cover a good length ball from Larwood, it was two for 7. 'Mutt and Jeff' had gone to the Notts' flyer inside a quarter of an hour for a joint contribution of two."

Australia had begun late in the second afternoon on a good, if grassy, wicket.

It was when Australia was four for 44 with the sun shining from a cloudless vault of Capricornia that George Hele "copped the lot" from the crowd and from English critics, who included Surrey and England captain P. G. F. Fender. George still regards Percy as more of a scimitar than a fender. Having lost Woodfull (0), Ponsford (2), Kippax (16), and Kelleway (8), and being partnered by Hendry, Australia's captain, Jack Ryder, appealed against the light at 4.48 p.m.

Hele and Elder granted the appeal "because of the brilliance of the sunlight." The sun, with the help of the grandstand, was cutting a shadow half way down the wicket. Balls were emerging from shadow into sunlight, and vice versa, from Larwood and Tate.

In his tale of the tour, *Turn of the Wheel,* Fender wrote: "Such an appeal would not have been given any consideration at all in England, because the sun was still shining and there was not a cloud in the sky."

Hele's comment: "Elder and I were on the pitch and Fender was not. In dealing with this session of play he referred to a decision of mine in favour of Hendry in critical terms. This decision was made during the Second Test at Sydney, *not* in the First at Brisbane. It was after the 1928–29 series, of course, that Fender declared Bradman 'wouldn't get a run in England in 1930.' His facts and his forecasts appear to have been on a par, yet Jardine regarded Fender, his Surrey County captain, with awe and idolatry as a cricket authority and I should not be surprised if he consulted him while planning his Bodyline campaign of 1932.

"Ryder had reserved Don Bradman for the third day, probably because of the tremendous stint he had done along the boundary during England's innings and also because this was his first Test. I believe Jack was wrong in doing so. Don had scored 87 and 132 not out against Larwood and Tate a fortnight previously in Sydney and followed these scores there with 58 not out and 18 against them for an Australian XI. Larwood had not dismissed him while he was scoring these 295 runs for twice out. Tate had got him l.b.w. for that 18.

"The ordeal Bradman had to face on the Monday, when Hendry left, l.b.w. to Larwood 30, and with the score at five for 71, was of no lesser magnitude than appearance at four for 40 on the Saturday evening would have been. Demotion denoted lack of confidence in the lad who was to become known as 'The Don.'

"Ryder rode the crisis commendably—concentrating, in the main, upon defence in an effort to help Bradman settle in. Larwood and Tate were using the grassy surface of the Exhibition Ground wicket far more effectively than Gregory and Kelleway had done, but Bradman began to bat in much the same manner as he had in that first Sheffield Shield innings of 118 at Adelaide the previous summer. To me, he looked sound and confident. Fender, however, wrote, 'Tate bowled twenty-six balls to the youngster and had him completely at sea all the time. During those twenty-six balls he made one scoring stroke, the ball going off the inside edge of his bat to long-leg for four.'

"Eventually Tate dismissed Bradman, again l.b.w. 18. Ryder scored 33 in eighty-three minutes and, with Gregory unfit, Australia was all out 122 from 50·4 overs 399 behind. Larwood had taken six for 32 on what, as England had proved and was now again to prove, was a batting wicket. Chapman's decision to bat again on so substantial a lead was to teach the youngest member of the Australian side a lesson he never forgot."

England led by 741 when Chapman, in the words of another English writer, "was merciful enough to declare," at eight for 342. Even Grimmett 84·1/10/298/9/33·1 was happy to desist.

Don Bradman did a lot more running about the boundary than between wickets during that Test. While he was running, a certain amount of iron appears to have entered his soul. It turned to steel when he was caught Chapman bowled White for a single in the second Australian innings and heard Tate reprimand the Taunton pastoralist with these words, "What do you mean, getting one of my rabbits?"

"Don has a long memory," George Hele says. "I don't think he ever forgot that remark and Tate was not the only Englishman to suffer in consequence of it. Tate was only joking, of course, but Don failed to sense the humour of the situation—particularly after being relegated to twelfth man for the Second Test."

Australia had lost Ponsford to Larwood for 6 on the fourth evening. During the night heavy rain fell, enough to make the wicket difficult, but not enough to affect the bowling approaches of Larwood and Tate. Under the thick surface mat of grass the soil was soft. The wicket was not a crusted top Melbourne "sticky," but perhaps even more difficult for batting. Larwood and Tate were able to deliver at full pace and the ball jumped occasionally and bounced with erratic velocity.

"I could have taken wickets myself," George says, "and I was a wicketkeeper, not a bowler." In the conditions prevailing Bill Woodfull's feat in batting through the innings for 30 was beyond praise. The only other batsman to reach double figures was Kippax (15) and Australia, 122 and 66, had lost by a margin of 675. This remained the record deficiency until England won the Oval Test of 1938 by an innings and 579.

Dr Roley Pope, Australia's cricket-watching Marco Polo, had given the Australian players and both umpires a white washing hat before the Brisbane Test. When it ended he asked George Hele for his hat. "I'm sending them all down to Sydney for the Second Test," Pope said.

"Thanks all the same, Doc," replied George, "but I'm keeping mine. I may not be appointed for Sydney." "I'll go and find out," Pope said. When he came back he said, "I've found out, but I'm not allowed to tell anyone. Give me that hat."

Thus ended the only Test ever played at Brisbane's Exhibition Ground.

The Great Hammond

WALTER HAMMOND WAS BORN IN JUNE 1903. ON 15 DECEMBER 1928 at Sydney, he began a sequence of Test scores never matched by an Englishman. His 251 there was followed by 200 and 32 run out at Melbourne, by 119 not out and 177 at Adelaide, and 38 and 16 at Melbourne, bringing his contribution for the series to 905 runs from nine innings at 113·12.

Only Don Bradman, scoring 974 at 139·14 against England in 1930, surpassed this. Hammond said his record could be beaten only in a series played in Australia. Within eighteen months he was proved wrong—by the man who proved so many wrong.

Hammond was as handsome a batsman as he was a man, the most perfect, beautiful, and powerful player to the arc between mid-on and point there may ever have been. Perhaps nobody, not even Nureyev or Nijinsky, moved more gracefully.

Yet to a sixteen-year-old Australian, watching those 1928–29 Tests with patriotism high in his heart, Hammond was of the stuff of nightmares. No batsman can have given less promise of losing his wicket. He was the prophet of automation as well as the barb for Bradman.

Rarely can an Australian cricket captain have been confronted by so dispiriting and difficult a situation as was Jack Ryder on 14

December of that summer of 1928–29. His team had lost the Brisbane Test by 675 runs; both his new-ball bowlers, Gregory and Kelleway, had broken down and retired from big cricket. No replacements of comparable class had emerged. The average age of the men he led in Brisbane was thirty-three, and it showed in their fielding. One of his opening batsmen, Bill Ponsford, had scored 133, 437, 202, and 316 the previous December towards a month's return of 1,146 at 229·20 in first-class games. This summer in the Brisbane Test he contributed 2 and 6 and showed a fatal fallibility before the fire of Larwood. A new partner for Woodfull seemed essential.

Later, Ryder was to select Australian teams himself—for more than forty years, from 1930 to 1970. He cannot be said to have received the help he needed, as a captain, from the men who chose Australia's side for the Second Test at Sydney—Dr Charles Dolling (South Australia), Jack Hutcheon (Queensland), Warren Bardsley (New South Wales), and Ernie Bean (Victoria)—those less-than-just men who won immortality by omitting Don Bradman.

Understandably, none of the four ever admitted individual responsibility for this omission. Each sought sanctuary in collectivity.

One, as we have seen, disclaimed responsibility directly to George Hele four years later. George's reaction was to turn on his heel.

From the thirteen players originally named, the selectors omitted brilliant cover fieldsman and proficient funeral director, Tommy Andrews, and made equally brilliant boundary fieldsman, Bradman, twelfth man. In came Vic Richardson, who had scored 231 against Larwood at Adelaide, to partner Woodfull, Dr Otto Nothling for Gregory, and Don Blackie—stovepipe trousers, black socks, and all—for Kelleway.

Richardson was thirty-four, Nothling twenty-eight, and Blackie, born in 1882, the year of the Ashes Test at the Oval, forty-six. Up went the average age of the Australian team by 1·5 per man.

If anyone deserved blame for England's subsequent eight wickets victory and eventual four-one series victory surely it was those selectors, not Ryder, who contributed 492 runs at 54·66 and took five for 180. Little more than a year later Ryder was to receive the crowning blow from a selection committee which included himself. His colleagues omitted him from the 1930 tour of England without taking him into their confidence.

Says George Hele, who saw the five-act play unfold, "Jack Ryder

42

showed, during that series, many of the superb qualities for which his home town, Collingwood, is famous at football. His main mistake, in my opinion, was to keep bowling Don Blackie to a predominantly off side field against so magnificent an off side player as Hammond."

The first day of that Sydney Test provided one of the most controversial incidents in cricket history—the Kippax incident. It happened soon after Woodfull and Richardson had begun gallantly with an opening stand of 51 against Larwood and Tate.

Geary was bowling, and George, who was at the bowler's end, now, for the first time, tells the whole story.

"Alan Kippax's sportsmanship was as immaculate as his flannels and proved so on this occasion. Geary, an above-medium swing bowler, delivered a straight ball, one straight as an arrow in flight, directed on a line just outside the right-handed Kippax's legs. The ball did not alter course. It passed outside Kippax's pads and the wicketkeeper moved across to intercept it. Kippax had made no stroke at the ball. Duckworth did not take the delivery in his gloves; it appeared to strike his pads.

"It was the sixth ball. I called 'Over' and walked to square-leg. Geary made no appeal to me. I was standing at square-leg with my arms folded in front of me when I heard a voice ask, 'How was that for bowled?' It was the voice of Jack Hobbs.

"I immediately said, 'Not out.' Hobbs had been fielding at cover during Geary's over and was now about five yards from me at square-leg. No other fieldsman appealed to me. I looked to the far end of the wicket and saw two or three English fieldsmen sitting on the ground and Kippax leaving the wicket. I noticed Hobbs had moved to the far end of the wicket.

"Bill Ponsford came in and the game went on with Australia two for 65—Richardson 27, Kippax 9. The incident occurred ten minutes before the luncheon interval. As Dave Elder and I walked off together Dave said to me, 'He was out, George.' I replied, 'You gave him out stumped, Dave?' 'No,' said Dave, 'I think he was bowled.' 'But you had no right to give him out bowled from square-leg,' I said.

" 'Good gracious,' said Dave. 'What have I done?'

"The crowd had given us merry hell, of course, and I knew the Press would be on to the incident. 'Johnny' Moyes came to me during the luncheon interval and asked for the full story. I replied,

'No comment.' He kept pressing me, saying, 'I've got to write the truth in my paper, George.' I repeated, 'No comment "Johnny." '

"I was hungry and went to lunch, leaving Dave, who wanted to stay, in our dressingroom. I did not discuss the incident at lunch. When I returned to the dressingroom Dave was sitting alone. 'You should have some lunch, Dave,' I said. 'I don't feel hungry,' he replied.

"It was then that I heard a noise outside the closed door of our room. I put my fingers to my lips and tiptoed to the door. When I opened it a man almost fell into the room. He had a notebook and pencil in his hand. He was a stranger to me. I don't know who got the bigger shock, he or I. All I know is that he scampered from sight as if Frankenstein were after him.

"Dave was looking even more worried now and had good reason, as we learned from that evening's and next morning's papers. I shall always regard Dave as a magnificent umpire. All of us are human and we make the odd mistake. Dave, as an associate of Bob Crockett's in fourteen Tests, had proved his worth. He was retained for two more Tests of the 1928–29 series. He was sixty-four then.

"He and I were staying with friends of mine at Abbotsford during that Sydney Test. Abbotsford is near Five Dock. We took a train home and heard two characters sitting opposite us discussing the incident.

"One of them said, 'If I could get my hands on that Elder I'd cut his bloody throat.' Dave ducked his head further behind his paper. 'Don't let on, George,' he whispered. I didn't."

In his book, *The Vic Richardson Story,* Vic has given his account of the Kippax incident. It reads:

"George Geary delivered a ball to Kippax which was a half volley about the line of his pads. Alan had a habit of lifting his left leg to such balls and flicking them fine of square-leg. This time he failed to connect and the ball went through to Duckworth, who was standing up to the stumps. Duckworth moved to the leg side and stopped the ball without taking it cleanly.

"The next thing we saw was that the bails had fallen from the stumps. An appeal, apparently for 'bowled,' was made to George Hele, the umpire at the bowler's end. Hele shook his head and walked towards square-leg to take position for the next over.

"With Jack Hobbs as their spokesman, several members of the English team crowded around Dave Elder, the other umpire, and

44

kept haranguing him to give Alan out. Elder had the right to give a decision against Kippax from square-leg, only if he had hit his wicket, or had moved from his crease and been stumped. But Alan had not budged from his crease at any stage and clearly had not touched his wicket.

"Dave gave him out, however, for some reason or other and the only presumption possible was that he believed he had been bowled. An umpire at square-leg can only give a batsman out 'bowled' when appealed to by the umpire at the bowler's end to clarify some point which he was in a better position to observe.

"Hele had made no request for assistance from Elder. Elder had exceeded his authority. Alan was entitled to continue his innings, but he decided to leave the field.

"I suggested to Jack Ryder that he intercept Alan and persuade him to go to Hele who, I was sure, had ruled him 'not out.' Hele later confirmed that this is what Alan should have done.

"But Jack replied, 'Wait till Alan comes off and we'll find out exactly what happened.' This, as the next batsman would have begun his innings, would clearly be too late.

"When Alan joined us and we asked him what had happened, he said, 'I don't know. It all took place behind my back.' 'Well, were you out?' 'I don't know,' he repeated.

"I then took him to task for leaving the field without knowing why he was out and he said, 'It's all very fine for you experts up here. But you'd have walked off, too, if Jack Hobbs had said to you what he said to me.'

" 'What did he say?' we demanded. He said, 'What sort of a sport are you for staying here when you're out?'

"My reply to Alan was, 'If he'd said that to me they'd have had to carry me off the field to get rid of me.'

"This was the only time an umpire gave a batsman out 'bowled' from square-leg in a Test match on his own initiative."

The version of the incident given by Percy Fender, Surrey and England captain, in *The Turn of the Wheel*, is diametrically opposed to Hele's and Richardson's. It reads: "Geary had a stroke of fortune in his second over, which he bowled to Kippax, for the batsman tried to swing round and sweep a ball outside his legs to the boundary, but, failing to connect with the bat, partially stopped the ball with the inside of his leg and guided it into his wicket. It was bad fortune for

Kippax but, watching through the glasses, as I was doing at the time, I must say I thought he courted disaster by the wild way his leg swung round. For a moment I thought he had kicked his wicket down."

I wonder where Percy bought those glasses. Possibly from a coster cart in Portobello Road?

Fender's memory appears to have been even worse than his eyesight. On page 370 of *The Turn of the Wheel* he writes: "George Hele (who in reply to Hobbs' appeal gave Kippax 'not out') has given me permission to publish in these pages the fact that he is now convinced that, had his decision been allowed to stand, it would have been a wrong one."

Hele's reaction to this statement of Fender's is an unequivocal denial. He also denies Fender's claim that the umpires were called before the authorities concerning the Kippax Incident.

Hele tells how the issue was closed: "What *did* happen was that, after the Test, Ernie Bean, a national Selector and member of the Board of Control, asked the conductor of the Sydney–Melbourne Express, on which I was also travelling, to tell me he wished to see me in his compartment. I went and he said, 'George, tell me about the Kippax Incident.' I replied, 'I have nothing to say, Mr Bean.' 'But you know I'm a member of the Board of Control?' 'Yes.' 'Will you tell me what happened?' 'No.' 'Well, let me tell you this. You have been appointed for the Third Test in Melbourne. Had you told me what happened to Kippax your appointment would have been cancelled.'

"I learned later that Mr Bean had also called Dave Elder to see him. Dave told me his reply was, 'It's all over, Mr Bean, and I have forgotten about the incident.'

"Dave was also retained for the Melbourne Test and the Fourth in Adelaide."

He was replaced for the Fifth in Melbourne by A. C. Jones.

It is perhaps pertinent and politic to state that, in the first innings of the Leeds Test of 1930, Hobbs was caught by Ted A'Beckett close to the wicket off Grimmett for 29, that he stood his ground and that an Australian fieldsman, remembering Sydney 1928, said, "If you were a sport, you'd go."

History *can* be repetitive.

Australia suffered further misfortune after lunch when Ponsford

46

groped forward to Larwood. The very fast ball rose from a good length, struck him on the back of his left (top) hand and splintered a bone. Ponsford played no further part in the series, adding to Ryder's jinx.

As belief has grown, and lingered, that Ponsford did not relish fast bowling, George Hele's views on this point are important. He says: "If that belief is well-founded, it is not supported by his performances during the years before Bodyline. He got a great number of runs against Jack Gregory and Jack Scott in the early 1920s when both of them were classic fast. He was a sick man during the 1926 tour of England and played in only two Tests."

There was also a belief that Ponsford was drinking heavily in 1928–29. George puts paid to this tale. "I knew Bill well," he says, "and never saw him have more than a shandy at one sitting."

Geary took five for 35 in Australia's 253. He bowled well but gained the bonus of Kippax's wicket, as he must have known. He did not appeal for it and walked to his position when Hele called "Over."

The Englishmen had recovered their normal good humour by the time the forty-six-year-old Don Blackie and forty-five-year-old "Dainty" Ironmonger became associated at eight for 251. All ten of them asked Chapman for a bowl—even Duckworth. Chapman gave Larwood the ball, however, and with his second delivery he had Ironmonger caught at the wicket.

Between innings an old man came to the umpires' dressingroom and asked for George Hele. He had an autograph book in his hand. "This belongs to a young boy. Could you get the two teams' autographs?" he asked. Hele obtained the autographs and returned the book to the old man. "Got a book of your own?" the old fellow asked. "Yes." "Well, go and get it."

George has always been thankful he got his book. The old man signed it "Charles Bannerman." This scorer of the first of all Test match centuries and the first by an Australian in England, New Zealand, and Canada, died less than two years later, on 20 August 1930. Like Joe Travers he also umpired in Tests.

England's reply of 636 was remarkable chiefly for three factors: Hammond's great 251 in 461 minutes with 30 fours, Vic Richardson's *nonpareil* fielding, which earned him an editorial to himself, and the consistency of the English batting—only one scored less than 20.

Of Hammond's innings Hele says: "His strokes to the off side have never been equalled, let alone excelled, by an English batsman in my presence."

Ronald Mason, in his excellent biography of Hammond, wrote: "England were 65 for two when Jardine joined Hammond. This was the moment of truth, this phase of uneasy equilibrium when two great orthodox batsmen settled resolutely into place to impose on the situation the authority of character and style.

"I stress the orthodoxy because Hammond, for all his Herculean moments of devastating action, never departed from the rules, but merely adorned them and fleshed them out with the authority and beauty of his interpretation of them. I find it appropriate that this partnership (not a long one by Test standards, 83 only) between Hammond and Jardine should have stood at the head and source of Hammond's phenomenal flow of success that these Tests were to bring him.

"For Jardine, a player with a natural beauty of style and all the aggressive strokes in the calendar, was so imbued with a kind of Scottish Covenanter's discipline that you could read it in the line of his very nostril: his cricket was rigid with it, and there was no better time to make this manifest than here in Sydney at a moment of mild crisis.

"And at the other end Hammond, born to destroy and ravage, read the superb civilising message in Jardine's impeccable circumspection and took note. Perhaps not from this moment alone came the decision to curb his voracity; but from this innings dates the fully-matured Hammond of all our honour and it was Jardine with his modest innings of 28 who saw him finally to his maturity."

Cricket, as Sir Robert Menzies has said many times, can evoke very beautiful literature. Little of it is more beautiful, I suggest, than those paragraphs of Ronald Mason's I have taken the delighted liberty of quoting. Hammond will never be forgotten; Mason may be. Despite what my old Western Australian friend, Kirwan Ward, has been contending on radio, actions *do* speak louder than words in certain fields of human activity—one of them being cricket.

Possibly Hammond's army-trained father deserved praise for the degree of discipline his son applied to this innings. Walter Hammond was born at Dover, but spent some of his formative years in Malta, where his father's regiment was posted until the outbreak of the first World War. Hammond's earliest cricket was not played in England, but on a grassless patch of a foreign field close to Valetta. From this strange stage he stalked his imperious way to 7,249 runs at 58·45 in eighty-five Tests, to eighty-three wickets at 37·83 and the record number (until Colin Cowdrey beat it in 1970–71) of 110 Test catches for a fieldsman, as distinct from a wicketkeeper.

When, in the late 1960s, Gary Sobers was being classed by so many, including Sir Donald Bradman and Keith Miller, as the greatest all-round cricketer of all time, Stan McCabe quietly said to me in his little sports store in Cricket House, Sydney, "Have they all forgotten Wally Hammond?"

Stan gave considerable weight to Hammond's impeccable appearance and I was reminded of an occasion in Johannesburg in the early 1960s when the captain of the Natal University team informed me that Wally was its coach and manager at the South African Universities Tournament at the Wanderers Club ground. That captain said: "Mr Hammond even tied our bootlaces for us correctly, saying, 'You may as well look like cricketers, even if you aren't.'"

The sixty-year-old Hammond had not changed, it seemed, from the man of whom London *Times* tennis, soccer, and (in 1953) cricket writer Geoffrey Green wrote: "My fondest memories of cricket are of Frank Woolley driving lyrically through extra-cover and of Walter Hammond striding down the pavilion steps at Lord's like a stately white galleon in full sail."

Victor York Richardson's fielding in the covers and at silly-point throughout that ordeal by 636 runs won him a leading article in Australia's oldest newspaper, the *Sydney Morning Herald*. The article was entitled "Is Richardson Human?" and read:

"If we were Greeks and permitted long Test matches at our Olympiads, Richardson would be a demigod this morning with precedence over satyrs and all other earth gods. We would send maidens of shapely and charming proportions to weave flowers in his hair, to anoint him with rose-water and glycerine and to offer him morsels of roast pork and devilled peanuts. But the Greeks have gone, alas, and we do not deify our heroes now to the same extent as they did. So Richardson must be content with the thought that last night numerous schoolboys slept with cigarette cards bearing his countenance under their pillows."

It is George Hele's opinion that the young Don Bradman learnt a great deal from watching that 251 of Hammond's. Don, as we have seen, had done far more running along the boundary than between wickets while England scored 863 and he 19 runs at Brisbane. At Sydney, due to the injury to Ponsford in Australia's first innings, he was to field as a substitute for 636 more runs without gaining an opportunity for reprisal.

"Certainly his greatest moment as a bowler," George says, "must have come four years later at Adelaide when he bowled Wally for 85 with a full toss in the last over of the day—the perfect fluke."

Of Richardson's fielding at Sydney, Hele remembers a little contretemps between Vic and his friend Alan Kippax, whom he always called "Kelly." Ryder gave Kippax five overs of the 272·1 which Australia required to dismiss England. During those five overs Richardson was at silly-point. After the third he called to Alan, "Pitch 'em up for God's sake, Kelly, they're stinging my hands." During lunch Kippax drew Richardson's attention to his bowling analysis, which he had taken the trouble to reproduce on a slip of paper.

"Have a look at that: 'Hammond 87 not out, Kippax 5–3–11–0.' "

"They must," retorted Richardson, "be the three hardest maidens of all time."

George Hele believes that, had Richardson fielded like an ordinary mortal, Hammond, and not Gary Sobers (365 not out), would hold the record individual score for Test cricket. "Being Adelaide-born and reared," George says, "I watched Vic field in almost every first-class game he played, also in club cricket Saturday after Saturday. I never saw him field better, if as well, for so long a period as he did on that day at Sydney.

"I saw Learie Constantine, Percy Chapman, Jack Gregory, Neil Harvey, Jack Hobbs, Walter Hammond, Tommy Andrews, Johnny Taylor, 'Nip' Pellew, Paul Sheahan, and Don Bradman, who was the best outfieldsman Australia has had—better even than the brilliant Jack Rymill. I saw all of them, except Harvey and Sheahan, from *on* the field. I also saw Gary Sobers, Russell Endean, Roy McLean, Jackie McGlew, and Colin Bland from beyond the boundary.

"Of them all, Vic Richardson was the finest all-round fieldsman, as he was the bravest. Bravest of all on Saturday 15 December and Monday 17 December 1928. Vic could field well in any position

50

though, because he was so often captain, he rarely went to the boundary. One of these rare occasions occurred while Clarrie Grimmett was bowling for South Australia at the Adelaide Oval. Three outfield catches had gone down. 'Never mind, Clarrie,' Vic said, 'I'll go out there next over.' He did and he held the catch. Then he came in to Clarrie and handed him the ball with the words, 'There you are, Scarl.'

"He wasn't boasting. Vic didn't have to boast."

Arthur Mailey, that irrepressible raconteur, also told George Hele a tale of Vic Richardson, the fieldsman, that so far has not been preserved for posterity.

"Do you want to get Don Bradman out cheaply, Vic?" Arthur asked.

"Naturally, what do you think?" Vic replied.

"Well you've got the most accurate spin bowler of all time in Clarrie Grimmett. Go up to silly-point for Don."

Vic did and caught Don in the first innings of the match. When Don came out to bat in the second innings he noticed that Vic was standing back at mid-off, not silly-point.

"What are you doing back there, Vic?" Don asked.

"I've had a good think—*and so have you*," Vic replied. He was an older and wiser man then and this was not a Test match.

On that third day of the Second Test at Sydney the whole Hill stood and cheered Vic after every session of play. At stumps he was carried shoulder-high from the ground and right up into the pavilion. George Hele has not seen a tribute such as this paid to any other fieldsman. Nor have I, not during half a century of watching cricket.

Life can be cruel even to heroes, however. After England's 636, Australia had to bat a second time from 383 behind. It was just before 5 p.m. when Vic Richardson came out with Woodfull to face Larwood and Tate. His hands were puffed and sore. But, as Ponsford, the alternative opener, was injured, Woodfull had no option but to ask Richardson to partner him.

As George recounts: "This Vic willingly did, but he got a sharp riser from Maurice Tate before he had scored and Hendren held the catch inches from the turf at forward short-leg. Anti-climax, indeed, and the roughest of justice. But as he came in the crowd gave Vic the greatest reception I've ever heard for a man who had scored a 'duck.'"

Hunter Hendry, who was known as "Stork" because he had legs

that would have satisfied any self-respecting flamingo, shared in a stand of 215 for the second wicket—Woodfull 111, Hendry 112—and Australia was only 168 behind with eight men to bat at that stage. Ryder and Nothling produced a century stand for the fifth wicket to make it six for 348, but hope had donned a mocking sneer and England was left with only 16 to score in the fourth innings.

Larwood on a fast, true pitch and unaided by the Bodyline field, be it noted, completed the match with the analysis 61·2/9/182/4 and "Dainty" Ironmonger, that "rabbit" of all "rabbits," was one of his four victims.

In the Third Test at Melbourne, Australia saw what George Hele regards as "the most beautiful innings Alan Kippax, indeed probably any batsman, ever played in a Test match."

Kippax had scored 50, all told, in his four innings of the first two Tests. He had suffered from that mistake of Elder's in Sydney. But he came into the Third Test a superbly confident batsman. During the week he had batted for five hours with New South Wales Number 11, Hal Hooker, on this same M.C.G. to amass 307 for the tenth wicket, still (and probably for eternity) the all-time record. Kippax contributed 260 not out from late Monday to midday Wednesday. He returned to the middle of the M.C.G. at about noon on Saturday 29 December to face Larwood and Tate on the fieriest of pitches with Australia two Tests down and two wickets for 15.

Australia's selectors had seen fit to bring Don Bradman back in place of Ponsford and Ted A'Beckett and Ron Oxenham for Nothling and Ironmonger. Hele regards the omission of Ironmonger for a Melbourne Test in an era of uncovered wickets as worthy of an Oscar for idiocy. And so it proved.

England, following victories by 675 runs and eight wickets, retained her Sydney side.

George Hele saw Victor Trumper score his 214 not out in 240 minutes for Australia against South Africa at Adelaide in 1910–11. This and Vic's 185 not out against England at Sydney in 1903 are said to be technically his two finest Test match innings.

This exact 100 of Kippax's at Melbourne, according to Hele, was "truly a Victor Trumper innings." I also watched it as a boy of sixteen, and I have seen no knock that approached nearer to perfection both in defence and attack. From the moment he entered to defy the

52

hostility of Larwood and Tate, whose deliveries were whipping consistently fast and stump-high from the shiny surface, Kippax moved back on to his wicket, making use of every inch of his crease. He stood like a swordsman at bay during the early stages of a duel in one of those old black and white films of Rudolph Valentino and Douglas Fairbanks Senior. When he had converted the bowling to a playable length, he moved on to the offensive with the most glorious cover hits and hooks my memory still holds. I can see them, like framed masterpieces of the art of batsmanship, even today, forty-six years later.

Eventually, as he and his captain gained some command of the crisis, he began to hook the bumpers of Larwood so devastatingly that Chapman stationed three men on the leg boundary—one behind and another forward of square and the third behind mid-wicket.

I can see those fieldsmen still, cannoning into one another along the white rails, in vain endeavour to cut off those hooks which travelled with the flat trajectory of a rifle bullet.

When Ryder tried to emulate Kippax he flicked a bumper from Larwood from the back of the shoulder of his bat full on to the cream tarpaulin behind fine-leg. This was one of only three sixes ever hit from Larwood's bowling in Australia. The other two were struck by that "Guy de Maupassant of cricket," Herbie Gamble, of Queensland in 1932–33 and by Vic Richardson at Adelaide Oval earlier in 1928. Gamble's six travelled over cover, Richardson's into the rear row of seats in the George Giffen Stand from a hook stroke.

Ryder's six was equally as memorable because it came from the back of the shoulder of his bat and almost took his left ear along with it. He has endured a deal of chaffing on the score of that stroke ever since, but blandly replies, "I hit the ball and it went for six."

Patsy Hendren struck another freak six during his 169 at Brisbane in the First Test. The ball landed in a drain pipe on top of the pavilion. Hele and Elder called for another ball as the original one seemed unretrievable in reasonable time. Later a Queensland official asked Hele for a ball as a souvenir. He told him he could climb up and collect the one in the drain pipe on top of the pavilion, but fancies it is still there.

Before the second Australian innings of the Second Test had begun Herbie Collins, always a gambler and eventually a bookmaker, had bet one of his cronies Australia would total 400. Australia scored 397.

53

Collins doubled his bet before this first Australian innings at Melbourne. Australia again scored 397. "And they call me 'Horseshoe' and 'Lucky' Collins," was Herbie's comment.

Kippax (100) and Ryder (112) took Australia from three for 57 to four for 218. Then Bradman came in, bent upon personal redemption mixed with revenge. He had watched the sixes of Ryder and Hendren, but he was playing for his career as well as for his country and he showed no disposition to emulate them. On New Year's Eve of 1928 he set about laying the foundation for the phenomenal Test match career that was to bring him 6,996 runs at an average of 99·94. Those unpredictable selectors were not to receive a second opportunity of omitting him, or diverting him from his ambition—not if he could help it. He batted very soundly and circumspectly for 195 minutes for his 79. His innings read like a New Year's resolution.

Assisted by A'Beckett (41), he took Australia well on its way to that second 397 in succession. England had a score to chase this time and a more varied attack to overcome. Thanks to Hammond's second consecutive double century and another vital innings of 62 from Jardine, she totalled 417 and led by 20 on the first innings. Don Blackie's six for 94 from forty-four overs on a perfect pitch was a noble performance from a tall and spindly man of forty-six.

Significant centuries from Woodfull (107) and Bradman (112) in Australia's second innings 351, following those from Kippax and Ryder in its first, suggested our batsmen were finding confidence together.

"When Don reached his first Test hundred," says Hele, "I've never seen a man more pleased than he was. Ron Oxenham walked down the pitch to shake his hand. While he was doing so a number of the Englishmen sat on the ground. Even at this stage of his career they seemed to have taken a dislike to 'The Don.' This, I believe, was because of his demeanour, because of his sheer enjoyment in success. I think they mistook Don's manner for conceit, whereas he was never conceited—merely a realist who loved batting and never tried to conceal it.

"I wondered even then, though, if he remembered that remark of Maurice Tate's and, today, feel sure he did. Eventually Dave Elder and I had to order the Englishmen to get up and get on with the game. Jardine was not among the players who had gone to ground. He was in the outfield and I should like to stress right now, in view of what is to come later, that Douglas was immaculate in his sportsmanship in 1928–29 and a delightful person to deal with throughout that series.

"On one occasion when Dave Elder and I had taken the field following an interval on an extremely hot day, Jardine walked to the stumps which, in those days, had brass ferrules (since banned). He took hold of the stumps by the ferrules and pulled his hands away quickly.

"'My goodness, George,' he said, 'it must be 100° or more judging by the feel of those stumps.'"

"Farmer" White had delivered fifty-seven overs, including thirty maidens, of slow left-hand orthodox spinners in the first innings. He bowled 56·5 more, twenty of them maidens, in the second innings to finish with a match analysis of 113·5/50/171/6. According to Hele, his extreme economy came from subtle variation of flight rather than the ability to spin the ball. He flighted the ball more cleverly than his successor Hedley Verity, but gained less turn. White had perhaps the finest off side cordon in Hendren (mid-off), Hobbs (cover), Chapman (gully), and Hammond (slip), that England has fielded.

John Cornish White was born in Somerset in 1891, the same year as Ron Oxenham and Clarrie Grimmett. He began playing for Somerset in 1909. He was a farmer, as his nickname suggests, and as formidable a poker player as Herbert Collins.

Farmers are prone to spend a great deal of their time alone. Possibly, according to George Hele, that is why White rarely spoke to anyone on a cricket field.

"During the Fourth Test at Adelaide, Jack Ryder cocked up a sitting return catch to White. White incomprehensibly dropped it. Then he just stood there like a statue with the ball at his feet. Ryder returned to his crease, thinking all his Christmases had come at one and the same time. White still stood transfixed. Eventually, after what seemed an age, Percy Chapman strolled over from point and picked up the ball. Handing it to White, he said, 'What's the matter, Jack?' White took the ball and said, 'I dropped it.' Those are about the only words I ever heard him utter."

At stumps at Melbourne on 3 January, the fifth night of the Third Test, Australia, 397 and eight for 347, led by 327. Heavy rain fell during that night, rain that did a great deal of good to "Dainty"

Ironmonger's beloved garden down at St Kilda, but little to improve his mood over breakfast when the sun was shining on his agapanthus.

One of Melbourne's dreaded crust-top, soft sub-soil "stickies" seemed a certainty and old-timers at the ground, including Joe Darling, Hugh Trumble, Monty Noble, Clem Hill, and Jack Worrell, were in splendid unanimity that "England would be lucky to get between 75 and 100."

I was staying with my favourite uncle, Norval "Pat" Dooley, at Ivanhoe. We had watched every ball of the Test. My uncle, however, loves taking long walks more than most things in life. When he suffered a mild coronary in his late seventies, his family had to dissuade him from climbing Mount Kosciusko the week after his release from hospital.

"It'll all be over before lunch, let's go for a hike," my uncle said. And, as he *was* my host, we walked forty miles that day, and returned to Ivanhoe to become involved with friends of my uncle's, who were on their honeymoon, but discovered from the groom that England was one for 171, that the wicket had recovered, and that 162 runs were needed on the morrow.

Thus did I miss seeing the most classic exhibition of batting on a Melbourne "sticky" (the worst kind of wicket in the world) that Test cricket can have produced.

But George Hele, whose uncles resided in Adelaide, remembers the day's play well.

"I umpired both this Test and also the one in 1931–32 when South Africa scored 36 and 45—Ironmonger five for 6 and six for 18—and can say without hesitation that the one on which England scored seven for 332—Hobbs 49, Sutcliffe 135, Jardine 33, Hendren 45, and Hammond 32 run out—was the more difficult of the two.

"Australia was all out 351 and led by 331. The pitch began to improve between 3 p.m. and 4 p.m. on that Friday and continued to do so after tea. The difference between the situation that day and three years later was that Ironmonger was absent in 1928–29 and present in 1931–32 and that the England batsmen showed superior ability on a sticky wicket.

"England faced only two overs before lunch, owing to the delay in resumption that morning. In the first over after lunch Hobbs gave an easy chance to Hendry in slips off A'Beckett. Then he began to play the finest innings I've seen on a bad wicket. He concentrated

56

on defence. This was no time for division of intention. Blackie bowled, for the most part, at the line of the stumps, turning towards the leg. Hobbs contrived to make his bowling look almost unplayable, which it was not. It was during this period that Ryder, I believe, made his most costly mistakes of the series. He did not experiment with Grimmett until the wicket had passed its worst. When Grimmett was brought on to bowl it was too late for him to be dangerous. In the outcome he took two for 96 from forty-two overs. I also believe Ryder should have bowled himself much earlier instead of Hendry, who concentrated on and outside the off stump, but gained no lift. For A'Beckett the ball kept popping erratically and unpredictably. If Ryder, a fast-medium, had come on and bowled at the stumps I believe Australia would have won the Test comfortably.

"Ryder was thirty-nine years old, I realise, but ten overs at his pace would have done the trick. Hobbs and Sutcliffe played the dead bat game to perfection—favouring top or left hand, as they call it now. Ryder crowded his fields close to both batsmen—the closest at short square-leg about ten feet from the bat, the other two behind square.

"At tea England was none for 78. Just before tea Hobbs signalled for a new bat and gave the bat carrier a message for Chapman. This was to send Jardine in at the fall of the first wicket. Hobbs kept the bat he was using, I noticed. Jardine was not needed before tea. It was 5 p.m. before Hobbs left, l.b.w. to Blackie, playing forward. As cutting was far too dangerous, he and Sutcliffe had gathered their runs mainly in front of the wicket, running the short singles for which they were famous.

"When he did come in at one for 105, Jardine began shakily. The wicket was less dangerous now and he improved, playing with great courage and assisted by the odd stroke of luck. Sutcliffe and Jardine added 66 and at stumps it was one for 171.

"Just prior to stumps being drawn Sutcliffe executed three full-blooded drives off Grimmett, forcing Vic Richardson to vacate the silly-point position. I sensed the significance of those gestures at such a time.

"Sutcliffe stayed on the seventh day, the second Saturday, until England needed only 14 for victory. The pitch had rolled out well in the morning. Sticky wickets of the type the Englishmen overcame are exclusive to Australia. England's sun is not hot enough to bake the surfaces of pitches hard above the soft sub-soil. More praise,

57

therefore, to Hobbs, Sutcliffe, and Jardine, who batted when the pitch was at its most unpredictable.

"It is inexcusable, however, that six Australian bowlers, considered worthy of Test selection and averaging more than thirty years of age, had not learned to bowl on a wicket such as this one in an era when pitches were not covered in any class of cricket."

The best they could do was:

Grimmett 42/12/96/2
Oxenham 28/10/44/1
Blackie 39/11/75/1

All the honours and the Ashes were with England. The forty-six-year-old Hobbs had outwitted the forty-six-year-old Blackie, but it is appropriate and significant to emphasise that during the first two Tests Oldfield had allowed only two byes while England scored 1,510 runs. During England's second innings at Melbourne he allowed 15 byes and 14 leg-byes came, too.

These sundries vouch for the state of that wicket.

Batting's Rupert Brooke

GEORGE HELE HAS WATCHED EVERY TEST MATCH PLAYED AT THE Adelaide Oval since 1903–04 except those of 1958–59 between England and Australia and 1973–74 between New Zealand and Australia. The most memorable innings of these twenty-three Tests, to him, are Victor Trumper's 214 not out against South Africa in 1910–11, Don Bradman's 299 not out against South Africa in 1931–32, and Archie Jackson's 164 against England in 1928–29.

It was during Trumper's knock that Springbok googly bowler R. O. Schwarz, who claims to have helped invent the bosie with B. J. T. Bosanquet on a billiard table during a game at Cambridge University just before the turn of the century, said to his skipper Percy Sherwell, "I don't know how to bowl to him."

"You're not trying to get him out, are you?" replied Sherwell.

"Of course. What do you think I'm trying to do?"

"Forget it. When the time comes he'll get himself out."

On this occasion Trumper didn't. He remained 214 not out after 240 minutes. During these four hours he struck 26 fours.

It was during the 1932–33 Bodyline series that Sir Pelham Warner told Hele another story of Trumper. "Plum" was England's captain in that first of the Tests Hele watched at Adelaide Oval, the Test of 1903–04. In it Trumper scored 113 and 59 as an opening batsman.

59

When Len Braund was bowling, Trumper kept striking fours through cover. Warner kept reinforcing his off side field to narrow the gaps between mid-off and cover and between cover and point.

"Put another man there, Mr Warner, and see if I can get the ball through," Victor said.

Warner stationed his fifth man in the off side cordon. Trumper cover drove the next ball for another four. Warner put an extra man in the covers and ordered Braund to bowl wider of the off stump. Braund pitched the next ball about 18 inches outside the off stump and Trumper pulled it over mid-on for four.

Archie Jackson's maiden Test century, also as an opening batsman, ranks next in Hele's opinion to that 214 not out of Trumper's in 1910–11 and the 299 not out of Bradman's in 1931–32. We shall come to it chronologically.

England's victory in the Third Test of 1928–29 at Melbourne decided the series in her favour and meant she had retained the Ashes. Interest in this "Series of the Masters" had not declined in Adelaide, however.

Known as the "City of Churches," though its hotels outnumbered its cathedrals, churches, and synagogues by at least two to one, Adelaide was lucky, in the 1920s, if it saw one Test match every four years. The Fourth Test of 1928–29, played from 1 to 8 February, was to give the people of Adelaide their first chance of watching Walter Hammond and Don Bradman in this class of cricket. It also was to provide their first and last chance of watching Hobbs, Sutcliffe, and Hammond in one England side.

England made no change in its team; Australia dropped Adelaide's cricketing and footballing hero, Victor Richardson, and brought in the nineteen-year-old Archie Jackson to open with Woodfull. After Chapman won the toss, Hobbs and Sutcliffe began with a stand of 143, but England slumped to four for 179. Though Chapman 39 and Hendren 13 alone supported him, Hammond, 119 not out, steered England to 334, a total which seemed within Australia's reach.

The Scotland-born Jackson leaned forward to the first ball he faced from Maurice Tate, one directed in line with his leg stump. Believing the ball had struck Jackson's pads, Tate threw up his arms and appealed for l.b.w. The ball had flashed to the boundary at fine-leg. When Tate realised the youngster had glanced it, he turned to Hele and said, "This kid'll get 100."

60

Woodfull had left, caught Duckworth off Tate for 1. Hendry had followed in the same fashion to Larwood and Kippax was bowled "Farmer" White for 3 with the total three for 19. When Ryder joined Jackson he gave him constant encouragement.

"That's it, son." "Stick to it, son." "You'll be all right, son," he kept saying—between overs and between boundaries. His words were not wasted.

Jackson and Ryder took the score to 145 before Ryder was l.b.w. to White for 63. The twenty-year-old Bradman joined the nineteen-year-old Jackson, who was within a boundary of his century, with Australia four for 201 at lunch on the third morning.

At that time only two Australians, Charles Bannerman in 1877 and Harry Graham in 1893, had scored a century for Australia in the *first* innings of their first Test.

The total had reached 200; Chapman had the right to take the new ball. Behind the George Giffen Stand during lunch Jackson came to Hele. "George, get him to use the old ball," he said. Hele replied, "First the answer is 'No' and secondly why should you worry what ball he uses?"

On their way to the crease Bradman had what he calls the "temerity" to offer Jackson advice. Larwood *had* taken the new ball.

"There's no hurry. Take your time and the century will come," Don said.

Larwood's first ball to Jackson after lunch was about eighteen inches outside the off stump, and just short of a length. Hele declares he never saw it until it rebounded about fifty yards from the pickets behind point. Jackson 100 or 101—neither George nor Don, according to the latter's *Farewell to Cricket,* are certain.

Jackson's 164, Bradman's 40, A'Beckett's 36, and Oldfield's 32 helped Australia to 369, a lead of 35.

By the end of Australia's innings, Larwood was down to half pace, and taking snuff! White had delivered sixty six-ball overs to take five for 130. In the second innings, he delivered 64·5 more for a reward of eight for 126, making his match analysis 124·5/37/256/13. In two Tests he had now bowled 237·5 overs, eighty-seven maidens, to take twenty for 425 and, at the end of this double stint, was heard to break his silence: "I used up a few shirts and one or two whiskies and sodas," he confessed.

During a quiet spell in this Australian innings a barracker called,

"Bowl him a piano and see if he can play that." Walter Hammond picked up a wandering sheet of newspaper, brought it to George Hele, and was told, "Put it in your own pocket. I'm not a garbage tin."

Four years, almost to the day, after his debutant century, Archie Jackson died of tuberculosis at the age of twenty-three, the very day that Australia lost the Ashes to England in the Fourth Test at Brisbane. The pall-bearers of this young Rupert Brooke of Australian batsmanship included Bill Woodfull, Vic Richardson, Bill Ponsford, and Don Bradman.

England lost its great opening batsmen Hobbs 1 and Sutcliffe 17, before Hammond and Jardine became associated in a third-wicket stand of 262. Hammond, who finished with 177, should have been out before he reached his second century for the match. Grimmett was bowling from Hele's end at the time and Hammond spooned the ball back towards Jardine, who was positioned on the leg side end of the popping crease. Grimmett ran to catch the ball, but Jardine stood fast where he was, left hand on hip and elbow pointing towards Grimmett. Clarrie collided with the elbow and, according to Hele, was thus prevented from making an easy catch. The ball dropped to the ground in front of Jardine.

According to George, Grimmett was angry and said to him, "He did that on purpose." Hele ignored the remark but, when Grimmett passed him at the end of the over, he said, "That was deliberate." Hele still said nothing.

After play that day Vic Richardson, who had watched the incident from a good vantage point in the George Giffen Stand, approached Grimmett in George's hearing and asked, "Did you appeal for that interference by Jardine?" Clarrie replied, "No, but it *was* deliberate." Vic retorted, "You bloody fool, Grum. Why didn't you appeal in the correct way?"

At this moment Percy Fender approached and asked "Had there been an appeal, George, who would have been out?" Hele said, "There was no appeal." Fender repeated his question and Hele repeated his answer. George doesn't give much away—except at a bar in the form of beers.

We gathered there had been a discussion in the Press Box, where Fender was covering the tour for the London *Star*. Had there been an appeal, he would have given Hammond out because, under Law 40, the striker is out. The Law reads: "Either batsman is out

'Obstructing the field'—If he wilfully obstructs the opposite side; should such wilful obstruction by either batsman prevent a ball from being caught it is the striker who is out."

If and when they revise the Laws of Cricket they could pay some attention to punctuation. The bowler does not benefit from the wicket when a batsman is given out for obstruction. Heaven knows why. Grimmett *would* have got the wicket in the Hammond–Jardine–Grimmett case but for the obstruction and, had he done so, should have had it credited to his analysis.

Grimmett could have done with the bonus. He took twenty-three for 1,024 in the series at 44·52 and failed to take Hammond's wicket once. Wally added another 100-odd runs after his escape before being caught and bowled by Ryder at 177. His innings took 440 minutes and Jardine's 98 lasted 345 minutes.

In the outcome, thanks to a brilliant but brief display by Maurice Tate, who hit 47 from Number 10, England reached 383—a lead of 348. Grimmett's failure to appeal for that obstruction probably cost Australia the match. England won it by 12 runs.

A section of the crowd gained the wrong impression regarding Bill Woodfull's motives when he and Archie Jackson began Australia's second innings. Woodfull was giving his young partner the same kind of encouragement Ryder had in the first innings. The crowd thought he was trying to restrain his stroke-play. They heckled Woodfull after he had walked down to Jackson and said, "Keep it up, Jacko." Jackson lost his wicket to George Geary soon afterward when his aggregate for the Test was an exact 200.

Woodfull took another heckling in consequence and it may have had something to do with his own departure for 30 at two for 71. Australian barrackers do not always help their own side.

Hendry's quick dismissal made it three for 74 but Ryder, partnered by Kippax, played another fine captain's hand for 87, following his first innings 63. It was during this fourth-wicket stand of 137 that White dropped that "dolly," as George calls it, of a catch from Ryder. It was an easier one than that which Hammond returned to Grimmett in the first innings. Kippax did not interfere with White.

When Kippax left for 51, Australia, four for 211, needed only 138 to gain its first victory of the series, its first against England since February 1925.

The climax came when Bradman and Bert Oldfield were associated

63

and the total was transcending 300. Oldfield played a ball towards Hobbs at cover. Hobbs, Hele is certain, deliberately fumbled the ball to induce Oldfield to call Bradman, who had shown himself to be thoroughly in control of the bowling and the situation. Hobbs retrieved the ball swiftly but, for once, made a bad return to Duckworth. The throw came well to the off side of the stumps as Bradman dashed at his fastest pace for sanctuary. Duckworth gathered the return brilliantly and swept the stumps down in one and the same action.

Hele was standing at square-leg and in a first-class position to judge. He says, "Don was out by at least two yards when the wicket was broken. It was one of the simplest run-out decisions I've ever had to give, sad as I was to see Don go—being an Australian as well as the umpire."

Don had made 58 and Australia needed 29 runs with only Grimmett and Don Blackie to bat. White finished the innings with the help of catches by Tate and Larwood. Blackie's lack of resistance was particularly pathetic. With 13 needed for victory he skied a cross bat pull towards where the Victor Richardson Gates now stand and Larwood went down on one knee to make certain England would lead four-nil. Perhaps it was appropriate that Blackie was wearing long black socks under those stovepipe trousers of his. White's eight for 126 from 64·5 overs warrants the use of that much-abused word "marathon."

It was Lord Byron who wrote: "The mountains look on Marathon and Marathon looks on the sea." The Australians were now looking upon Melbourne and their last chance of claiming a win.

Our selectors at long last awakened to the need for youth and life in Australia's opening attack. They brought in Tim Wall, Percy Hornibrook, and Alan Fairfax, whose ages averaged twenty-five, in place of Hendry, Blackie, and A'Beckett, whose ages averaged thirty-three. As a forty-six-year-old, Blackie had taken fourteen wickets at 31·71 from 210 overs, fifty-one of them maidens, a performance even "Rowdy" Mallett might envy.

The oldest Test players to take part in Anglo-Australian Tests have included:

Dr W. G. Grace—fifty years and eleven months and captain in the Trent Bridge Test of 1899. He scored 28 and 1 and in Australia's first innings delivered twenty overs for 31 runs.

64

Wilfred Rhodes—forty-nine years and ten months at the Oval in 1926. Rhodes took six for 79 from forty-five overs and scored 28 and 14.

Herbert Ironmonger—forty-nine years and ten months (don't believe *Wisden*) in the Fifth Test of 1932–33. He bowled fifty-seven overs, eight-ball overs at that, to take two for 96.

Jack Hobbs—forty-seven years and eight months in the Oval Test of 1930. He scored 47 and 9. In his last Test in Australia, the Test we are about to describe, he scored 142 and 65 at the age of forty-seven years and two months.

Frank Woolley—forty-seven years and three months in the Oval Test of 1934. Woolley scored 4 and 0 and, as substitute wicket-keeper in Australia's second innings 327, allowed 37 byes.

More modern Australian champions like Keith Miller, Richie Benaud, Bobby Simpson, Neil Harvey, Norman O'Neill, Alan Davidson, Graham McKenzie, and Bill Lawry either retire or are dispensed with when they are comparative "chickens."

I suppose it's all part of an age in which a "typical teenager," profiled in the *Queen* Magazine in April 1962, was reported as saying, "I expect I'll be dead by the time I'm thirty. We all will. It's the strain, you know."

It is, indeed, a miracle that cricket has survived the 1960s. Perhaps it is a change for the young, nowadays, to find something which fundamentally has not changed.

In 1928–29 England had played the first four Tests with only one alteration in cast—Geary for Mead, following the first match. Its captain, Percy Chapman, suffering from influenza, and Herbert Sutcliffe, ordered to rest owing to an injured arm, were replaced by Ernest Tyldesley and Maurice Leyland in the Fifth Test at Melbourne, Jardine partnering Hobbs as an opener.

There was a change, too, in the umpiring cast, Alf Jones coming back to a fold he had joined first in 1903–04 to replace Dave Elder. Jones officiated in one Test in each of the 1903–04, 1907, 1911–12, 1920–21, 1924–25, and 1928–29 seasons. He must have felt like Dame Nellie Melba or that less imposing, but equally ubiquitous personage "Off agin, on agin, gone agin" Finnegan. Dave Elder was sixty-five years of age and had umpired fourteen Tests, beginning in 1911–12. Alf was nearly seventy.

Hele and Jones had a comparative holiday in the Fifth Test as only fourteen wickets fell during the first four of the eight days play, and only three of the fourteen required a decision on appeal.

The match was also remarkable in that Hobbs scored the last of his twelve centuries against Australia in this his last Test in Australia and Leyland scored the first of his seven centuries against Australia in the same match, his *first* Test in Australia. Patsy Hendren was unfortunately dismissed for 95 in *his* last Test in Australia. Few Australians who watched and knew him would have begrudged him those five runs.

When England began with 519, nobody could have foreseen her defeat—especially her defeat by five wickets. It was during that innings that Hugh Trumble, Clem Hill, and J. C. Davis ("Not Out" of the *Referee*) asked George Hele whom he regarded as the greatest outfieldsman of his experience. The three of them spent some time over the question. When Hele replied "Bradman," Davis said, "We three have just reached the same conclusion."

It was a tribute to Don because Trumble had played in thirty-two Tests and Hill in forty-nine. Hill was a great outfieldsman himself. Davis was generally acknowledged to be Australia's most respected cricket writer of the years between the World Wars. Hele still regards Bradman, even post-Sheahan, as the finest out-fielder he has seen, "because of his anticipation, speed of foot in interception, and the phenomenal accuracy of his throw from any distance."

Hobbs played one of his most masterly innings until, when the shadow of the grandstand cut the wicket in two (this time sideways) towards the close, he lost sight of a ball and was bowled by Ryder. Hobbs' 142 came out of 235 and it set a golden seal upon his unparalleled performances as an opening batsman in Australia.

On four tours of Australia extending across seventeen years Hobbs batted thirty-seven times in Tests to score 2,191 runs at the magnificent average of 60·86. His average was assisted by only one not out. His Test figures for the four tours are:

	Innings	Not out	Highest score	Aggregate	Average
1911–12	9	1	187	662	82·75
1920–21	10	0	123	505	50·50
1924–25	9	0	154	573	63·66
1928–29	9	0	142	451	50·11

Top left: "The Old Firm", Sutcliffe and Hobbs, going in to open for England in the Second Test of the 1928–29 series. *Top right:* George Hele, as caricatured by Arthur Mailey. *Bottom:* With characteristic grace, Hammond drives a ball on the Sydney Cricket Ground

To
George

Arthur
Mailey
'53

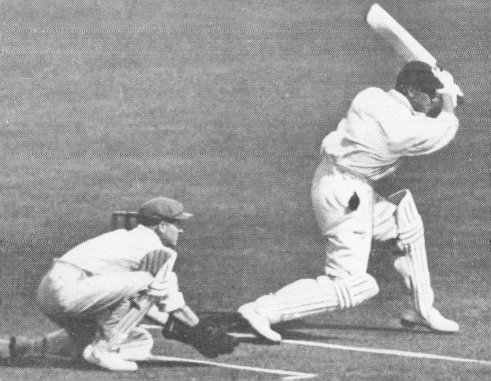

No more convincing argument for the advantages of copy-book correctness can have been catalogued than this monument John Berry Hobbs left for our admiration and wonder.

Only R. E. Foster, 287 at Sydney in 1903–04, W. G. Grace, 152 at the Oval in 1880, and George Gunn, 119 at Sydney in 1907–08, scored centuries on debut for England against Australia before Maurice Leyland got his 137 from Number 7 in this innings. When Australia batted, Leyland celebrated by gulping down beers offered him through the rails along the boundary, establishing a precedent which Denis Compton was not loth to follow in Brisbane in 1950–51. The broad beam of Leyland's backside was equalled by his Yorkshire smile and he became, and remained, one of the most popular cricketers England has sent to Australia.

For Australia Woodfull, a well-deserved 102, and Bradman 123, led the resistance movement. Bradman's was a classic innings, the one that really put him on the map of Test match cricket. Of this innings, however, Percy Fender wrote: "Bradman is such a curious mixture of brilliant and very mediocre batting. He will make a number of glorious shots and then, in attempting another, he will fluke the ball in some totally different direction to that intended, and practically always just out of a fielder's reach."

Later Fender was to say of Bradman: "He will always be in the category of the brilliant, if unsound, ones . . . he does not inspire one with any confidence that he desires to take the only course that will lead him to a fulfilment of that promise . . . he does not correct a mistake or look as if he were trying to do so."

Fender played in thirteen Tests for England, captained Surrey for many years and was regarded as one of the outstanding judges of the game in the land which gave it birth. But his predictions concerning "The Don" read like those of an ancient weather prophet who predicted droughts on the eve of Noah's flood.

In my opinion, the difference between Bradman's batting and that of the more graceful Kippax, Jackson, and McCabe, was that Bradman did all the work himself when executing his strokes; the other three allowed the ball to do some of the work for them. Bradman's was the sounder method, as his results reveal. He left far less to chance and this, ironically, is where Fender went wrong.

Modern curators may wonder how a Melbourne Test wicket could play almost perfectly for eight days with an intervening Sunday.

Top: Chapman caught (as well as stumped!) by Oldfield in the Brisbane Test of 1928. *Bottom:* Hobbs steps out to drive Grimmett during the Second Test of the same series

The answer, of course, is in the soil. The M.C.G. used Merri Creek soil in 1928–29. The first deliveries to behave at all erratically came on the seventh day of play. One of them hit Kippax in the chest, and the other hit wicketkeeper Duckworth in the neck. Then all life went out of the pitch.

In the meantime England increased its 28-run first innings lead to 285. Tim Wall followed his first innings 49/8/123/3 with 26/5/66/5, despite Hobbs' 65 and Leyland's 53 not out.

During his second innings Leyland said to Wall within Hele's hearing, "You're a certainty for England in 1930." "I wish you meant it," replied Tim. "I'll bet you a tenner if you like," responded Maurice.

Though Leyland scored 190 runs for once out in that Test, those were the only words George Hele heard him utter throughout the eight days.

It was towards the end of the sixth day that Ryder sent Oldfield and Percy Hornibrook to open Australia's second innings with 287 needed for victory. These night-watchmen, normally Number 8 and Number 11, were still together until the last ball before lunch on the seventh day, though Larwood and Tate did their utmost to dismiss them. When Australia was 51 without loss, Hornibrook fell, bowled by Hammond. Hammond also bowled Oldfield 48, and Woodfull 35, but Larwood and Tate went wicketless through Australia's five for 287.

Larwood's figures for this Test were one for 168 from 66·1 overs and suggest very strongly that he benefited tremendously from the Bodyline field four years later.

Hornibrook, be it not forgotten, scored 26 from Number 11 in his first innings and Umpire Alf Jones, in his 70th year, stood through the eight days without a shooting-stick.

Fittingly, Jack Ryder was 57 not out in partnership with Bradman, 37 not out, when victory came after 707 overs and two balls. Of these White 93·3, and George Geary 101, contributed 194·3. Geary's eighty-one overs in Australia's first innings remained a Test record until Fleetwood Smith eighty-seven, and O'Reilly eighty-five, surpassed it at the Oval almost ten years later.

During the entire series John Cornish White, almost invariably under that white washing hat for which he will be remembered, took a wicket every 97·6 deliveries while establishing an analysis of

68

406·4/134/760/25/30·40 and the all-time low-frequency record for wickets in Tests.

Marathon upon marathon perhaps best describes the rubber.

After the series, the M.C.C. manager Sir Frederick Toone invited Hele to be his team's guest on the Adelaide Express for dinner at Ballarat and breakfast at Murray Bridge. At breakfast George congratulated Walter Hammond on his 905 runs for the series.

"Thank you, George," replied Wally, "that will remain a record for a long while. It must be broken in Australia, where matches are played to a finish. You couldn't do it in England."

Within eighteen months, as we have seen, Don Bradman was to aggregate 974 runs in five Tests on his first tour of England.

On arrival at Adelaide on the Sunday morning, Hele was met by his wife Matilda and his son, Ray, later to become a first-class match umpire in Melbourne. Several yards along the Adelaide Railway Station he was encircled by a group of friends.

"Are you ready, George?" one of them asked.

"Ready for what?"

"You promised to umpire our game on the parklands today—our final."

The match was the final of the Hotels' Association competition and George had forgotten all about it and his promise. Matilda raised no objection. Two hours after the arrival of the Melbourne Express George was behind new sets of stumps and he stayed there for six more hours.

His fee for that one day's umpiring was ten pounds—exactly the sum he had received for standing through the eight-day Test.

He consoles himself with the thought that, tragically, Archie Jackson was never to play for his country in Australia again and that he would not have missed umpiring for that beautiful 164 of Jackson's at Adelaide if he had had to pay for the privilege.

Constantine and Company

T HERE IS A PHRASE IN ITALIAN WHICH FORTUNATELY IS LARGELY true of human nature: *Non rammentare che le ora felici*. In English this means "Remember only the happy hours." Perhaps this is why George Hele and I are strongly of the opinion there was far more depth and delight in Australian cricket in the 1920s and 1930s, particularly the late 1920s, than has existed since the second World War.

Lesser-light South Australian Sheffield Shield players such as Jack Nitschke, Jack Rymill, Gordon Harris, Brian Hone (later Oxford University captain), Roy Lonergan, Tom Carlton, and that aesthetically satisfying stroke player, Colin Alexander, to us seemed, and still seem, superior to their 1972–73 successors like McCarthy, Jeff Hammond, Barnes, the Causbys, and Curtin.

They certainly had more colour, or what is now called "charisma."

The same, we believe, can be said of Victoria's "Bull" Alexander, Keith Rigg, Hector Oakley, Jack Ledward, and Jack Ellis; New South Wales' Hal Hooker, Hughie Chilvers, Alan Marks, Arthur Allsop, and Bill Howell; and Queensland's Leo O'Connor, Roy Levy, "Pud" Thurlow, Herbie Gamble, and Frank Thompson.

Only a few of these gained their Australian caps and none of them wore them long, unless perhaps nostalgically in their gardens.

70

Of all these "second-string" Australians the most colourful were Jack "Slinger" Nitschke, Tom Carlton, Jack Ellis, "Bull" Alexander, Hal Hooker, Arthur Allsop, and Herbie Gamble.

Jack Nitschke is nationally famous today as a breeder of bloodstock horses and the owner of the 1972 South Australian, Victorian, Western Australian, and Australian Derbies winner, and 1972 Perth Cup winner, Dayana. Had he taken his batting as seriously as he takes his horse breeding he might have become one of Australia's outstanding left-handed batsmen. But he played in only two Tests, scoring 53 runs in two innings at 26.50. In 1932–33 Jack hooked and cut Harold Larwood in an opening stand for South Australia with Vic Richardson in a manner that only Stan McCabe was to emulate that summer. Nitschke took deep delight in lofting those left-handers Bert Ironmonger and Hedley Verity into the Creswell Gardens, near where the Victor Richardson Gates now stand.

Many Adelaideans still wonder why Holmesdale Charles Nitschke is invariably called "Jack," or "Slinger." He gained the first nickname during his first innings against Victoria. George Hele was one of the umpires and Jack Ellis the wicketkeeper.

"What's your name?" Ellis demanded when he took post behind Nitschke for the first time.

Nitschke was none too proud of his Christian names. His parents had been pretty unorthodox in allotting names. Two of his sisters had been christened Vestalia and Corinna. He ignored Ellis' question. Ellis repeated it and again received no reply.

"My name's Jack. I'll call you Jack," Ellis said, and the "Jack" stuck.

Even Nitschke's wife Ann (née McTaggart) was unable to tell me definitely how her husband came to be called "Slinger" when I asked her in his presence in the Windsor Hotel lounge one evening. She suspects it arose from the way he threw a cricket ball. "Jack" again maintained a pixy-like silence.

Any chance "Jack" had of inclusion in Woodfull's 1934 team to tour England ended at Brisbane during the 1933–34 Australian summer. He was determined to make the side. An onslaught upon "Dainty" Ironmonger at Melbourne, which saw several sixes soar into the old treble-decker stand beyond long-on, hadn't helped his cause as a substitute opener for Woodfull and Ponsford; the selectors were looking for soundness and solidity, not pure slogging. "Jack"

71

regained ground with a superbly played century against O'Reilly at the S.C.G. Unfortunately he was seated at the same table as former Queensland captain, Leo O'Connor, at a reception for the South Australian team on the eve of the following Shield match at Brisbane.

O'Connor spent what seemed hours extolling the virtues as a new-ball bowler of his son, Brian. "He's another Maurice Tate," said Leo. The next morning Nitschke hit seven fours from this Tate-in-embryo's first over and repeated the performance in the second innings. Unfortunately for his chances of going to England, "Jack" was dismissed from the last ball of each of those overs. Ernie Bromley got the left-handed batting slot in the Australian team.

"Jack" Nitschke is reputed to be a millionaire today, some say a multi-millionaire. But he was a superior batsman to Bromley and most of his friends feel he would sacrifice at least half his fortune to have been a member of Woodfull's side.

Jack Rymill, another left-hander, was as brilliant and fleet an out-fieldsman as South Australia has owned. Don Bradman had retired to the infield when he came to Adelaide in 1935–36. Rymill's most memorable batting performance was his 146 run out against Maurice Tate at the Adelaide Oval in March 1925. Tate took thirty-eight wickets in Tests against Australia that summer. No Australian Test batsman treated him as contemptuously as did Rymill that March.

There is little doubt that Rymill would have won his Australian cap had his employer not given him the choice between seeking Test status and promotion in Goldsbrough Mort. Jack chose his work and was rewarded when he became managing director of the amalgamated Elder Smith and Goldsbrough Mort pastoralist giant in the 1960s. Of his fielding along the boundary Charlie Macartney once said, "He runs so fast and so far during a day cutting off fours he'd run out of breath in England before the end of May."

Tom Carlton was a tall left-hand new-ball and spin bowler who hailed from Victoria. In our opinion, he was at least as good a bowler of his type as Percy Hornibrook, who represented Australia in six Tests.

In a game between South Australia and New South Wales in the late 1920s Carlton managed to get a leg-break past Don Bradman's bat. It grazed the off stump.

"Don't bowl it again, Tom,—not that one," his captain, Vic Richardson, warned.

Carlton did, the very next ball, and it landed on the mound.

Another South Australian left-hander was always having difficulty with his set of false teeth. Almost every time this bowler shouted an appeal, his teeth came to rest on the wicket. And he *was* one of cricket's most ambitious appealers.

"If you appeal frivolously again," called Vic Richardson, "I'll kick those teeth of yours the length of the wicket." The bowler paid no heed to the warning. He appealed again next ball. His teeth dropped in front of him. He dashed to retrieve them before Vic could honour his threat. Vic kicked at the teeth but contacted the bowler's hand and put him out of action for the match.

George Hele says he took great trouble to ensure *his* teeth were in trouble-free condition throughout his umpiring career.

Roy Lonergan, who scored twin centuries against Victoria just before the 1934 team to tour England was chosen, was one of the least-confident outfield catchers Adelaide ever owned. Roy made sure that any catch he held along the boundary looked like a miracle. He would judge the flight of the ball to ensure he was never right under a catch. He dallied in his movement towards the ball so he could reach it only with a last-second dive. If he caught it, the crowd cheered him loudly; if he dropped it his alibi was there. Not with Vic Richardson and other members of the team, who had got to know Roy and his ruse, however.

"Bull" Alexander, bowling for Victoria, was as fast through the air as most Australian bowlers. As his name suggests, he also created awe among batsmen, many of whom looked upon him as they looked upon film ogre Boris Karloff. Alexander's immortality rests on the bumper he bowled at Douglas Jardine in 1932–33 and the time he failed to appear when Victoria were nine for 103 before lunch at the M.C.G. against New South Wales—with Bill O'Reilly five for 22 at an average of 4·40.

Learning that Woodfull had won the toss, "Bull" left the ground and departed on what "Tiger" O'Reilly has described as a "mysterious mission." Returning from it ninety minutes later, he boarded a tram at the corner of Flinders and Spencer Streets. Victoria had a powerful batting side in 1932–33. It began with Woodfull and Ponsford.

"What's the score, Connie?" Alexander enquired of the conductor. ductor.

"We're all out," he replied.

73

"I mean the match at the M.C.G."

"We're all out, sir."

"We can't be all out," said "Bull." "*I'm* the last batsman!"

The conductor did his utmost to hurry that tram along Flinders Street and Wellington Parade. "Bull" was there for the first over of the New South Wales innings. Watchers, however, remarked upon the mysterious decline in his hostility and speed. He'd lost at the races.

Another player of that era who possessed considerable flair was New South Wales all-rounder Alan Fairfax. Had he been on deck in the 1960s, he might have played in many more Tests than the ten he did.

A tall, stately batsman and a lively late-lifting new-ball bowler, Fairfax literally walked out of cricket after being persistently barracked from the Hill on the Sydney Cricket Ground. He stalked off the field in high dudgeon, following a word to his captain Alan Kippax.

Transferring to England, he became proprietor of the first of several cricket coaching schools that sprang up before and after the second World War. Alf Gover followed his example in Surrey and Barry Knight now operates a similar establishment in Sydney.

His State captain, Alan Kippax, was the last person who would have expected Fairfax to succeed in a coaching capacity. Kippax' main trouble was getting him to stand in his appointed position in the field. Fairfax was prone to wander like a nomadic Afghan hound and Kippax came over and drew a circle about two yards in diameter on the turf. "Stay in that," he commanded. "What if the ball comes outside the ring?" Fairfax asked. "Still stay inside it," Kippax said, and Fairfax obeyed.

Herbie Gamble, of Victoria and Queensland, was, as we have seen, one of only three batsmen to strike Harold Larwood for six in Australia. Gamble was an eccentric; the six he hit from Larwood travelled over cover-point. As I was to discover on my first trip to Brisbane, he was also a devoted believer in the philosophy of Guy de Maupassant. Following my first dinner at Brisbane's Carlton Hotel, I was flirting (harmlessly of course) with a particularly pretty receptionist when an arm came round my shoulder. "Join me for a beer," ordered, rather than requested, Gamble.

At a table in the lounge he asked, "Haven't you read Guy de Maupassant?" "A little," I replied. "Well you haven't taken in very

74

much of him. His cardinal maxim was, 'never despoil your own doorstep.' " It was a lesson I've tried not to forget.

It was possibly because Australia had such a galaxy of talent at the close of the 1920s and felt more players should be tried in Tests, that the Board of Control invited the first West Indian side to Australia in 1930–31 and the second South African side here in 1931–32.

Cricket had not been made the plaything of politicians and racialists then. Apartheid, though it had existed naturally for 250 years, was still part of posterity in the statutes of South Africa and should have remained so. It was possible to invite a West Indian side one summer and a South African one the next without drawing a barrage of fire bombs on to the field or bedevilling the nation with strikes.

Australians were more mature, better informed, and more rational then. They believed that in a country professing democracy, individual citizens should have the right to decide for themselves whether or not to attend matches in which a team representing South Africa took part. They believed that this democratic choice should not be prejudiced and denied by the kind of people whose main criticism today of the Nationalist Government in South Africa rests upon that Government's denial of democratic rights to the majority of *its* own people.

How paradoxical—and all, apparently, to no avail.

A series of Test matches between Gary Sobers' 1968–69 side to Australia and Ali Bacher's Springboks would have produced one of the most exciting contests of all time. Imagine Barry Richards, Graeme Pollock, Mike Proctor, Eddie Barlow, Ali Bacher, Dennis Lindsay, and Lee Irvine batting against Wesley Hall, Charlie Griffith, and Lance Gibbs. Imagine Gary Sobers, Rohan Kanhai, Clive Lloyd, Seymour Nurse, and Basil Butcher batting against Mike Proctor, Peter Pollock, and Atholl McKinnon.

They would have provided a spectacle for the gods. The players of both the West Indies and South Africa were ready to meet one another. Politicians, greedy for votes, and young men and women, anxious for notoriety, have denied us cricket of a kind we have rarely had the privilege of watching.

Apartheid remains, and will remain, until someone can advance a viable alternative. Neither Sir Robert Menzies nor the late Adlai Stevenson, both of whom spent time in South Africa seeking a solution, were successful. Both admitted failure. In the meantime, the relatively ignorant rule out international matches with Springbok cricketers teams. Have any of the protestors lifted a finger to help non-white cricketers in South Africa in a practical way—by sending financial aid, for instance? The answer, of course, is "No." They are exploiting the sad situation in which South Africans need help not hate.

Mike Proctor, whose main role is fast bowling, scored six consecutive centuries in first-class cricket, in the years 1971 and 1972. Only Sir Donald Bradman and Charles Fry have performed this feat. Australia never saw Fry bat; she could have seen Proctor.

George Hele found the West Indian cricketers of the early 1930s different from any he had known and contends their successors of the 1950s and 1960s—the "Three Terrible Ws," Worrell, Walcott, and Weekes, and Sobers, Kanhai, and Conrad Hunte and company— were in the same category.

"A more popular group than Jack Grant's 1930–31 side," George says, "I have not met or umpired for. The most electrifying cricketer I have ever watched was in that side. His name was Learie Constantine. They called him 'Old Electric Heels' and he was a great fast bowler, a devastating stroke-player, and a phenomenally brilliant fieldsman. Sensation was his speciality.

"One day against South Australia at the Adelaide Oval he was bowling at his fastest. A batsman cocked the ball up towards square-leg. Learie caught the ball alongside the square-leg umpire after a total dash, including his run-up, of more than fifty yards at full gallop. He had to veer at the end of his follow-through to chase the falling ball, but he made the catch look easy while the other leg side fieldsmen stood paralysed in their positions."

On another occasion, Constantine threw the wicket down unsuccessfully from cover, chased the ball to mid-wicket, picked it up and ran the batsman out at the bowler's end. On a third occasion he ran forward from slip to hold a catch at silly-point.

The First Test of the 1930–31 Australian summer was played at Adelaide in December. George told Stan McCabe of that catch by Constantine in the game against South Australia. McCabe laughed incredulously. "He changed his mind about my veracity," Hele says, "when Constantine caught him in almost identical fashion when he was 90 and in full flurry during a fourth-wicket stand of 182 with Alan Kippax."

Constantine could field brilliantly anywhere—at slip, cover, silly-point, silly mid-on, along the boundary, *and* when bowling. The nearest approach George saw to those catches of his at Adelaide Oval was Gregory's attempt to catch Larwood in the Brisbane Test of 1928–29, the time Jack broke down.

Hele saw Grant's 1930–31 side in only three matches—the Adelaide Test and the two games against South Australia. The Great Depression had hit Australia. The Australian cricketing authorities had not realised what attractive cricketers the West Indians were. They decided to economise by using local umpires in the Tests in each State.

George Headley, in Hele's opinion, was one of the three finest batsmen in the world at the time—Bradman and Hammond being the others. Headley had scored four centuries against England—one at Bridgetown, two at Georgetown, and one at Kingston—in the West Indies in the 1929–30 series. He was to score 169 not out against England at Manchester in 1933, 270 not out against England at Kingston in 1935, and become the only batsman who had scored twin centuries in two Tests by making 106 and 107 against England at Lord's in 1939. All told, in forty Test innings, he scored 2,190 at 60·83 with ten centuries.

Early in the 1930–31 Australian tour Headley had difficulty in picking Grimmett's wrong-un. In the five Tests he scored 334 runs with two centuries at the average of 37·11. Grimmett dismissed him twice in the First Test, but not thereafter.

According to Hele, "Headley was a sound and a glorious stroke-player, mostly to the on side. Occasionally bowlers and fieldsmen said something out of place and undiplomatic to Headley. He would reply by awarding them the 'raspberry' so audibly it could be heard beyond the boundary. Headley was being playful, of course."

Headley gained great respect for Australian cricket in 1930–31, as he revealed in 1955 when he tipped Ian Johnson's underdog side to win the series in the Caribbean against a team including Worrell. Weekes, Walcott, Collie Smith, Ramadhin, Valentine, and Gary Sobers. The West Indians were highly confident of victory that year. Headley's prediction proved right, but unpopular.

"You may be surprised that I should class Headley above Ponsford, Kippax, McCabe, Woodfull, and Jackson as a batsman, but I was not alone in my judgement. I'd like to have had Ponsford, Kippax,

77

McCabe, Woodfull, and Jackson batting against Derek Underwood on that fungus fusorium at Headingley in 1972, but I'd have preferred Headley to any one of them," George says.

In that Adelaide Test of 1930–31 Kippax scored 146 and McCabe 90. After dismissing Ponsford 24 and Jackson 31, West Indian fast bowler George Francis was put out to browse along the boundary and stayed there all day. Hele fancies the reason for this was that Francis "performed" when refused an l.b.w. appeal against Kippax. The decision appeared almost to have broken his heart. Hele gave it.

Francis stood on the pitch with the ball at his feet. His captain, Grant, walked across and picked it up. He handed it to Francis, patted him on the shoulder and said, "Never mind, George. Try again." Francis remained unconsoled. "Was he out, George?" Grant asked his fast bowler. "No, the ball was pitched outside his off stump, but it would have bowled him," replied Francis. "Well, the umpire was right," said Grant. "Yes, but he shouldn't have had his leg there."

Francis still refused to be comforted and took post along the boundary when badly needed in the attack. Perhaps he believed Georges should stick together. Kippax simply sat on his bat and laughed.

This odd incident is reminiscent of one in which Bill O'Reilly figured in 1932. "The Tiger" beat a batsman with a vicious wrong-un and lifted the clouds with his appeal for l.b.w. The umpire declined the appeal, explaining that the ball had hit the edge of the bat before contacting the pad. "I know he hit it," growled O'Reilly. "That's where the bloody rule's wrong."

The coloured members of the 1930–31 West Indian side were an exceptionally temperamental bunch—on top of the world one minute and in deep despair the next, but always lovable.

George Hele believes Alan Kippax, on his showing that day at Adelaide, was an even more stylish stroke-player than Stan McCabe and he had the opportunity of watching them performing together from behind the stumps and from square-leg. George says, "The stroke-play of both was glorious to watch. They were different and yet the same. McCabe could be brutal in his batting, as he showed that day and at Sydney in 1932–33, Johannesburg in 1935–36, and Trent Bridge in 1938. Kippax, in my vision, rarely departed from sheer style. Except when hooking, he caressed rather than cracked the ball. He hooked like a fusilier."

Australia scored 376 in reply to the West Indians' 296. Grant followed his 53 not out in the first innings with 71 not out in the second and the visitors led by 169, when Australia began its fourth innings.

Archie Jackson and Bill Ponsford were again the openers. As they walked out together, Jackson said to Ponsford, "I see the skipper is padded up. We won't give him a hit."

They didn't. Jackson scored 70 and Ponsford 92 of none for 170 while Woodfull dallied in the dressingroom.

Whenever Don Bradman failed, it was time for his adversaries to beware. Don scored only 4 of Australia's 376 at Adelaide and followed this with 25 of Australia's 369 at Sydney on New Year's Day. This scarcely pleased the young man who had returned triumphantly from England in September with just about every record an Australian could break in England in his bag.

Alan Kippax had scored 146 in the Adelaide Test and Stan McCabe 90. At Sydney, Bill Ponsford followed his 92 not out at Adelaide with 183. As the West Indies were dismissed for 107 and 90 in reply to that 369, Don again received no second chance. By the time he reached Brisbane in mid-January he was raring to go. Archie Jackson's duck brought Australia's two most prolific scorers Ponsford and Bradman together at one for 1. Before they were separated it was one for 230.

For reasons nobody has satisfactorily explained, Don and "Ponnie" had not succeeded in partnership before and were not to do so again until the last two Tests of 1934 in England, when they produced those incredible partnerships of 388 for the fourth wicket and 451 for the second wicket at Headingley and the Oval.

Watching them together in this Third Test against the West Indians was like watching those great Spanish matadors Luis Dominguin and Antonio Ordonnez engaging in what Spanish aficionados call *para suo manu*, each striving to outdo the other in brilliance in order to win the louder plaudits of the crowd. Matadors engaged in this kind of contest fight alternate bulls. If one of the swordsmen excels the other with the cape consistently, his adversary has to take greater physical risks, get closer to the horns, to win cheers and approbation and this, in the long run, can lead to his death or serious wounding.

Cricket is a friendlier game except, as we shall see, when desecrated by Bodyline tactics.

In this great partnership at Brisbane in 1930–31 Ponsford was the first to go. He left, caught Birkett bowled Francis 109. Bradman went on to 223 in partnership with the consistent Kippax, 84. His 223 was scored in 300 minutes at almost 45 runs an hour and it contained 25 fours. From this onslaught our old friend George Francis emerged with the analysis 26/4/76/3 and he was bravely supported by his fellow fast bowler Griffith 33/4/133/4.

In Hele's opinion Francis, Griffith, and Constantine formed one of the finest pace attacks ever sent to Australia. It is a view Don Bradman supports. Of Constantine's fielding Don has written: "Without hesitation I rank him the greatest all-round fieldsman I have seen. Gregory may have been his superior in slips, Percy Chapman excelled him near the wicket in specialist positions, but the phenomenal agility and anticipation of Constantine made him a perpetual danger in any position."

Australia won the First Test by ten wickets, the Second by an innings and 172 and the Third by an innings and 217. Thanks to Bradman's 152 (his "customary hundred," as English statistician, E. L. Roberts, described it) and Bert Ironmonger's match analysis of 37/11/79/11, she took the Fourth Test by an innings and 122 at Melbourne.

It speaks highly for the West Indians' heart and resilience that they won the Fifth Test at Sydney by 30 runs. In this match their captain, Grant, who won the toss and batted first, established a still extant record for Tests in Australia by declaring both his team's innings— the first at six for 350 (Francis four for 48) and the second at five for 124.

In the return State game at Adelaide Philip Keith ("Perka") Lee, the cricketer with the chewing gum initials ("Slasher" Mackay please note), took five for 57 with his off-spinners and then scored 106. This performance must have helped towards his selection in the Fifth Test of the Bodyline series two summers later. Lee, one of the closest cricketing friends of Vic Richardson and "Jack" Nitschke, can still be seen in the seats in front of Adelaide Oval's Mostyn Evan Stand watching big games with his hamper of food and wine beside him. He's a keen and excellent golfer nowadays and, if the tempo of play doesn't please him, he slips off unostentatiously to Kooyonga Golf Club.

We have given Sir Donald Bradman's opinion of Learie Constantine as a fieldsman. Of Don in 1930–31 Constantine said to Hele, "I don't worry about him. I accept him and his hundred. It's the six other brilliant batsmen besides Don that make dismissing Australia such a handful."

George Hele saw two of the 1960–61 Tests between Australia and the West Indies. Of that series he says: "The two Tests in Melbourne, played under the leadership of that chevalier of the game, Sir Frank Worrell, and one of Australia's finest captains, Richie Benaud, showed how cricket should be played, how it was designed to be played. That is why 90,000 Australians watched one day of the Fifth Test and why 92,000 of them lined what was once Australia's most beautiful city street, Collins Street, Melbourne, to cheer the West Indians goodbye.

"I stood among those 92,000 that day," said Hele, "and felt, as did many of those around me, that I was waving farewell to royalty. I only hope I live to see another team of West Indians on the cricket fields of Australia."

George, now eighty-three, gives splendid promise of seeing this wish granted. He is a remarkably durable old man and walking proof that twenty years as an umpire, even one as a Bodyline series umpire, is no barrier to longevity and love of life.

Dingaan's Day at Melbourne

GEORGE HELE RECEIVED $20.00 FOR UMPIRING THAT ADELAIDE TEST against Grant's West Indians in 1930–31. For each of the five Tests between Australia and "Jock" Cameron's 1931–32 Springbok side he received $16.80. This represented a saving to the Australian Cricket Board of $3.20 per Test per umpire, making a total saving for the series of $32.00.

George's comment today is: "The Board of Control must have needed the money even more than George Borwick and myself. And we needed it badly. There were no planes in those days. We travelled by train. I spent three days in the train between Adelaide and Brisbane for the First Test and, looking back, I am thankful they played no Tests in Perth at that time.

"We had to be in the city of play twenty-four hours before matches began. For a Test in Brisbane I had to spend six days travelling and the day before the Test and the duration of the unlimited match away from home. In addition to that $16.80, I received $3.00 a day to cover my hotel tariff, my food, and what have you. George Borwick and I also had to pay our own laundry bills and they included the cost of a clean starched white coat for each day of the match.

"To umpire for this reward could, I suppose, be called dedication,

Top: Larwood bowls to Woodfull. Kippax is the non-striker, with Hammond and Hendren at square-leg and silly mid-on respectively. *Bottom:* Jackson drives White to the boundary on his way to a score of 164 in Australia's first innings of the Fourth Test in Adelaide, 1929

especially when one remembers those voluble and volatile characters on the Brisbane mound, on the Sydney Hill, at the Richmond end of the M.C.G., and in front of the scoring board bar at Adelaide. Nor do I forget those, at times, not-so-kindly critics in the Press.

"I realised, of course, that we were in the middle of a Depression, the world's greatest Depression. But what we received was frugal reward for being members of a 'race apart' and for having to keep more secrets than a Prime Minister's confidential adviser or Richard Nixon's private secretary."

That First Test of 1931–32 at Brisbane lasted six playing days so the two Georges (Hele and Borwick) received $2.80 per day of unflagging concentration lasting 330 minutes.

Authoress Freya Stark has described dedicated service as "The rose in the first desert, which still makes life possible for nurses, government officials, men in offices whose work might otherwise be arid beyond their capacity to bear." She claims that: "It endows humble people with their chance of the greatest of the worldly luxuries, since it makes their labour, which is the only commodity they have, a thing that can be given . . . Its secret of happiness is made manifest in any crisis when men forget to care about their rights and think of service only."

I hope umpires and referees will feel happier having read all this. It is particularly apposite in present-day Australia.

The first Springbok side to tour Australia came here in 1910–11. Hele saw some of the matches played by that team of Percy Sherwell's. George was nineteen then and today ranks Sherwell equal to Oldfield, Strudwick, Evans, and Tallon as a wicketkeeper.

South Africa has been happily blessed with "Aunt Sallys" who could bat. Between them, Sherwell, Cameron, and John Waite dismissed 223 batsmen behind wickets in Tests—Sherwell 36 in thirteen matches, Cameron 51 in twenty-six, and Waite 136 in forty-eight. Waite scored four Test hundreds, Sherwell one, and Cameron a 90.

Before dealing with this Springbok tour, George is insistent upon indulging in a friendly argument with Sir Donald Bradman about a statement he made concerning Gary Sobers' 254 for the Rest of the World XI against Australia at Melbourne in 1971–72.

After Sobers' dismissal Don said, "That is the finest innings I have watched in Australia."

Top: McCabe hits out during an innings of 187 not out in the First Test match of the 1932–33 series. *Bottom:* In the same Test, Sutcliffe had a lucky escape at 43 when a ball trickled from his bat on to the wicket without dislodging the bails

But Hele disputes this: "Don did not see Victor Trumper's 214 not out at Adelaide Oval against Sherwell's side. That was as great an innings as I've been lucky enough to watch. Nor did Don see his own 299 not out, of course, against Cameron's side, also at the Adelaide Oval. This, in my opinion, was perhaps the most brilliant innings, in the technical sense, that I have seen him play.

"I also saw Don score his 226 against South Africa in Brisbane that summer, his 103 not out against Larwood and Bodyline bowling at Melbourne in 1932–33, his 270 against England at Melbourne, his 212 against England at Adelaide, and his 169 at Melbourne in 1936–37. All these innings which Don did not see I saw, some of them from twenty-two yards.

"Like him, I saw Sobers' 254. Unlike him, I saw Bill Ponsford score 214 out of a total of 315 for Victoria against South Australia in an innings which Ponsford himself regards as technically his finest. Nor can I forget Jack Ryder's 295 with 33 fours and 6 sixes against New South Wales at the M.C.G. in 1926–27. Jack scored that 295 in 245 minutes against an attack that included Arthur Mailey.

"Don *did* see Stan McCabe's heroic 187 not out against Larwood at Sydney in 1932–33 and he was at the far end of the pitch for part of Archie Jackson's 164 at Adelaide in 1928–29. He has too fine a memory to have forgotten two of Lala Amarnath's great innings here in 1947–48 and one or two of Rohan Kanhai's in 1960–61.

"I think it would be harder to name a World XI from all cricket history than to distinguish between these great innings, but not much harder."

George and I believe Sir Donald was being generous to Gary Sobers, modest about himself, and conscious of the need for encouraging more interest in contemporary cricket when he uttered that eulogy at the New Year of 1972.

We believe the greatest innings played in Australia must have come either from himself or Victor Trumper somewhere along the line, the most beautiful from Victor Trumper, Alan Kippax, Archie Jackson, or Neil Harvey, the most correct technically from Hobbs.

Percy Sherwell's 1910–11 Springbok side included a galaxy of googly bowlers in Schwarz, Vogler, and Pegler. Bruce Cameron's attack depended mainly upon pace and swing—including, in Neville Quinn, probably the outstanding left-handed new-ball bowler Hele has seen, high praise from an umpire who has watched Frank Foster,

84

Bill Whitty, Bill Voce, Alan Davidson, and "Big Bill" Johnston.

George's deep regret so far as the 1931–32 series is concerned is that H. W. "Herbie" Taylor, the Springbok who scored 518 at 51·8 in the series in which England's Sydney Barnes took forty-nine wickets at 10·93, was beyond his best. Taylor, forty-two years old in 1931–32, scored 314 at 31·4 in ten Test innings. The dance had deserted his feet and the loss of it did not help him against Clarrie Grimmett.

"Taylor," says George, "was a shortish right-hander with a sound and correct defence. Even in his early forties, when his reflexes were slowing, he gave glimpses of the great batsman the world recognised him to be."

Fortunately that fine South African cricket writer, Louis Duffus, painted Taylor's best batting in beautiful language in his books.

In forty-two Tests Taylor batted seventy-six times for 2,936 runs at 40·77, scoring seven centuries and seventeen fifties—most of them in a losing cause.

Australian captain Bill Woodfull either gained or justified his name "The Unbowlable" during the First Test at Brisbane of 1931–32. He and Ponsford opened against that jolly Rhodesian farmer, "Sandy" Bell, and Quinn. A ball of Quinn's first over contacted Woodfull's off stump. The ball proceeded to the boundary; the bails did not drop. They did not even move from the grooves on the tops of the stumps. Woodfull, 0 at the time, made 76.

As the series developed Quinn produced a complex in Ponsford similar to the one Alec Bedser created in the mind of Arthur Morris after the second World War.

Says George Hele: "Ponsford's superbly correct technique began to come asunder at the seams as Quinn had him moving across his stumps, instead of backward and forward as he previously had done. This, I believe, was the main cause of the decline in Ponsford's performances and it was capitalised upon the following summer by that other pacy left-hander, Voce."

Ponsford did not fall to Quinn in the First Test but was bowled by him in the Second and Fourth Tests. In the other games Quinn destroyed his confidence. In four Tests Ponsford scored only 97 for five dismissals. The only batsman who has scored more than 400 twice in first-class innings averaged 19·4 for the series. Had he played in the final Test his average might have been lower.

If Don Bradman had a weakness it was early in an innings against an outswinging new ball. He was troubled for a time by Quinn's superbly late and sharp outswinger.

Springbok opening batsman Bruce Mitchell usually played his cricket in a silence that would have satisfied Dean Maitland. He fielded at first slip. When second slip dropped Bradman early in his innings Bruce was heard to emit an expletive which few of his friends believed part of his vocabulary. This short (four-letter) word had scarcely escaped him before he dropped Don himself. He must have felt almost as embarrassed as he did one day when captaining Old Johannians in a club match in Johannesburg. On this other occasion Bruce was fielding at slip. Russell Endean was the wicketkeeper. An opposing pair of batsmen were proving particularly hard to dismiss. Strolling the pitch between overs alongside Endean, Mitchell was moved to remark, "Wouldn't you think the skipper would change the bowlers, Russell?"

"You *are* the skipper, Bruce," replied Endean.

"Good heavens, so I am," said the woolgatherer.

Bradman, as usual, took full advantage of his luck. He soon found his finest form and set about establishing an ascendancy over this South African attack that was to take him to 226 in this innings, 112 at Sydney, 167 at Melbourne, and that 299 not out at Adelaide.

Bradman also scored two centuries for his State against the Springboks that summer. Towards the end of it the bowler who suffered perhaps most from his bat, "Sandy" Bell, was sitting in A. G. "Johnnie" Moyes' office in Sydney when Don got up and left. Bell looked after him as he went through the door and said in his resonant voice, "That's the first time on this tour I've seen his back."

Bradman's 226 formed more than half Australia's first innings 450 (Oldfield 56 not out) at Brisbane. On the Saturday night Bruce Mitchell was not out. On the Sunday night a tropical downpour began and play proved impossible until 4.00 p.m. on the Wednesday. Two days and two sessions of play were lost.

On the Wednesday, Woodfull and Cameron inspected the wicket and decided to look again at 3.30 p.m. At the appointed time they disagreed, leaving the decision to Hele and Borwick, who agreed to resume play at 4.00 p.m.

After stumps that day Grimmett came to the umpires dressing-room, for which by some oversight they were not charged rent, and said to George Hele, "You were wrong to begin at 4.00 p.m. Hours of play are 12.00 to 1.30 p.m., 2.15 to 4.00 p.m., and 4.15 to 6.00 p.m." Hele and Borwick emphasised that, where there was no previous play for a day, there was no adjournment. Grimmett replied, "'Woody' would have objected to beginning at 4.00 p.m. had Australia been batting."

Hele tells the story: "George Borwick and I saw Woodfull and he confirmed what Clarrie had told us. I then said, 'I'm going to "Jock" Cameron to tell him I'll write to the Board of Control and that, if George Borwick and I are selected to umpire the next Test and the same position should occur, we would do the same again, in the absence of an instruction to the contrary from the Board.'

"Both Woodfull and Cameron agreed this to be fair. I received a letter from the Board *after* the Second Test. It stated: 'In the opinion of the Board you and Umpire Borwick erred in not delaying play till 4.15 p.m., but provision has been made for future Tests so that, if the same thing occurs, your decision will be a correct one.'

"I spoke to Board secretary, W. H. Jeanes, about the matter. He told me the caterers had to be considered. I replied, 'Well, with two-and-two-thirds days lost how could you cater for six spectators?' This query stumped even Bill Jeanes, who was as unstumpable as Bill Woodfull was unbowlable."

The outcome of all this (and of some superb bowling from Ironmonger) was that Bruce Mitchell did not add to his overnight Saturday score until 5.31 p.m. the following Wednesday.

Mitchell was eventually run out for 58 in what, for Hele, are unparalleled circumstances. Bruce drove a ball towards mid-off, where Bradman was fielding, and called to his partner Herbie Taylor, "Come two." Taylor responded, Bradman sprang upon the ball and threw down the wicket at the bowler's end before Mitchell had run even one. He was two yards from his ground when the wicket was broken. As he passed Hele he said, "Tut, tut. What *have* I done?"

Mitchell must have agreed with Hele's decision because he gave him his Springbok cap at the end of the tour. That cap is now in the M.C.G. museum near those of Bill Woodfull, Jack Hobbs, Bill Voce, and Wally Hammond, which Hele was "lucky and proud enough to receive from their owners along the cricketing trail."

South Africa lost that Brisbane Test by an innings and 163 and reduced the margin by only eight runs in the second at Sydney.

After Stan McCabe (far more renowned for his batting than for his bowling) had taken four for 13 as against Clarrie Grimmett's four for 28 in South Africa's first innings of 153, he made a point of telling Grimmett that his average was 3·25 as against Grimmett's 7·00. After the match Clarrie said to Stan, "You never got a wicket in.the second innings. I got four more."

Keith Rigg, who played all too rarely for Australia, batted stylishly for 127 in Australia's 469, sharing a century stand with Bradman. It was in this innings that "Jack" Nitschke compiled his highest Test score, 47. Hele believes Nitschke might have fared far better against Bodyline bowling the following summer than some of the batsmen preferred to him.

South Africa, according to George, "were slowly getting Australia's measure." They reduced their losing margin to 169 runs in the Third Test at Melbourne in which Bradman scored 167 in 180 minutes with 18 fours. George emphasises that he has not umpired for finer fellows or better sportsmen than "Jock" Cameron's 1931–32 Springboks. The standard of sportsmanship they set was equalled by Jack Cheetham's 1952–53 side and Trevor Goddard's men in 1963–64. This should be remembered by those who have the chance to restore Test match cricket between Australia and South Africa.

Perhaps no visiting team has been confronted by so powerful a batting line as Woodfull, Ponsford, Bradman, Kippax, McCabe, and Rigg formed in 1931–32 or so gifted a spin combination as that of Grimmett, Ironmonger, and O'Reilly.

Of those three bowlers, Hele says: "I doubt whether any Australian side had a richer fund of spin. All three of them commanded such superb control and all of them were so different from one another in method and spin. Had Australia owned them in 1972 I don't believe they would have produced that pitch at Headingley. If they had, England would certainly have been out for a song and Underwood and Illingworth made to look third-class."

Australia were dismissed for 198 in the first innings of that Melbourne Test of 1931–32, Bell taking five for 69 and Quinn four for 42 against that frightening batting line on a good wicket.

Of South Africa's reply of 358 Ken Viljoen contributed 111, the only Springbok century of the series. When Viljoen returned to Australia as manager of Cheetham's side in 1952–53 he had a long talk with Hele. During it he turned the subject to Bodyline bowling and said, "You could have stopped it under the law relating to fair and unfair play." Hele replied, "Well, why was it necessary for the Imperial Cricket Conference to introduce a new law covering that type of bowling?"

Viljoen stuck to his ground. "I still think the unfair play law could have been used." Hele played his trump card by saying, "No umpire could interfere with the progress of a game except on appeal under the laws of cricket as they stood in 1932–33 and there *was* no appeal. Had Borwick and I decided Bodyline was unfair and interfered, Jardine would immediately have said, 'Has any Australian appealed?' Our answer must have been 'No' and Jardine's retort, 'Mind your own business, then, till someone does.' "

This seems to have silenced even the obdurate Viljoen, who had scored that 111 from Number 6 position in 210 minutes twenty years previously. According to Hele, this was a "slow and tedious but sound innings" and it certainly helped South Africa to a lead of 160.

Australia then roused itself with a reply of 554 (Woodfull 161, Bradman 167, McCabe 71, and Kippax 67), Grimmett, six for 92 from forty-four overs and Ironmonger, four for 54 from forty-two, made it three wins in a row.

It was during South Africa's second innings 225 that "Sandy" Bell and Neville Quinn, who were great friends, made a wager as to who would outscore the other. When Bell entered at nine for 225, Quinn had not scored. Bell said to George Hele, "Mind you give him out before me." Quinn had won a similar wager on the first innings by scoring 11 to Bell's 10. This time they both scored 0. Grimmett needed no help from Hele. He bowled Bell neck and crop.

Hele was to notice none of this joviality and banter, this cricket through fun and joy, during the Bodyline series that was to follow.

Despite the discrepancy between the strengths of the two sides, interest was high in Adelaide before the Fourth Test, which produced compensation with some magnificent moments and the debut of the greatest bowler George Hele says he has ever watched—William Joseph O'Reilly.

In Hele's words, "O'Reilly had all the cunning of Clarrie Grimmett, equal powers of endurance and courage and, in addition, a tremendous competitiveness, one I have not seen paralleled by any other bowler. I saw Sydney Barnes have Australia reeling on four for 11 at Melbourne in 1911–12 after dismissing Kelleway, Bardsley, Hill, and Armstrong on a perfect pitch. At this stage a section of the crowd began to barrack Barnes and drove him into one of his black moods. If Bill O'Reilly had dismissed the four first English batsmen for 6 runs from his bowling he would have mesmerised those who followed them. Barnes finished with five for 44."

Of Bradman's 299 not out in the Adelaide Test Hele says: "I have watched no batsmen of any era so completely in control of an attack. This was one of the greatest innings, in a technical sense, that I have umpired for, or seen. Don really enjoyed himself. His unconcealed delight in his art was often misconstrued by opposing teams, who mistook his smile for gloating. Don was never one to gloat. I always found him most modest. What human being would not have been delighted to have been able to bat as he could? It was just one of those quirks of fate that saw his partner 'Pud' Thurlow run out while scampering for the run that would have given Don his 300."

During one of O'Reilly's early overs in this Test "Jock" Cameron, in Hele's opinion, nicked a ball which Oldfield caught. Neither Oldfield nor O'Reilly appealed. Hele would have given Cameron out, had an appeal been forthcoming. At the end of the over drinks were brought out. Oldfield walked to Hele and asked, "George, did he nick that one?" "You can always ask," Hele replied.

At this stage Bradman walked up and called, "Don't you fellers appeal when a man is out?" Oldfield then asked Cameron if he had nicked the ball and he replied that he had.

O'Reilly's feelings can best be imagined by those who know him. He was yet to take a wicket in a Test match then and, in the entire Test, delivered 81·4 overs for the reward of only four wickets for 155.

Australia was not to see another visiting South African side for twenty-one summers. Possibly what occurred at Melbourne on 12, 13, and 15 February 1932 had something to do with the delay.

Australia won the Fifth Test of that series in three days, by an innings and 72. Bradman did not bat and Grimmett was not called upon to bowl in either of the Springbok innings.

February 12–15 are remembered like Dingaan's Day and Rorke's Drift in South Africa.

Those days produced one of the most extraordinary matches in the history of all Test cricket. In the words of E. L. Roberts "It was South Africa's Waterloo—and there was no Blucher."

90

South Africa won the toss and batted. They were in and out in just over ninety minutes—Cameron and "sundries" scoring 19 of the team's 36. That great Victorian footballer, Laurie Nash, whom we have mentioned before, took four for 18 from twelve overs and Ironmonger five for 6 from 7·2 overs on a Melbourne "gluepot."

The Australians also were in and out before the end of that first day—for 153, of which Kippax scored 42 and Jack Fingleton 40. Bradman wrote "in jumping down from a form in the dressingroom, I twisted my ankle, which prevented me from batting."

Before stumps, South Africa had scored one for 5. A day's play was lost through rain and the wicket on the third morning was as bad as Melbourne, in those days of uncovered pitches, could produce.

As we have seen, the Australian selectors had not omitted Ironmonger this time. He proceeded to take six more wickets for 18 to finish with eleven for 24 for the Test. It had needed 23·2 overs to dismiss South Africa on the first day. 31·3 overs were enough the second time round and Australia 153, won by an innings and 72 from South Africa, 36 and 45.

George Hele went home to Adelaide with $84.00 in his pocket for umpiring twenty-two days of Test cricket, which works out at well under a dollar an hour.

That Angry Acrimonious Summer

AUSTRALIANS, EVEN TODAY—AFTER RORKE AND HIS DRIFT, MECKIFF
and his elbow, Bob Hewitt and his tennis tantrums—enjoy an
international name for fair play and good sportsmanship. My
wartime infantry battalion's padré, Reverend Whereat, born and
educated in England, gave me his opinion that Australians exhibited
a sense of fair play which he had not encountered among the men
and women of any other nation.

The English, let's face it and let the English face it, do not enjoy
quite the same reputation abroad, *whether or not they deserve to do so*.
The reasons are not easy to pigeonhole but this truth is indisputable.

England, of course, built her nationhood in the tough school of
Europe. Australia, for her first 100-odd formative years, had only
herself to oppose and nurtured only one Ned Kelly.

Anglo-Saxon, Nordic, and Norman toughness rubbed off, no
doubt, upon England's sportsmen and rose like a New Zealand
geyser in cricketing characters such as Dr William Gilbert Grace,
Douglas Jardine, Harold Larwood, William Voce, Raymond
Illingworth, Geoffrey Boycott, and John Snow.

We realise that the Arthur Gilligans, Percy Chapmans, Patsy
Hendrens, Denis Comptons, Billy Griffiths, and Douglas Wrights
were exceptions to this toughness during the 1930s and 1940s, as

were Archie MacLaren, Sir Stanley Jackson, Gilbert Jessop, and Frank Woolley before them.

During the angry, acrimonious summer of total cricketing war, 1932–33, the "grand old English game" was waged more ruthlessly in and against Australia than at any other time in cricketing history— and so waged by Englishmen, led by an English amateur. The mask came off and under it there was little but malevolence.

My collaborator George Hele has read a score of books about the Bodyline summer, books written by Douglas Jardine himself, by Harold Larwood, Bruce Harris, Jack Fingleton, Alan Kippax, Arthur Mailey, and others. He has read scores of chapters devoted to the events of that Donnybrook in books by Sir Donald Bradman, Victor Richardson, Nottinghamshire's captain A. W. Carr, Sir Pelham Warner, and Sir John Berry Hobbs.

George Hele watched Bodyline bowling from behind the bowler's arm and from square-leg at distances of no more than twenty-two yards from the batting or "popping" crease. He stood throughout the five Tests of that unpleasant summer.

"Much of what I have read," says George, "makes me wonder whether I was really there, sharing those box seats with my old comrade George Borwick."

George regards Victor Richardson's, Jack Fingleton's, and Alan Kippax's accounts as the most accurate. The others, he believes, were too coloured by personal interest and patriotism, which bordered at times upon chauvinism.

At the end of the series, which England won by four Tests to one and 100 or so bruises to none, an Australian who chose to call himself Man in the Street, compiled a ninety-page account of and commentary upon that summer of 1932–33. He concluded it with these paragraphs:

"Let a mere Australian hint in an undertone that an Englishman could be 'unsportsmanlike' and you fire a magazine of high explosives.

"Well may the Liturgy of the Church of England enjoin the supplication:—'From all blindness of heart; from pride, vain-glory and hypocrisy; from envy, hatred and malice, and all uncharitableness.'

"And well may Australia fervently echo the set response:— 'Good Lord deliver us.' "

93

In this book, which received limited circulation, Man in the Street made some forthright points. They include:—

1. "We Australians are at a loss to understand why we alone, of all the Empire, are singled out for these continual attacks and assaults by Englishmen. We claim to be loyal to the Throne, and to uphold the traditions of the British race. Also, we pay our debts and are England's very best customer within the Empire. When danger threatened we were the first to respond to the call to arms by the Motherland. Well then ... I know that from Cairns to Kalgoorlie, and anywhere in between, Australians are deeply resentful of the unjust, unsportsmanlike, and malicious slanders that have been hurled at us by the English."

2. "I believe that every Australian has a very vital and clear-cut conception of what constitutes fair play and sportsmanship and that the Australian has a more vivacious and dynamic mind than those 'sportsmen' of a colder clime who stagnate in a mould of stilted phraseology, and who talk so glibly about 'playing the game' and such-and-such a happening as 'really not cricket, what?' We have had a wealth of illustration during the just-ended series of England versus Australia cricket matches to demonstrate that our Australian idea of sportsmanship is as different from the English conception, as the Marquess of Queensberry's code is from the rules of the famous Mr Rafferty."

3. "I think that when Mr Jardine was in Australia he would have made himself more popular if he had pasted in his harlequin cap this sound dictum of Emerson: 'Life is not so short but there is always time for courtesy.' Certain it is that wherever the English captain spoke in public his every utterance either chafed a wound or was a challenge to good taste. It was an American observer who said: 'The ordinary Englishman is a man of few words, and these are generally disagreeable.'

"Mr Jardine had a bitter word for Australia and the Australians. And so had Mr Larwood. 'When Australians come to England they are treated as gentlemen,' declared the waspish bowler. 'They are treated as gentlemen!' Just think of that. And, when all is said, when Australians *do* go to England they *behave* like gentlemen."

4. "A leading member of the M.C.C. (Mr T. A. Higson) said

94

at the Lancashire County Cricket Club's luncheon in April (1933) that Bodyline bowling 'had served its purpose in winning the Tests.' Thus, by implication, it was not to be used in dear old fair-play England. Mr Higson also said: 'Bodyline bowling is detrimental to cricket and I hope it will not be pursued.' He also said: 'Jardine had been subjected to indignities in Australia which no Englishman should have suffered.'

"No Englishman! Any indignities Mr Woodfull and the members of *his* team were made to suffer don't count, it would seem. Only W. S. Gilbert could have done justice to Mr Higson's smug appreciation of that sacrosanct prodigy, 'an English gentleman.' "

5. "The capture of the Ashes at all costs seemed to be the one and only object of Jardine. The object of this new form of attack was not merely to bowl on the leg side with a packed leg field, but to direct bumpers at the batsman's body and head and so disconcert him that he must, of necessity, be more concerned about protecting himself from serious injury than about guarding his wicket. Obviously, if a fast bowler sends down four balls at a batsman's body and two at the wicket, the wicket is more likely to be hit than if the whole six balls were bowled at the wicket. It is quite evident that Larwood, Voce, and Bowes were selected with the definite object of carrying out this carefully formulated plan. Larwood, bowling on orthodox lines, is undoubtedly the best bowler in the world, but when he sends down his Bodyline delivery with the batsman dodging the ball or ducking his head, he is practically unplayable on Australian wickets."

Man in the Street then quoted the Sydney *Referee* (the leading sporting paper in the southern hemisphere in those days), of 25 January 1933. The *Referee*'s report was headed, "Menace of the Body Theory. Future of Cricket in Danger." *Inter alia*, it read:

"Who shall say that the Australian players in the first Test were a team of cowards? Yet to hear the inanities spoken and the utter drivel written in many English quarters, one would think that some of them were arrant curs. And it is all because they have not succeeded in smashing this pernicious body-battering attack of England's fast bowlers—an attack utterly foreign to our batsmen, because it is utterly foreign to true cricket.

95

"Let it now be openly declared that Mr Pelham F. Warner, manager of the English XI, and Mr Douglas R. Jardine, the captain, have deliberately acquiesced in a campaign of attack that is at once ruinous to cricket, a direct and emphatic negation of the principles and traditions of cricket and an alarming danger to batsmen called upon to face it.

"Mr Warner seems a double personality. What is abhorrent to him in English County cricket is, presumably, the essence of true sportsmanship to him in Australia. Only four months ago at the Oval he watched the Surrey batsmen being 'Aunt-Sallied' by the Yorkshire fast bowler, Bowes, who is with the England XI in Australia. The English crowd at the Oval shrieked its disapproval. Hobbs, one of the batsmen, also protested. Mr Warner himself protested. These words were attributed to him: 'Bowes must alter his tactics. Bowes bowled with five men on the on side and sent down several very short-pitched balls which repeatedly bounced head high and more. Now that is not bowling; indeed it is not cricket . . . These things lead to reprisals—and, when they begin, goodness knows where they will end. I *do* love cricket and on Saturday Yorkshire fell from her pedestal and her great reputation was tarnished.' "

These words of Sir Pelham's appeared under his byline in the London *Morning Post* of 22 August 1932.

One of Jardine's fast bowlers, G. O. Allen, refused to bowl Body-line during the 1932–33 series on threat of omission from the last four Tests.

Before proceeding with George Hele to our position behind the stumps at the bowler's end and square with the stumps at the other, we should remember two further comments made by two prominent English cricketers—Sir Stanley Jackson and Elias "Patsy" Hendren.

Speaking at a Yorkshire County Cricket Club annual meeting, Sir Stanley, who led England to victory in the 1905 series of Tests and topped England's batting and bowling averages to boot, said: "In all my long experience I have never known an Australian cricketer with whom I could find fault. The Australians always observed the written and unwritten rules of cricket."

Patsy Hendren, who played in twenty-eight Tests for England against Australia and made three tours of this country, wrote in the

London *Sunday Express*: "Don't tell me that the Australian umpires don't know the game. They do! There are constant complaints regarding the umpiring when our men are in Australia, yet in my whole experience I have never heard the Australians criticise our umpires here."

George Hele has already recounted how happy was the atmosphere which prevailed during the Tests of the 1928–29 (Chapman–Ryder) series of Tests between England and Australia, how friendly on the whole were the relations between opposing players and between players and umpires. He has told how, after the Fifth Test, he was the invited guest of the England captain and manager during the train journey from Melbourne to Adelaide.

It is not because George is an Australian that, forty years later, he condemns Bodyline bowling unequivocally. He does so as an umpire and, in the written words of Douglas Jardine, he was one of the two finest umpires in the world.

He says at the age of eighty-three: "Given the chance I would not walk across the street to watch Bodyline again. The damage done to senior and junior cricket by emulation of the Bodyline tactics was tremendous. The game could not afford or survive their repetition."

It is his firm opinion that, had the manager of Chapman's 1928–29 side, Sir Frederick Toone, cricket's first knight, been manager of Jardine's 1932–33 side, Bodyline bowling would not have been seen in Australia. "Toone was a grand man. He was also a strong man, a man of tremendous principles. He would not have countenanced Bodyline for a moment and he would have made even Douglas Jardine bow to his beliefs and orders."

But Sir Frederick Toone, the Secretary of the Yorkshire County Cricket Club, had died, aged sixty-one years and eleven months, on 10 June 1930.

According to Hele, no inkling of the Bodyline plot leaked to him during the early stages of the 1932–33 summer. South Australia's captain, Vic Richardson, did not communicate to George the conversation he had with Bill Voce during October in Perth. "What kind of team have you brought to Australia, Bill?" Vic had asked. "Not a bad side, and if we don't beat you, we'll knock your bloody heads off," Voce had replied.

Sealed lips was the set rule for the Englishmen during the early

97

November game at Adelaide between the M.C.C. and South Australia. At its conclusion, word was dropped to George that something strange could happen during the following game between the M.C.C. and Victoria. Nothing untoward did. Larwood did not play in this match. The English plan in the match appeared to be for Walter Hammond to knock Victoria's left-handed googly bowler, Leslie O'Brien Fleetwood Smith, from Test considerations. This task Hammond discharged by scoring 203 with one six and 23 fours while "Chuck" took two for 124 from twenty-five overs.

Before the succeeding game in Melbourne between the M.C.C. and an Australian XI, a friend of Hele's disclosed to him that "something might happen" this time. Hele's friend said he had the information "on good authority."

The Australian team for this game included Don Bradman; the M.C.C. fielded their full battery of fast bowlers, Larwood, Voce, Bowes, and Allen.

The M.C.C. batted first and totalled 282. The Australian XI replied with 218. The Bodyline field was not set and only a few bumpers were bowled. Bradman was l.b.w. to Larwood for 36. It was in the M.C.C.'s second innings that Lisle Nagel, bowling at between medium and fast-medium pace, took eight for 32 from ten overs. M.C.C., 282 and 60, led by 124.

Back in England during the English summer the Press had roundly condemned the composition of Jardine's team for the Antipodes. The Press had nominated a team it believed would defeat Jardine's best Eleven. The challenge was accepted. During the match in the south of England, The Rest led Jardine's side on the first innings. According to South Africa's great batsman, Herbie Taylor, Bodyline bowling was then "let loose among the oaks and elms and horse-chestnuts of some of England's most lovely southern countryside." The initial recipients of it were some of England's own most revered batsmen—among them the "pride of Kent," Frank Woolley.

Said Taylor, "When I came in to bat about the fall of the fourth wicket, Jardine's bowlers refrained from bowling Bodyline at me. My batting partner was taking it from lower wind to high water. We agreed that I should face Larwood and the other fast bowlers as much as possible and that my partner should stay at the non-active end. Despite a certain amount of success with this ruse, Jardine's side dismissed us cheaply enough to run out eventual winners."

A similar situation had now arisen in this 18 to 22 November match of the same year in Melbourne. Jardine's team was in danger of defeat.

Nagel had bowled Sutcliffe for 10, had Bob Wyatt caught Ben Barnett for 3, Pataudi caught O'Brien for 5, bowled Leyland for 6, had Allen l.b.w. 6, bowled Paynter 12, had Larwood caught O'Brien 0, and Duckworth l.b.w. 4.

"But for this freak performance of Nagel's, I believe Bodyline would have been reserved for the First Test at Sydney a fortnight later," Hele says.

"Bodyline began with the new ball from one end—Larwood's end. From the other end 'Gubby' Allen would not bowl it. Now it was on. I've never seen more vicious bowling than Larwood's, who dismissed Woodfull 0 and Bradman 13 that afternoon. When I saw the Bodyline field set for the very first ball of the innings I knew my friend's information was right. I was glad I was there, but horrified at what followed. The very first ball to Woodfull was a bumper and he was out in Larwood's second over, caught by Duckworth from a flyer. The crowd's reaction was one of stunned silence. I was sitting alone behind the wicket in the Members' Stand of the M.C.G. Larwood's speed was phenomenal. I don't think he ever bowled faster than he did that day.

"Fortunately the rain came and ended the match with the Australian XI's score two for 19. Len Darling, due to bat at the fall of either 'Mo' O'Brien's or Keith Rigg's wicket, said to me, 'I was bloody pleased I didn't have to face it.' Back in Adelaide, Vic Richardson said to me, 'It'll be on, George, for a certainty in the Tests.' Vic remembered what Bill Voce had said to him in Perth and he knew the Englishmen were out to get Bradman for far smaller scores than they had in 1930 in England."

In his book *The Fight for the Ashes 1932–33,* Jack Hobbs had this to say of the M.C.C. bowling during the Australian XI's second innings:

"On the Tuesday the wicket rolled out pretty well, with a certain amount of damp from rain on the previous day. Larwood and Allen bowled at a terrific pace . . . When Bradman came in the bowling, if possible, became even faster—really demoniac—in an attempt to shake Don's wonderful confidence. It seemed that

99

this had been done. For the fourth time on the tour Bradman failed to make a big score. The violently rapid bowling of Allen and Larwood was too much.

"Off Allen, Bradman put one between second slip and gully, a lucky shot. In the same over the ball hit Bradman's glove, flew to Duckworth, who knocked it up with hand above his head, and Sutcliffe just failed to make the catch. Allen's next ball was splendidly cut to third man for a single. This brought Don in front of Larwood. The first ball was enough. Bradman, drawing away to cut a shortish delivery, completely missed the ball, which hit the top of the off stump. And, once again, silence fell upon the crowd . . . Larwood and Allen were able to make them absolutely fly. The bowling looked very dangerous stuff . . . These were real shock tactics . . . Most of all I was impressed with the form of Larwood. I don't think he has ever bowled faster."

No mention of the Bodyline field setting for Larwood, one notes.

The two Georges, Hele and Borwick, were appointed to umpire the First Test in Sydney from 2 to 7 December. Hele stayed with Borwick at Glebe and told him of what he had watched in Melbourne.

This was to be George Borwick's first English Test. The previous summer, the two Georges had gone to see Alan Kippax, who had been ill in hospital during the Test against the Springboks in Brisbane. Kippax asked Borwick, "How do you like umpiring in Tests, George?" "It's beautiful—easier than in State games," Borwick replied. "Wait till the Poms come out, eh George?" Kippax said, winking at Hele. Those words were to prove prophetic indeed.

The two Georges had long discussions about the Bodyline bowling and the legality, or otherwise, of the field before they took the tram to the S.C.G. on the morning of 2 December 1932.

The First Test

Bill Woodfull won the toss from an obviously irked Douglas Jardine and decided, as captains almost invariably did in those days, to bat first. Don Bradman was not playing owing to illness, but he was present to watch what happened. Bradman did not play in a Test against England at the S.C.G. until 1936–37. He was dropped in 1928 and ill in 1932.

"Neither Woodfull nor his players," Hele remembers, "discussed Bodyline with me before play began. If they had I would have replied,

'We'll judge events as they occur on the field.' George Borwick and I had done our homework on the laws, however.

"When Jardine and his men came on to the field at high noon that December morning they did so in a conspiracy of silence. They were not chatting to one another. While Larwood measured his twenty-six yard run, not one of them greeted the umpires with an amiable 'Good morning, George,' as they had in 1928–29.

"Harold Larwood," recalls Hele, "was not only the fastest bowler I have watched. He also had the most beautiful action. While he was running in behind me I never heard him. He glided towards the wicket until the last three yards. Australian fast bowlers dragged their right or left toes as they gathered themselves into the delivery stride; Larwood dragged his entire right foot and at right angles to his course. He placed a tremendous strain upon that foot and his ankle. I have not seen a bowler gain greater impetus from his left and guiding arm. From here came his exceptional speed and exceptional accuracy. There was nothing loose, untidy, or wasted about Larwood's action. It was copybook, classic, and utterly direct.

"When he glided in to deliver the first ball of the Test the atmosphere was terrific. The Press and Radio build up for the match had brought 30,000 to the S.C.G. to watch the first ball. Bradman had only been pronounced unfit to play on the previous (Thursday) afternoon. Many of the crowd did not know he would not be playing and news of this produced a sensation.

"The black Bulli soil pitch was not as fast at the start as I had expected, but it had sufficient pace for Larwood to be able to implement Jardine's orders. Woodfull took strike with Bill Ponsford his partner. Larwood's first ball to Woodfull was about five yards faster than any I had seen him bowl in the 1928–29 series. Woodfull let it pass and it went from a goodish length over the top of the off stump. I would describe a truly good length ball from Larwood as one that didn't bump, even though some of these did. Harold could get the ball up from a length, despite his stature of only five feet eight inches. He didn't have to bowl short to make the ball bounce. This ability of his was astonishing to me. I had umpired for the giant Jack Gregory, for Ted McDonald, Jack Scott, Maurice Tate, Learie Constantine, Neville Quinn, 'Sandy' Bell, Harry Howell, Bill Hitch, and for the West Indians, Francis and Griffith. None of them could make the ball lift so sharply from a length as did Larwood.

101

"Jardine did not dally long before moving the Bodyline field into position for Voce, but maintained a 50–50 on and off side setting for Larwood.

"Voce virtually had nine fieldsmen on the leg side, for wicketkeeper Ames took position at first leg slip, knowing where the ball would come. Duckworth was a better keeper, in my opinion, than Ames, but a man who could stump batsmen was not needed for the tactics we were now to watch."

Voce, not Larwood, was the first bowler to deliver Bodyline in its full fury *in a Test match*. Bowling to the full leg side field, Voce bumped many of his deliveries about halfway down the wicket, some even shorter. All of them bounced head-high, or higher. Woodfull was particularly uneasy against these deliveries. The Australian captain was not fast on his feet or in his other reactions. Bill was a back-to-the-wall batsman, a pillar of courage, but no swordsman. He was out for 7 with the total 22, fending at a bumper he could have ignored.

Larwood continued to aim mainly at the wicket. He delivered two short spells before lunch, being relieved quite early by "Gubby" Allen. It was shortly after lunch that Larwood struck down Ponsford 32, Jack Fingleton 26, and Alan Kippax 8, during a glorious spell of extremely fast bowling which lasted an hour and cost England only 14 runs. According to Kippax, Larwood hit Number 6 batsman Victor Richardson several times during this spell but "with the fairest type of delivery," striking between knee and hip. Though a strong leg side field was set at times for Larwood, he never bowled to the full Bodyline field in Australia's first innings. He bowled in the main at the wicket.

He bowled Ponsford and had Kippax l.b.w. As the day wore on, with Stan McCabe and Richardson together, Larwood's pace abated slightly. Richardson hit Larwood freely and McCabe was equally severe with Voce.

Stanley Joseph McCabe was twenty-two years old, weighed ten stone and stood five feet eight inches high in December of 1932. When he came in to bat, Australia was three for 82 and without Bradman. But there was courage in the McCabe family tree. His grandfather, Edward James McCabe, was first a member of the famous Irish constabulary and then of the Victorian Police Force.

As a young man Edward James McCabe rode alone the 400-odd miles from Melbourne to Grenfell, in central New South Wales, through bushlands virgin of all but bushrangers, to stake a claim on the new goldfield at O'Brien's Hill. His pretty young wife, Catherine, made the same long, arduous, and frightening journey three weeks later in a single horse-drawn wagonette. She had their three young children with her and only a rifle, which her husband had trained her to use, for protection.

One afternoon, when her children were asleep behind her, three bushrangers rode out of the scrub and held up the wagonette. They stared for some time at the pretty young woman, examined the inside of the wagonette, saw the sleeping children, and rode off into the bush.

Heroic loneliness, indeed, on the part of this woman whose obituary notice was to read: "Mrs Edward McCabe was one of the greatest of the pioneer women of the Australian bush, possessing all the qualities of self-sacrifice, resourcefulness, industry, determination, and courage that left their mark on the Australian race and laid the foundation of the nation."

And "heroic loneliness" was the way in which Sir Neville Cardus described the 187 not out of Australia's 360 that Catherine McCabe's grandson played at the Sydney Cricket Ground on 2 and 3 December of 1932.

While his team proceeded so bravely to two for 65, Stan McCabe sat with his father and mother in the seats below what is now the S.C.G.'s M. A. Noble Stand. When the second wicket fell McCabe left his seat with the following words to his father, "If I happen to get hit out there, Dad, keep Mum from jumping the fence and laying into Larwood and Voce."

There was to be no need for Mrs McCabe to behave so dramatically. In George Hele's words, "Stan gave Voce all he was bargaining for. He and Vic Richardson took all the English bowlers could hurl at them. This innings stamped Stan as one of the world's greatest batsmen. He stepped into the bowling, he hooked, pulled, and did what he liked with it. The faster they bowled the more he seemed to enjoy it. Several times he could have been out—one stroke to midwicket went through Larwood's upstretched hands, another just too high for gully to clasp. His hook strokes travelled mainly square of the wicket, or forward of square. Some of them landed between

103

the fieldsmen and the leg fence. He did not knock the pickets from that fence as has so often been claimed, however. The pickets were nailed from the inside. He was 120 not out on the Friday night."

Richardson was dismissed on the Friday for 49 of a stand of 129. Oldfield was also out for 4 before stumps. Grimmett left for a gallant 19 early on the Saturday. When Lisle Nagel followed him without scoring, in came McCabe's closest cricketing pal, William Joseph O'Reilly, the total eight for 300. Before he left the dressingroom Woodfull said to "The Tiger," "The only instruction I have to give you is don't get hit." As O'Reilly approached the pitch McCabe crossed to him and said, "You just get behind him, 'Tiger.' He won't bounce one at you. All the bouncers Lol's got left he'll bowl at me."

Bill got right behind the first bumper from Larwood. "I watched it from behind my bat," he recalls. "It hit the middle thereof. I hadn't seen a great deal of it on the way down but I'd seen Larwood running in and that was more than enough. I looked up at Stan and shook my head. I had decided to obey my skipper's orders, not Stan's. He smiled back at me and said 'Okay.' "

Exit W. J. O'Reilly—bowled Voce 4. Nine for 305.

In came Tim Wall, the tall, dark South Australian schoolmaster and fast bowler. A ball from Larwood's first over to Tim hit the bottom edge of his bat. Wall saw it again only when it cannoned into the fence at fine-leg. The next 50 runs all came from McCabe and they came in twenty-eight minutes. All told McCabe batted 242 minutes for his 187 not out—exactly 100 of his runs in fours.

Says Hele: "The reception he got from the Saturday crowd of 58,000 as he left the field was the most magnificent and heartfelt I have ever known. The members just stood and clapped and cheered Stan right into the dressingroom. Those packed on the Sydney Hill stood like guardsmen and cheered till he was out of sight."

It is important to emphasise at this stage that Larwood delivered thirty-one overs to take five for 96 without ever resorting to out-and-out Bodyline tactics. He should have had six for 91. Wrote Alan Kippax, "Had Larwood reproduced his bowling of this innings throughout the other Tests I have not the slightest doubt that his performances would have received the wholehearted acclamation of the crowds, as did this performance at Sydney. Critics were unanimous in dividing the honours between McCabe and Larwood and, though many enthusiasts wrote to the newspapers at this stage

104

condemning the bowling of Voce, they had nothing to say against Larwood. In the second innings, however, Larwood fell from his high estate. After his preliminary overs the whole field was changed to the leg side and placed as it had been for Voce in Australia's first innings."

George Hele says, "The Australian batsmen dived and ducked for cover as much as possible against Voce in the first innings. Both George Borwick and I were of the opinion that, if this attack continued, let alone intensified by application from both ends, somebody would be killed or seriously maimed during the remaining Tests. Borwick and I sensed this. The crowd had sensed it and its demonstration against this form of attack was, to my mind, utterly justified. While Voce was bowling in the first innings and Larwood and Voce in the second innings, an almost continuous demonstration, particularly by those on the Hill, did take place. On our tram journey home on the Friday and Saturday nights Borwick and I listened to plenty of criticism from passengers who, thank goodness, failed to identify us.

"During Australia's first and second innings Fingleton stood up straight to Voce and Larwood and took some bruising. Occasionally he had to stoop and weave. Woodfull stood up to the bowling and so did Vic Richardson. Kippax weaved like Ian Redpath did to Snow. None of the batsmen ran away from the line of the ball. This is why I believed someone would sooner or later be seriously injured. Ponsford did not turn his back to the ball in these innings as he was to do later in Adelaide.

"None of the Australian players discussed the tactics of Voce with me or George Borwick. Nor did any of the Australian cricket officials. The Pressmen knew we were forbidden to speak to them. Throughout this Test there was no communication between the players of the opposing sides. The game was conducted in silence within the boundary and uproar beyond it."

So far this summer, five English batsmen had scored eight centuries against State and "Combined" Elevens. They were: Nawab of Pataudi 166 and 129, Herbert Sutcliffe 169, 154, and 182, Maurice Leyland 127, Douglas Jardine 108 not out (and a 98), and Walter Hammond 203.

Against the M.C.C. attack only Victor Richardson 134, and Jack Fingleton, who batted through the New South Wales first innings for 119 not out, had reached 100 until Stan McCabe scored his 187 not out in this Test.

In England's first innings Sutcliffe 194, Hammond 112, and Pataudi 102, emphasised the power and consistency of the imposing batting machine which Tim Wall, Bill O'Reilly, and Clarrie Grimmett, later reinforced by Bert Ironmonger, had to subdue.

When Sutcliffe was 43 he played a ball from O'Reilly on to his stumps but the bails did not fall. George Hele claims he did not hear the "Tiger" make any remarks. Sutcliffe's eventual 194 was the highest of his seven centuries against Australia and his highest score in Tests.

The Nawab of Pataudi was bent upon equalling the feat of his fellow countrymen, Ranjitsinhji and Duleepsinhji who scored centuries in their first Test matches against Australia. His 102 occupied 302 minutes as compared with Sutcliffe's 194 in 436. After "Pat" had been batting four hours for 80, Vic Richardson suggested he might consider getting a move on. Pataudi replied "I'm trying to gauge the pace of the pitch." Richardson snorted. "It's changed pace five times since you came in," he said.

Hammond's 112 was described as "a beautiful innings" by the one English batsman who is considered to have been his superior, Jack Hobbs.

Of that innings George Hele says, "I cannot speak loudly enough in my praise of Hammond. This great batsman was at his greatest and Sutcliffe also played superbly."

As a result England was not dismissed until before lunch on the fourth day, for 524 runs—a lead of 164.

Discussing Woodfull's refusal to retaliate with Bodyline tactics Hele says, "Three of England's greatest batsmen, Sutcliffe, Hammond, and Leyland, were professionals and I believe they would have shown a distinct distaste for some of their own medicine—even from Tim Wall. I have sound reasons for saying this as I shall reveal later."

Hele continues, "Australia's second innings was dismal, to say the least. In this innings Larwood delivered only two overs to the orthodox new-ball field, then moved his entire field to the leg side. Larwood and Voce, also using the Bodyline field, bowled a great number of short bumping balls straight at the batsmen. While this truly vicious attack was in operation Australia's recognised batsmen collapsed to eight for 113. We prayed it would all be over on that

106

fourth day but had to come back for the *coup de grâce* the next morning because Lisle Nagel 21 not out and Tim Wall 20 hung on. The last two Australian wickets added 51 runs to bring the scores level. This was because the Bodyline attack was not aimed at these batsmen."

Alan Kippax, who was l.b.w. Larwood 8 and bowled Larwood 19 in this Test, wrote: "Bodyline was undoubtedly successful in undermining the morale of Australia's batsmen." In a similar vein, Victor Richardson, who scored 49 and 0, wrote: "We retired to lick our wounds, both real and psychological."

The Nawab of Pataudi wanted a souvenir of the match in which he scored a century on Test debut. As the players and umpires were leaving the field on the fifth morning after England's ten wickets win, Pataudi asked George Hele for one of the bails. Hele refused to give him one. "I have something better for you than a bail," he said. "I have the ball against which you completed your hundred. It has to be handed to the secretary of the New South Wales Cricket Association."

"How can I get it?" enquired Pataudi.

"It's in the left-hand pocket of my coat."

The Nawab quickly encircled George and extracted that ball, while his benefactor did his utmost to look like a man who was not being burgled. By the time the Test trail reached Adelaide, Pataudi had been omitted. He came to Hele behind the Press seats and handed him a gold wristlet watch of considerable value. This was an act of gratitude, not a bribe.

"I thanked my lucky stars Pataudi did not play in another Test," says George.

Though Jardine and Pataudi were known as "Fish and Chips," following their partnership in the first match of the tour at Perth, Pataudi had no time at all for his captain.

There was only one spectator on the Sydney Hill, indeed in the entire outer ground, when Sutcliffe and Bob Wyatt scored that solitary single to give England victory. George Hele suspects he was the famous barracker "Yabba," whom he met between the Brisbane and Sydney Tests of 1928–29 at a game between Balmain and Glebe.

On their way home to Glebe that night of the 1932 Test Hele and Borwick discussed the events of the previous four days' play. Hele said, "If you and I go through the whole series, George, we

107

are going to see something that no other two men in the history of cricket have seen from umpiring positions and which I'm certain no two other Test umpires will ever see."

Hele is adamant that the Bodyline plot was hatched to harness Bradman and that it was used in the Sydney Test because the Englishmen knew Don was watching and wanted to show him what he would receive if he rejoined the Australian ranks.

George lost a stone in weight during that First Test. Bradman was ordered "complete rest" in the hope that he would be fit for the Second Test due to begin in Melbourne in twenty-three days' time.

The Englishmen were sent to Wagga Wagga and Tasmania for matches at these venues. At Wagga they encountered dust storms and more flies than there are in all the British Isles. A wag advised Jardine to cease swatting the flies on the ground because they were his only Australian friends.

One of the members of my platoon hailed from Wagga Wagga. While in Palestine, as it then was, he went on leave to Bethlehem. On his return he wrote a letter home to his mother. It began, "Dear Mum, I've just been to Bethlehem, where Christ was born and I wish to Christ I was in Wagga Wagga where I was born."

Down in Hobart Jardine encountered trouble again. During the game against Tasmania, which was played over Christmas and which might have been expected to produce some Christmas goodwill, a dispute arose between the two captains regarding the fitness of the ground for play. The matter was referred to the umpires, whose decision under the laws was final.

Jardine would not accept their ruling, however, and saw the chairman of the Tasmanian Cricket Association. The chairman correctly supported the umpires. During the remainder of the Tasmanian innings the only ball delivered by a recognised M.C.C. bowler was one from Hedley Verity to complete an over. For the rest of the Tasmanian innings Jardine bowled Eddie Paynter, wicketkeeper Leslie Ames, and himself. Paynter delivered twenty overs to take three for 40, Ames ten overs for none for 26, and Jardine ten overs for none for 21.

I asked George Hele how Jardine bowled. "With a leather ball," he replied.

On 27 December the Hobart *Mercury* saw matters in a less humorous light. In a leading article it said:

108

"For seventy years at certain intervals, cricket teams representing the best that England can send, have visited Tasmania in the course of their tours of Australia. They have received such hospitality as they would accept and the matches with Tasmanian teams have always been played in a friendly spirit of good sportsmanship. It has been left to Mr Jardine to break that honourable tradition.

"His conduct will, we are afraid, go far to destroy the good impression which his predecessors left, and an amount of mischief has been done which cannot easily be measured.

"Perhaps we can best describe the conduct of Mr Jardine as that of a sulky schoolboy who, not being given his own way, snarls, 'Then I won't play.' But, lest it seem that we are unfair, we should put the other side, which is that Mr Jardine, through a lack of something which is expressed in the useful French phrase, *Je ne sais quoi,* did not realise that he was levelling a deliberate insult, not only at the crowd of Tasmanians who had come from all parts of the island to see cricket played as it should be played, but, even more, at his opponents.

"Apparently he did not realise that his action was gravely belittling and offensive to Mr Atkinson and his team."

Atkinson showed what he thought of Jardine's action by declaring the Tasmanian innings closed at five for 103.

Commented Colonel L. M. Mullen, chairman of the Tasmanian Cricket Association, "I consider Jardine's action an insult to Tasmanian cricket and the matter will be officially brought to the notice of the Board of Control. I also did not agree with the attitude of the English captain in endeavouring to induce me to override the decision of the umpires as to the fitness of the ground."

The Hon. Joe Darling, former Australian cricket captain, said, "The Australians have played on far worse wickets in England in Test matches. I have never witnessed a bigger farce in first-class cricket. I was sickened and disgusted by it and, considering that the M.C.C. visits are made only once in four years, our players and the public were entitled to greater consideration."

The comment of another Australian, G. Crosby Gilmour, is even more interesting. It read: "The English captain, speaking to a Launceston audience, congratulated himself on being an old Winchester boy. Winchester was founded, I think, about 1387 by William of

Wykeham. 'Manners maketh the man,' was the immortal motto of that illustrious personage. Presumably the aphorism is unknown to Mr Jardine. Certainly his conduct at Hobart was not what one would have expected from an English gentleman.

"Whatever other impressions Mr Jardine leaves in Australia, he will always be remembered as the undertaker and gravedigger of the traditions of English cricket."

After the Tasmanian captain declared at five for 103 the English batsmen "used every device to waste time, such as frequently appealing against the light, altering the position of the sightboards, which had not previously been moved, continuous patting of the pitch, etc."

Of Jardine's tactics in Tasmania Sir Jack Hobbs, in his *Fight For The Ashes 1932–33,* tactfully wrote, "When you read the scores at Hobart you will be surprised to see how much bowling was done by Jardine, Ames, and Paynter. The wicket there was so wet and soft that Jardine considered it unwise to risk his strongest attack."

Tasmania, of course, had developed a little since Dutchman Abel Tasman discovered its western shores in 1642, even since it was "settled"—"deliberately in order to relieve the over-crowding of English gaols"—by the English some 150 years later.

This development appeared to have escaped the admittedly narrow horizons of Douglas R. Jardine.

The mood prevailing in the rival cricketing camps when the Englishman came to Melbourne for the Second (New Year's) Test, could certainly have been more cordial. The words of Alfred Lord Tennyson's *In Memoriam* could hardly have been more appropriate:

> *Ring out, wild bells, to the wild sky . . .*
> *Ring out the old, ring in the new.*

Bradman's Bravest Innings

GEORGE HELE WATCHED THE CLOSELY-FOUGHT SECOND TEST AT
Melbourne from twenty-two yards. I listened to it, ball by ball,
squatting on the carpeted staircase at Mount Breckan, Victor Harbor,
which looks across the long causeway to Granite Island and to
Encounter Bay, where in 1802 Matthew Flinders and the French
explorer Nicolas Baudin, had their historic meeting.

While play progressed it was almost impossible to ascend or
descend those stairs. One had either to stay put or to whisper a score
of apologies as one strove to find a way through. The staircase was
sardine-packed from oak bannister to oak bannister by boarders at
that old castellated summer holiday sanctuary of "accepted" Adelaide
society, packed like the dress circle of Adelaide's Theatre Royal on
Nellie Stewart or Gladys Moncrieff first nights.

Had roll calls been taken, no resident would have been found
missing, with or without leave. Bradman was back in the Australian
team, reportedly fit, and we all believed that Bradman would find
the answer to Larwood and Voce and their Bodyline. Bradman was
at that time Alexander the Great, Samson, Horatio Nelson, and
Houdini combined, in the eyes of his compatriot Australians—and
deserved to be.

On this occasion a wicket had been pitched out on the spacious,

111

sloping lawn before the rather sinister two-storey, greystone building so during breaks in play, we could demonstrate just what "The Don," McCabe, Hammond, and Sutcliffe should have done, or should be doing, at the M.C.G.

When she sighted the six stumps on the buffalo grass lawn, an eighty-year-old dowager with blue-grey bouffant hair and gold-rimmed pince-nez asked just what purpose they were intended for. We told her. "Oh," she exclaimed, "is *that* what they are for? Since I was a girl I've always wondered."

I was regarded as one of the more enlightened listeners to the events of the Test. Had I not caught Harold Larwood off Mervyn Waite at silly mid-on earlier that summer at Adelaide Oval, caught him from the skier of all skiers?

That was my first catch in an international match. Vic Richardson ran from mid-off while I staggered forward and back under the flight of the ball, trying, as I had been taught by S.A.C.A. coach "Patsy" Hendren, to allow myself room to run in to the catch at the ultimate moment, instead of having it fall embarrassingly behind my back.

I retreated so far from the line of its descent at one stage that Richardson told me afterwards, "I nearly ran you down and bumped you to the ground so I could catch the ball myself." Larwood was 81 at the time and the M.C.C. eight for 599.

"I thought you were going to drop it," Vic said. It was an opinion I shared.

When we left the field at the end of the Englishmen's innings, my cousin, Bob Thomas, accosted me below the George Giffen Stand. "Why didn't you drop it?" he demanded. "Larwood gave us the only exciting batting of the innings." This *was* true. "Lol" hit up his 81 in forty-two minutes, at 120 runs an hour, with 2 mighty sixes and 10 fours; Sutcliffe took 223 minutes over his first 85, on the way to 154.

Drop it, indeed!

Those daily scenes at Mount Breckan demonstrate the intense interest prevailing in the Test series all over Australia. Cricket had gripped the continent. Bodyline was the national bogy. Attendances at the Sydney Test were 46,709, 58,058 (only 388 below the ground record), 27,938, 25,420, and, on the fifth day, only the solitary "Yabba." Total attendance was 158,128.

112

The crowd on the first day of the Melbourne Test was the then world record 63,993. Jack Hobbs wrote for the London *Star:* "The Melbourne Cricket Ground was one huge bowl of staring faces." The second day was watched by 36,944 people. On the third day the first-day world record was smashed, when a crowd of 68,188 people attended. A fourth and final day crowd of 31,460 raised the total attendance to 200,588 and the takings, in those days when you could watch Test cricket for about two "bob" (twenty cents), to $32,144.

Today, with admission averaging about eighty cents a head, these Tests may have reaped a fortune of some $300,000.

None of us on that staircase at Mount Breckan were too sanguine as 30 December reached its high noon. Before those unhappy boo-boos by Douglas Jardine at Hobart, Sutcliffe had notched his fifth century of the tour and Pataudi his third in the game against Tasmania at Launceston. Eddie Paynter, still unable to win a place in England's side, had scored 102. The strength of England's batting loomed colossal. To buttress her battery of fast bowlers, Jardine brought in Bill Bowes alongside Larwood, Voce, and Allen, omitting Hedley Verity.

"I remember," wrote Hobbs, "no Test match which opened in an atmosphere quite so tense and dramatic as this one." Hobbs played in sixty-one Tests before retiring after the Oval Test of 1930.

Australia brought in Bradman and the left-handed Leo "Mo" O'Brien as batsmen in place of Bill Ponsford, who was made twelfth man, and Alan Kippax. It introduced the left handed Bert "Dainty" Ironmonger for Ron Oxenham, to help Grimmett and O'Reilly. Australia had the three greatest spin bowlers in the world and hoped they would suffice.

Woodfull won a hastily conducted toss from Jardine and chose to bat first on a pitch which, to George Hele, "looked perfect." That toss was rushed, Hele says, because Australia's captain had not been informed whether or not he was playing, let alone captaining, Australia, when Jardine came to him at 11.45 a.m., a quarter of an hour before play was due to be called, with a view to tossing. Woodfull told Jardine of his dilemma and the unbelieving Douglas said, "Oh, tut tut."

A great outcry against Woodfull's inclusion had been raised by the Australian Press between the two Tests. The Press wanted a captain who would give England back as good as she gave, demanding Wall, "Bull" Alexander, and Laurie Nash to fling Bodyline back at the English batsmen, especially Jardine.

It was while Woodfull and Jardine were talking to each other outside the Australian dressingroom (the Australians would not allow him inside it) that the Australian selectors arrived with the team they had narrowed down from their previously named thirteen. Despite the discouraging and demoralising tardiness of their decision, the Test began on time—Woodfull taking strike to Larwood.

George Hele still regards the Melbourne Test as the most remarkable match of that sensational series. What was to become high drama, however, began in farce. The prospect of Bradman facing England's Bodyline attack had set up an incessant buzz of excitement among the great crowd. But an early boundary caused a piece to be cut from the new ball by one of the white iron railings that encircle the M.C.G.

"We then saw," says Hele, "the ridiculous spectacle of Jardine bowling underarms to Woodfull from a distance of about four yards. The damaged ball had to be replaced by one deemed to be in like condition of wear, if not tear. This operation occupied five minutes—Jardine's performance benefiting, perhaps, from the ten overs' experience he had gained as an overarmer in Hobart over Christmas.

"Except when tossing, I never saw 'Woody' and Douglas in such close proximity for the remainder of the tour as during this display of pat-ball on the pitch. Even the pat-ball was conducted in grim earnest. At one stage Jack Fingleton came down the wicket to join in the 'French cricket.' " Just imagine the perplexity and curiosity of that old dowager on the staircase at Mount Breckan!

"Play had hardly resumed," says Hele, "when Larwood split his right boot from toe to heel, left the field and borrowed a pair from wicketkeeper George Duckworth. These he split almost immediately and went off again. Donning a new pair of boots this time, he ordered the original pair to be dispatched post haste to a bootmaker for repair. The cobbler did an amazingly swift job and, when the boots were back in the dressingroom and a message was brought to Larwood to this effect, he went off yet again to retrieve them. Altogether the kingpin of the England attack was off the field four times during the first ninety-minute session of play. According to Hobbs, he was absent for a full hour of that hour and a half."

Woodfull struck by a ball from Larwood during the 1932–33 Test series. This photo clearly shows the packed leg side

In the meantime Allen, Voce, and Bowes did the bowling. Before play began Jardine had given Allen the option of bowling Bodyline or withdrawing from the Test. "I'd better get my golf bag from the Windsor then Douglas, hadn't I?" replied the Sydney-born "Gubby." For once in his life Jardine submitted. Voce and Bowes delivered most of the bumpers that morning.

Woodfull was first batsman out. He was bowled, unluckily, by a ball from Allen that contacted both of his pads before dribbling through them on to the stumps. Woodfull 10, Australia one for 29 at snails' pace, and O'Brien preceding Bradman.

Woodfull had scored 7 in twenty-seven minutes and 0 in ten minutes in the Sydney Test. He had now gone for 10 in just under an hour, including that five minutes of pat-ball. O'Brien had been included partly because he was a left-hander. The selectors believed bowling first to a right-hander and then to a left-hander would affect Larwood and Voce's control of line. "Mo," as he was known, was also something of a pugilist and known to have a quick eye and courage. If he could dodge punches from six inches or so, he would be able to evade bumpers pitched eight or ten yards from his feet. So it was thought.

"Mo" gained little opportunity of proving the selectors right or wrong. Fingleton, who had begun bravely after his bruising in Sydney, called for a short run after tapping a ball to short-leg. O'Brien tried to send him back, then generously sacrificed his wicket by running through.

Bradman came slowly to the wicket like some old-time warrior-hero striding out to do single combat with the chosen of the enemy. The great crowd clapped and cheered him all the way from the Grey Smith Stand to the wicket. George Hele was at the bowler's end, with Bill Bowes to bowl.

Hele remembers the occasion clearly: "Don took guard, asking for 'two legs,' which interpreted means 'middle and leg.' The Bodyline field was set—three leg side slips, Hammond, Voce, and Sutcliffe, behind them Pataudi at deep fine-leg, Jardine at leg gully, and Wyatt close to him, but squarer, Allen at suicide square-leg, Leyland at suicide silly mid-on (these two for the vertically played prop-shot to the bumper) and Larwood's substitute, the loneliest of off side fieldsmen, at cover.

"The crowd had quietened now. It waited in silence, as I imagine

Top: Woodfull and Jardine knocking the shine off a replacement ball during the Second Test of the Bodyline series. *Bottom:* Ponsford bowled by Larwood in the First Test of the same series

men await a hanging or the volley of rifle fire at a military execution. Bradman set himself. He always addressed the bowler like a statue, head erect between hunched shoulders, eyes steady, unblinking, and level, gloves close together about the middle of the handle of his short-handled bat, the back of his left forearm square to the bowler, bat an inch out and forward of the right toe. You could have drawn a straight and perpendicular line from the point of his left shoulder through his left elbow and wrist, left knee and heel.

"Bowes' first ball to him was short and well outside the off stump. Crouching a little Bradman stepped back a foot or more outside the off stump, his right leg bent almost at right angle as he pivoted almost square-on to the ball, now approaching his left shoulder. Swinging his bat horizontally and over the ball, he contacted it with the bat's lower edge and dragged it on to the base of his leg stump before he followed through. The bail on the middle and off stump did not fall.

"I don't know what was in Don's mind before he played that ball. I still don't know because I have never asked him. The ball asked to be hooked or, preferably, cut square to the off. I thought Don should have approached it more prudently. He had been out of cricket for some weeks. On his way to the wicket Sutcliffe had spoken to him of the wonderful reception he received from the great crowd and Don had replied, 'Yes, but will it be so good when I'm coming back?'

"He left the field, of course, in silence and I have always wondered whether this or his return to the old pavilion at Kennington Oval in 1948, when he was bowled by Eric Hollies for a duck in his last Test innings, was the longest cricketing walk of his life. He needed only four in that eightieth and last of his Test innings to have averaged an exact 100 in these games.

"Certainly he looked downcast as he turned from the crease at the Members' end with Australia's score three for 67. Of one thing I *am* certain. Many an English bowler has suffered at Bradman's hands since that December day at the M.C.G. because of that 'duck.' By the time he reached the boundary gate the crowd of almost 64,000 had recovered sufficiently from its shock to rise and applaud him sympathetically. I shall always regard that stroke as a rash one— Jardine called it 'daring.' Knowing Bradman's genius, I am confident he could have directed that delivery of Bowes anywhere he wished on the off side of the wicket through the virtually vacant field for

116

four. But that is cricket and that ball and stroke will remain immortal."

Joined by McCabe, Fingleton continued his splendid innings, taking runs through the leg trap. His on side play was, for the most part, perfect and he was unlucky not to reach his century, being bowled by Allen when 83 and Australia five for 156. In his three subsequent Test innings that summer Fingleton scored 1, 0, and 0. He was omitted from the last two Tests.

Hele believes Jack's limited repertoire of strokes and consequent lack of adaptability, rather than any lack of courage, left him pinioned. "No person," he says, "who stood so close to Bodyline as I did, would ever be so unfeeling as to condemn a batsman for not handling this bowling effectively or with orthodox technique. There *was* no effective, or orthodox, answer to it. Many suggestions were made, from safe positions beyond the boundary, as to how it should have been handled by the batsmen and by the umpires.

"But only two men, George Borwick and myself, saw from start to finish the five acts of this vicious drama from close quarters and George and I are still unanimous in our views regarding it. As I have said, I would not cross a street to watch it again, but in my seventies and eighties I have regularly watched District cricket in Melbourne and reflected as I did so that, if Bodyline had not been banned, there would have been no District, County, or other grades and classes of cricket to watch."

Stan McCabe tried to take control of the English attack again in the way he had at Sydney. He played well, but this was a different wicket, a much slower wicket, and what batsman could have played two innings of the calibre of that 187 not out twice in one month? McCabe lost his wicket to a catch by Jardine off Voce when he was 32 and when his dismissal was least expected. His great 189 not out at Johannesburg and even greater 232 at Trent Bridge were to come later—three and six years later respectively. Together with that 187 not out against Bodyline they stand like Parthenons on the Acropolis of batsmanship.

Stan said after his innings at Sydney, "I was lucky. I could never do it again." Nobody else ever did it even once.

George Hele does not believe (and Jack Fingleton agrees) that even Victor Trumper could have handled Bodyline bowling consistently. Though he saw Victor score that 214 not out at Adelaide in 1911, he is adamant that Trumper could not have conquered

117

this form of attack. Where Trumper would have failed and Bradman and McCabe *did* fail, what other batsman could have succeeded?

Vic Richardson, the most consistent batsman against Bodyline until he scored a "pair of spectacles" in the Fifth Test, scored 34 before being caught, late on the first day, by Hammond off Voce. Vic, in our opinion, was technically a lesser batsman than his grandson, Ian Chappell, and a far lesser one in this respect than his grandson, Greg. Like Ian and Greg, however, he had guts and, unlike them, he could hook a ball exactly where he meant to hook it—even from Larwood. He showed this when he scored 231 against Larwood in 1928 for South Australia and 134 against him in the corresponding game of 1932. He "murdered" Voce at Trent Bridge in 1930 and it was more because of Vic Richardson than any other factor that Voce, who made three tours of Australia with M.C.C. teams, never represented England in England.

Vic had proved he could handle Larwood when he was bowling to an orthodox field setting. He was determined to try to do so with the Bodyline field. He kept endeavouring to do so until the fate of the Ashes and the outcome of the series was decided at Brisbane.

Oldfield was as plucky as ever and Bill O'Reilly, adhering to captain's orders, kept at as safe a distance from the line of the bowling as his policeman grandfather did from *his* quarry, Ned Kelly, in the Riverina fifty years before. In a total score of 15, Bill struck three fours powerfully, through cover, before Australia was out early on the second morning for 228.

Hobbs wrote home to London, "I had never seen Australian batsmen surrender the initiative to quite the same extent as in this innings. I wondered, as we waited for our men to come out, what sort of a bullfight we should have seen if Australia, too, had a shock brigade. The short, bumping deliveries were by no means as frequent as at Sydney, but the batsmen always shaped as if they expected one. In some instances the batsman was in position for a bumper when something else came along and got the wicket.

"We were struck from the start by the astuteness and keenness of Jardine's captaincy, and I was left thinking that England had had no better man in the field since Warner's time. No bowler was allowed to tire (Ian Chappell, Dennis Lillee, and Max Walker please note) and no batsman saw too much of any one bowler."

In fact, as George Hele stressed and the figures reveal, the Australians

118

had done better against *three* Bodyliners in Melbourne than they had against *two* in Sydney. In Sydney, Larwood 31/5/96/5 and Voce 29/4/110/4 in the first innings; in Melbourne, Larwood 20·3/2/52/2, Voce 20/3/54/3, and Bowes 19/2/50/1. Possibly the slower, less responsive pitch at Melbourne and the recurring disintegration of Larwood's footwear before lunch best explains the discrepancy.

"Oldfield's ability to bat effectively against the bowling when the Bodyline field was not set," says Hele, "indicates what the recognised batsmen could have done if similarly blessed."

Australians have always regarded the imperturbable Herbert Sutcliffe as a lucky as well as a great batsman. He had played that ball from O'Reilly on to his stumps when 43 in Sydney without dislodging the bails. Now, when he was 30 in Melbourne, he was left two yards up the pitch by Grimmett's leg-break. Oldfield missed taking the ball and it went to McCabe at slip. McCabe's shy at the wicket from about three yards also missed and Oldfield had not turned to take the return.

Lining the hall of Grimmett's long-term home at Firle in the Adelaide suburbs hung a set of framed photographs of missed stumpings (mostly by Oldfield) from his bowling in Australian Tests. This was why, Clarrie asserts, his efforts in Australia against England were less successful than his endeavours on English wickets.

The M.C.C. had amassed totals of eight for 334 against Western Australia, seven for 583 against a combined Australian XI, nine for 634 against South Australia, nine for 408 against Victoria, 530 against New South Wales, England had scored 524 in the Sydney Test. Now, against Wall, O'Reilly, Grimmett, and Ironmonger, England was out for 169.

O'Reilly's 34·3 overs, seventeen of them maidens, for 63 runs and five wickets, which was to be followed in the second innings by twenty-four overs, five of them maidens, for 66 runs and another five wickets, remains for Hele, "the finest bowling performance I have seen." He says, "Bill showed that, when the wicket gave a spin bowler some assistance, he was the one who could take fullest advantage from it. He delivered every kind of ball he owned, from the above-medium-pace leg-break to the high-popping wrong-un. He used his faster straight ball occasionally. He had every batsman who faced him groping forward or scurrying back. They were great professional batsmen and they tried everything they knew. Bill's

119

control of sharp variant spin and his deceptive flight were just too much for them.

"The Englishmen contended that the Melbourne curator, acting on official instruction, doctored the wicket to reduce its effectiveness for pace and increase its responsiveness to spin. This was not so. It just happened that during this season, *before* this season, in fact, the Melbourne Cricket Club changed from Merri Creek to Glen Roy soil for the preparation of its pitches."

Jardine wrote: "Though every allowance be made for the fact that the wicket was tricky, and that it was even receptive of spin—a characteristic that had never been associated with a Melbourne wicket on the second day—there can be no excuse for our very feeble batting performances."

It was an old, long-term retainer of the Melbourne Cricket Club and Ground who told me, during the Melbourne Test between Len Hutton and Ian Johnson's teams, that Jardine locked a man in the England dressingroom during the Sunday of the 1932–33 Test to report any untoward tampering with the wicket.

Jardine was generous enough, in June 1933, to say of the Australian bowlers, "Where all were deserving of the highest praise, it is invidious to discriminate. It was this match which set the seal upon O'Reilly's fast-rising reputation. The rising of a new star is often the occasion for the disappearance of another below the horizon. The setting star was Grimmett's.

"Personally I am inclined to doubt whether the South Australian deserved the declination which was to be his, for though Wall and O'Reilly shared nine wickets between them, Grimmett played an important part in their success, bowling fourteen overs at a cost of 18 runs for the reward of one wicket."

Of the Englishmen only Sutcliffe 52, Allen 30, Leyland 22, Pataudi 15, and Wyatt 13, reached double figures and it is important to remember this when measuring the greatness of Bradman's second knock.

Down, or rather up, on that staircase at Mount Breckan we were pretty happy, if not assured, at that Australian lead of 59. Our eighty-year-old dowager was growing erudite regarding the function of stumps. She had by now heard them fly eight times in two days— the stumps of such illustrious batsmen as Woodfull, Bradman, Fingleton, Hammond, and Leyland among them. On the second

120

afternoon she disclosed that her paternal grandfather had been born in Cork and she was smugly satisfied about the success of the Irish-descended topscorer, Fingleton, and top wicket-taker for Australia, O'Reilly.

If this trend continued, we were hoping to find her out on that buffalo grass lawn keeping wicket before she was much older.

Vic Richardson, who at Durban in February 1936 was to catch five Springbok batsmen, three off Grimmett and two off O'Reilly, in one South African innings and so establish a Test fielding record that still stands today, caught Sutcliffe off Wall and Allen off O'Reilly, the two highest scorers of this English innings.

Vic once told George and me that he only dropped one catch in about fifteen years of first-class cricket. George insists that he'd forgotten two misses. He says he saw Vic miss three catches in sixteen summers, but he still classes him as the safest fieldsman he's seen. "Percy Chapman," George says, "was brilliant on his left side but a different proposition on his right. I would rank Neil Harvey next to Vic for all-round excellence and reliability when the big moment and big opportunity came. Neil had a far better throw. Vic took the catch that ended the England innings above his head at long-on like the champion Australian Rules footballer he was."

So far this summer Bradman had scored 3 and 10 for the Australian XI at Perth, 36 and 13 for the Australian XI at Melbourne, and 18 and 23 for New South Wales, plus his first innings 0 against this English attack. Verity and Allen dismissed him in Perth, Larwood got him l.b.w. and bowled him in Melbourne in mid-November, and he was l.b.w. to Tate and bowled by Voce in the State game in Sydney.

His average against the Englishmen, therefore, was 14·7 from 103 runs when he joined Woodfull, following the dismissal of Fingleton by Allen for 1 and O'Brien bowled by Larwood 11, at two for 27. Australia led by 86 and few expected O'Reilly and company to be able to dismiss England cheaply again.

A crowd of 63,993 had come to watch Bradman on the Friday. There were 68,188 at the M.C.G. for the same purpose on the Monday. Bradman knew why they were there.

Back to George Hele behind the stumps:

"Jardine experimented with Bodyline almost from the start of the Australian second innings, despite the unresponsive pitch. He soon

121

discovered he was bowling Larwood against the breeze. Though his partner Allen had dismissed Fingleton with the fourth ball of his first over and delivered three overs for 10 runs, he was taken off and Larwood transferred to his end. Neither Larwood nor Voce, who joined forces with him, could get the ball to rise as they would have wished and both reverted to orthodox fast bowling. They were very fast indeed. It was after Larwood's second ball had knocked out O'Brien's off stump that Bradman entered.

"Larwood's field for him was two leg side slips, three short-legs, and two long-legs, a mid-on very straight and close, one slip on the off side almost wide enough for gully. For Woodfull he had four short-legs and a strong off side slips cordon. Apart from that close mid-on, Larwood had no fieldsman forward of the batting crease for either batsman. Leyland, square with the wicket at point for each batsman, was the nearest to being so.

"It was now that a crowd of nearly 70,000 saw one of the greatest innings I myself ever watched. After Woodfull left for 26 at three for 78, only one batsman, Vic Richardson 32, gave Don any support. Together they took the score from 81 to 135. Bradman's defence and general tactics against this most difficult and dangerous of all bowling, a pot pourri of Bodyline and the orthodox, were superb.

"He played strokes against the bumpers, forcing them as often as he could to the vacant off side front-of-the-wicket field. He placed the good length ball magnificently, mostly to the on side between square-leg and mid-on. If he believed a ball was likely to hit him, he evaded it. Don had vowed that Larwood would never hit him. He kept hammering both Larwood and Voce, and Jardine seemed frightened to try Bowes, despite his first-innings success.

"Instead he used Wally Hammond, one of the finest bowlers of his type I have seen. On a wicket like this one Hammond was extremely hard to hit. The way in which he made the ball lift from a length on a pitch which did not help the fast bowlers was remarkable. This, I believe, was because he did not pound it into the wicket but allowed the pitch to provide the lift."

Of Bradman's innings Hobbs said, "Instead of playing ordinary defensive back shots, as most first-class batsman would, Bradman, by quick footwork, retreated slightly and either placed the ball hard past the bowler, or, when it pitched outside the off stump, cut it brilliantly.

122

"Perhaps Jardine might have placed a fielder at long-on to curb Bradman. Of course, it is really difficult to set a field for him, especially now, when his strokes are greater in number than when he was in England . . . A wonderful performance his, even if he did not have the cheeky shots of his previous big innings against us. This was probably due to the admirable direction of our bowling and to a natural desire on his part to make good after his failures.

"On only one point was I not quite satisfied. I was not convinced that Bradman had mastered our leg-theory, because the wicket was not ideal for it."

Of that performance Jardine wrote: "Bradman came in to play what proved to be by far his best and most worthy innings of the series. With the ball rising hardly more than stump-high, he was always at ease with the fast bowlers. Moreover, he adopted more orthodox methods. Why he ever deserted such methods will always remain a mystery to me for, relying on them on this occasion, he obtained the complete mastery which so many Australians associate with his batting. He was at the top of his form playing a great innings for his side."

When Australia was nine for 186 Bradman was 98 not out. "It was on this occasion, however many other versions of the tale you may have heard," insists George Hele, "that 'Dainty' Ironmonger, that ultimate in tailenders, received a telephone call in the dressing-room just as he was walking out of the door to bat. It was Mrs Ironmonger. The attendant said to her, 'He's just gone out to bat, Mrs Ironmonger. Will you hang on?'

"She did, for far longer than she expected.

"As 'Dainty' came towards the pitch Don walked to meet him. 'Dainty' was due to face Wally Hammond, who had just dismissed Tim Wall for 3 and Bill O'Reilly 0. Hammond was bowling from the Members' end, the one at which I was standing. I'm not sure whether Don spoke to 'Dainty,' but I heard 'Darkie,' as he was also called, say to Don, 'Don't worry, son, I won't let you down.'

"I have never seen two balls go closer to bowling a batsman, yet miss the off and leg stump, than did the last two of Hammond's over. Nor have I ever seen a look of greater anxiety on the face of a batsman at the bowler's end than the one which appeared on Bradman's. He breathed the sigh of all sighs of relief when I called 'Over.'

"Ironmonger had taken centre stump for his block and faced up

123

with his bat absolutely vertical. Bert had only three fingers on his left hand and the index finger of these ended with the first joint. It might amaze many people to know that he batted right-handed. Few cricket-lovers saw him long enough to find out."

His batting average in fourteen Tests in which he played twenty-one innings was 2·62, this with the help of five not outs. His highest score was 12 and his aggregate 42. But in those fourteen Tests he took 74 wickets at 17·97, all of them in Australia.

"As each of those deliveries from Hammond grazed the stumps," continues Hele, "the slips fieldsmen threw up their hands. Hammond made odd noises through pursed lips. No more. Voce then bowled to Bradman. Don played the first four balls carefully. He crash-hooked the fifth over the leg field to be 102 and, when the roar of the crowd subsided, steered a single from the sixth to be 103 in 185 minutes with 7 fours, 8 threes, 12 twos, and 27 singles. He scored most of the singles to retain the strike after the recognised batsmen had gone. His 103 came out of 164.

"Ironmonger had kept the faith, and had not let Bradman down. In the outcome he was run out 0, but could confront the impatient and puzzled Mrs Ironmonger on that dressingroom telephone with pride. Many of the cheers that had brought Don back undefeated had been aimed at Herbert Ironmonger, that rabbit (should we say ferret?) among all Test match batsmen."

Australia, 228 and 191, led England 169, by 250. England had 45 minutes that third night and then all eternity in which to get them.

As the Australian team took the field, Bill O'Reilly crossed to George Hele.

"How's your eyesight, George?" he asked.

"OK."

"The hearing?"

"OK, too."

"Good, you're going to need both of 'em."

"The Tiger" obviously was feeling as the "Demon" Spofforth had felt that August day of 1882 at Kennington Oval when England needed 85 in her second innings to win the game they still call "The Ashes Test." On that grey afternoon in Kennington Spofforth declared to his unconvinced comrades: "This thing *can* be done."

Thanks to Spofforth's 28/15/44/7 on top of his first innings 36·3/18/46/7, or 64·3/33/90/14 in all, it was done—by seven runs.

Jardine had placed his faith in Bob Wyatt as Sutcliffe's opening partner in the first three innings of the series. This time he chose two Yorkshiremen—Sutcliffe and Leyland—and they had 43 on the board without loss by stumps, leaving 208 needed.

Sutcliffe, in the words of his captain, "brought out his best batsmanship" during those forty-five minutes that Melbourne evening. "Whatever may be said about his batting in the first innings, there can be no two opinions about the 32 runs he made before the close of play. They bore the stamp and hall-mark of a master batsman," wrote Jardine.

Back to George Hele for the fourth and final day: "After Leyland had scored 19, Sutcliffe 33, and 1 sundry had come for England to be none for 53, O'Reilly bowled Sutcliffe with the best ball I've seen bowled in any class of cricket. It pitched on his middle and leg stump and hit the off stump about six inches below the bail. I've not seen a faster leg-break, *break* as distinct from *cutter*. The great Sydney Barnes was supposed to bowl this kind of ball and no doubt he did, perhaps even faster than O'Reilly.

"Despite this possibility, I rank O'Reilly as a greater bowler than Barnes. This is not because I am an Australian. It is because O'Reilly never gave up fighting. Barnes was a temperamental man and he did. He proved this at this same Melbourne Cricket Ground in 1911 12. After dismissing Kelleway 2, Bardsley 0, Clem Hill 0, and Armstrong 4 before lunch at a personal cost of six runs, Barnes finished with five for 44 from twenty-three overs. This was because the barrackers took to him unfairly and he sat on the ground waiting for the noise to subside. Had it been England at bat and 'The Tiger' bowling, he would have become even more malevolent and gone on with the business.

"Vic Richardson understood Bill O'Reilly better than any other captain, knew how to get his magnificent best from him. Once in South Africa he sent him out to the boundary and left him there for hours, fuming at being denied the ball. Then he brought him on with devastating effect. On another occasion on that tour Vic told Len Darling to try and hit Bill on the shin with his next return to the wicket. Darling managed to do so. O'Reilly had been taking matters easily. He ceased doing so next ball.

"For sheer bowling ability there was probably little to choose between Barnes and O'Reilly. Barnes was slightly faster through the air, but he didn't bowl a wrong-un. He bowled an orthodox off-break. He also developed spin swerve, as distinct from seam swerve. O'Reilly almost invariably bowled with the breeze at his back to gain greater pace from the pitch. Barnes varied ends.

"The pitch, as O'Reilly had demonstrated so indelibly, was now taking sharp spin. It was a rough top now. As the Australians took the field I had heard O'Reilly say to Tim Wall, 'If you get Leyland, I'll get Sutcliffe.' Tim replied, 'Is that all you want?' O'Reilly had been as good as his word. Now it was up to Wall. Tim was a trifle lucky with his part of the assignment, as I saw from square-leg. The shortish ball which did the trick hit Maurice on his right (front) pad, ricocheted to his left pad near his boot and trickled on to the stumps."

England two for 53, 198 needed, Hammond and Pataudi at the wicket.

"Hammond seemed assured, almost cocksure; Pataudi was on the brink of panic. Indians can be like this under pressure, and the pressure was extreme now. He probed indeterminately forward to Iron-monger and Fingleton held the soft catch—three for 70 and Jardine the next batsman in. Douglas faced 'Dainty' Ironmonger, who had relieved Wall. Using his tremendous reach, he strained forward to the first two. Both of them were pitched on the leg stump. They beat the bat and the off stump by a razor's edge. Again Jardine went forward and snicked a catch to McCabe. Four for 70 and Ames to join Hammond.

"After the match Jardine came to me and said, 'Those were the three finest balls I've ever faced in a row.' I replied, 'They *were* three magnificent balls.' Jardine used to talk to me quite a bit during the early part of this series, as he had done in 1928–29. He ceased doing so as the 1932–33 rubber wore on. He was a far more affable person, more relaxed, in 1928–29. He wasn't the captain then, of course. Nor was there any Bodyline bowling.

"Ames was the next to go, being brilliantly caught by Fingleton, one of the finest of all Australia's close-to-the-wicket fieldsmen, for 2. Five England wickets had now fallen for 24 runs from none for 53. Bill O'Reilly had dismissed three of the batsmen. In came the relegated Wyatt to join the still-confident Hammond.

"Hammond was giving the impression that he wanted to win the match before lunch. He off-drove O'Reilly, a lofted stroke, when he was 23 and 'Mo' O'Brien held the vital catch three-quarter way to

126

the white rails. Wally could hardly have chosen a safer fieldsman and England were six for 85.

"I had taken my wife, Matilda, to Melbourne for this Test," continues Hele, "and my sister-in-law had come too. My wife had a seat in the reserve enclosure for players and their wives, but my sister-in-law did not. Before the Test began Bob Wyatt came to me and said, 'George, I've just given a ticket for the special reserve to your wife's sister so they can be together. Now you won't be able to give me out l.b.w.' Wyatt had a 'thing' about l.b.w. dismissals.

"Despite the state of the wicket, which Douglas Jardine later described as 'treacherous,' Wyatt began steadily and convincingly against both O'Reilly and Ironmonger. The pitch did appear to have lost bite at this stage. England still had a chance. 'Gubby' Allen was an accomplished batsman and a superb fighter.

"Settling in together, Wyatt and Allen took England past the 100, on into the 120s and 130s. It was when the total was 135 that I gave Wyatt out l.b.w. to O'Reilly *for the second time in the match*. It was seven for 135, eight for 137 when Allen was beautifully stumped by Oldfield off Ironmonger, nine for 138, and all out 139."

According to Hobbs, "Our innings ended in a wrestling match between the Australian players and an umpire for stumps as souvenirs. This was followed by a great demonstration of joy by the crowd, who invaded the pitch, took pieces of the wicket away as souvenirs and howled loudly for Woodfull to come out and make a speech."

O'Reilly's match figures were:
    34·3/17/63/5 and 24/5/66/5 or 58·3/22/129/10 at 12·9.

Ironmonger's were:
    14/4/28/0 and 19·1/8/26/4 or 33·1/12/54/4 at 13·5.

Between them in that fourth innings O'Reilly and Ironmonger produced the figures: 43·1/13/92/9. Says Hele, "I've never seen a more difficult combination of spin in operation."

I asked George why Ironmonger was never taken to England and if he had been, how he would have fared. He replied, "No member of the 1928–29 or 1932–33 English sides ever queried Ironmonger's bowling action to me. Nor did I ever hear any of them doing so. I did learn that Patsy Hendren was supposed to have spread the story on his return to England in 1929 that the bowling action of 'Dainty' was questionable. When Woodfull and his 1930 team were on the ship on their way to England they cabled the Australian Board of

127

Control requesting that Ironmonger be sent to join them. The Board refused this request.

"I had talks with Bob Crockett, who umpired in thirty-three Tests from 1901 to 1925, concerning Ironmonger's action. He replied, 'George, you've never no-balled him.' 'No, have you?' I said. 'No, because he does not throw.' Ironmonger had no top joints on his left index finger, *the* most important finger for a spin bowler of his type. He had huge hands, however, and he used to push the stump of that finger into the seam and spin from it.

"In my opinion, Ironmonger might have taken 150 wickets in England in 1930 and we, with his help, could have won the five Tests. It was during the Bodyline series that Leyland demanded that 'Dainty' should empty his pocket to prove he wasn't using resin to assist his grip of the ball. 'Dainty' obliged, but he emptied the wrong pocket and Leyland never thought to insist he empty the other one."

Woodfull was carried from the field at the finish of the Test. They must have found O'Reilly too heavy. Wrote Jardine, "Both O'Reilly and Ironmonger bowled magnificently, exploiting the wicket for all it was worth, and without giving away any unnecessary runs. After the drubbing which Australia had received in the First Test match, her come-back in the second cannot be too highly praised. Throughout the match, Woodfull handled and captained his side magnificently." Douglas could take defeat like a gentleman and a sportsman, anyway.

When the two Georges, Hele and Borwick, returned to the loneliness of their dressingroom they decided Australia had a "pretty good chance of retaining the Ashes, provided the remaining pitches resembled the one at Melbourne."

Alan Kippax, who watched the Test, said, "Australia was no nearer to solving the Bodyline problem than she was at Sydney. In the first innings Fingleton's 83 stood out in lonely relief in a total of 228. In the second it was Bradman who played a lone hand with 103 not out of a total of 191. The win was due mainly to fine bowling, especially by O'Reilly, assisted by the unaccountable collapse of the English batting."

One all and three to go; and Bradman was himself again, or so it seemed. The Mount Breckan dowager at least appeared to think so for she put her Adelaide Oval Lady's ticket aside securely for use in ten days' time.

128

Adelaide Explosion

RETRACING THE TRAUMATIC EVENTS WHICH OCCURRED AT ADELAIDE
Oval on six of the last seven days of January 1933, in the coolest
light which forty years' reflection can furnish, we are thankful that
those events happened in the city of disciplined decorum which
Adelaide was then believed to be—under, indeed, the Gothic spires
of Australia's most graceful cathedral.

Had the Adelaide Test been at Sydney or Melbourne's cricket
grounds or at Brisbane's Woolloongabba, the Ashes series between
England and Australia might have ended with that 127th Anglo-
Australian Test. For this match between the teams of Douglas
Jardine and William Maldon Woodfull was the most dramatic of
all Test matches.

It was contested in an atmosphere of electric hostility—at times,
on the Saturday and Monday, of ill-concealed hate. Throughout
its course, a pall of sinister suspense and dread enveloped it. During
it, Bodyline and its purpose was unmasked, and Bodyline became
as horrid a word for Australians as the name Hitler was to be from
1940 to 1945.

Only by some miracle did the volcano, as English cricket historian,
Ralph Barker, called it, fail to produce its Pompeii.

On the Saturday and Monday normally peaceful, well-educated, and aristocratically-reared Adelaide octogenarians stood in rows in the Members' Enclosure, their faces scarlet with anger, contempt, and disgust. Together, and in chorus upon chorus, they counted Jardine and Larwood "out"—"one, two, three, four, five, six, seven, eight, nine, OUT."

On the Monday, when Oldfield was struck to the ground by a legitimate bumper from Larwood, who was bowling with the second new ball, a mature and experienced Police Inspector called to Adelaide barrister, Charles Sandery, at the base of the George Giffen Stand, "Why don't you jump the fence? I won't stop you." Thousands of spectators across the oval on the eastern mound almost did. At least one of them had his foot on top of the paling fence. Between forty and fifty mounted troopers were summoned to the ground to deter a mass invasion of the field.

During this Test, says George Hele, "the language of some members of the English team would have caused them to be reported by any self-respecting V.F.L. umpire. Oddly enough, Jardine, Larwood, and Voce were beyond reproach in this respect. Yet I learned more four-letter words during this match than throughout the remainder of my life."

Attendance at the Adelaide Test was 174,442, following 158,193 at Sydney and 200,625 at Melbourne, a total of 533,260 for just more than thirteen days' cricket. The 50,962 present on the Saturday at Adelaide produced another ground record, the fourth in three Tests.

Total attendance for the series was 765,249, during the Great Depression.

Between 4,000 and 5,000 people made their way to the Adelaide Oval on the Wednesday, two days before the Test, to watch the English and Australian players at practice. They, according to Jardine, "seized the opportunity to exhibit such a display of hooliganism as to make practice a farce."

At Jardine's request the ground was closed to the public while practice was in progress the following afternoon.

In the first two Tests Jardine had called "tails" when Woodfull tossed the coin. Before the Adelaide Test Maurice Leyland lent his captain a miniature black cat for luck. Jardine called "tails" again and third time proved lucky.

That great Australian and Adelaide left-hander Clem Hill then came to Jardine and said, "It should be a close match." Douglas

Bradman clean bowled as he attempts to hook Bowes during the Second Test, 1932

replied with the nearest thing he could produce to a smile, "Haven't you heard who won the toss?"

For this vital game Paynter replaced Pataudi and Verity replaced Bowes in the English side. The Adelaide Oval had earned its name as the "graveyard for pace bowlers." Jardine may also have feared Australia would produce another pitch that favoured spin in the way the Melbourne one had.

Australia restored Ponsford, who had been twelfth man in Melbourne following his 32 and 2 in Sydney, in place of O'Brien.

Wrote Hobbs, "I was struck by the luck we were having all through the tour with the weather. In my first Test at Adelaide (that of 1907–08), we were in the field two days with the Fahrenheit temperature at 114° in the shade and I could not remember any Test when the thermometer was not hovering round 100°. England touring sides now do not seem to get those long, gruelling periods of really scorching heat."

Maybe this was as well. The human heat engendered was more than enough.

Jardine joined Sutcliffe to open England's innings, despite Sutcliffe and Leyland's opening stand of 53 in the fourth innings of the Melbourne Test.

Two incidents, both of them instigated by Englishmen on the first day of this match, aggravated the ill-feeling which already existed between the opposing players. The first was Leyland's demand that Ironmonger turn his trouser pocket inside out to prove whether or not he was using resin. Leyland later apologised for his accusation. The second was Jardine's dispatch of a message to Woodfull requesting him to instruct Richardson, who was fielding on the leg side, not to move about behind the English batsmen who, he alleged, were being upset by such action.

Those who knew Vic Richardson will realise there was no substance in this accusation. Nor will they be surprised to hear that Vic's reactive comments were "forcible and free."

Showers on the Thursday caused the pitch to be sweating a little when Sutcliffe took guard to Tim Wall. Until the luncheon interval ninety minutes later, the occasional ball kicked from a good length.

"Before the Englishmen knew where they were," says Hele, "they were four for 30—Jardine 3, Sutcliffe 9, Hammond 2, and Ames 3. The wickets were shared by Wall (two), O'Reilly, and

Woodfull staggers from the wicket after being struck over the heart by a delivery from Larwood during the tense Third Test in Adelaide

Ironmonger. At lunch it was four for 39. The ball from Wall which bowled Jardine hit the back of his left pad and went on to take the leg stump. Wall began to appeal for l.b.w. but stifled his cry when he saw the wicket break.

"Jardine and I were still on amicable terms then. During lunch on the stairs of the Giffen Stand he said, 'George, had you given me out l.b.w. I would have thought it a wrong decision. I did not think I was that far across my stumps.' Douglas used to take block on 'two-legs.' Then he usually backed away to the leg side until his bat was grounded from nine inches to a foot outside the leg stump. From here he would shuffle in towards his wicket as the ball was coming to him. This time he shuffled too far to a ball that did not swing. Many people in the Members' Enclosure said to me, 'That ball from Wall must have swung a mile.' It did not swing at all.

"Before play had gone very far I began to think how lucky Woodfull was to have lost that toss. On this lively pitch before lunch Larwood and Voce would have been extremely dangerous. Sutcliffe went to a superb catch by Wall at silly-point off O'Reilly, his opening bowling partner. Wall held the hot catch with one hand, alongside his boot."

Soon afterwards occurred the incident which convinced Hele that the English professional batsmen would have been distinctly vulnerable to Bodyline reprisals.

"Several balls from Wall had whistled about Sutcliffe's ears. The first that Wall bowled to Hammond rose sharply outside his off stump. After he had scored 2, Hammond got another riser on the same line and he pulled his handsome head back swiftly from its path.

"Then," continues Hele, "I saw something I had never expected from so great a batsman. The very next ball rose in similar fashion outside the off stump and Hammond, in my opinion, steered it deliberately to Oldfield. It wasn't a snick so much as a purposeful glide and Wally walked out without waiting for Oldfield to take the catch. This convinced me that, even without a Larwood, Australia could have ended Bodyline right smartly by giving the Englishmen their own kind of medicine.

"We had in Australia at the time several fast bowlers besides Wall. They included 'Bull' Alexander, Laurie Nash, who had taken five for 22 against the South Africans the previous summer in his one Test, Eddie Gilbert, the Aboriginal, who could have made things

132

really nasty by bowling Bodyline to batsmen whose livelihood depended on their cricket."

Bill O'Reilly agrees with Hele. He says, "Retaliation would have wiped Bodyline on the spot. I say this because, when Hammond passed me after being caught from that ball of Wall's by Oldfield, he said, 'If that's what the game's coming to, it's time for me to get out.' The England batsmen of that summer would have demanded that Jardine abandon Bodyline. They would not have stood it themselves. They were mostly professionals. Cricket was their bread and butter."

Vic Richardson also agreed with Hele. He wrote, "Bill Woodfull steadfastly refused to retaliate with similar tactics throughout the series. Many said Australia was not equipped with fast bowlers fitted to use similar tactics successfully. This was not so. Any fast bowler could have belted them down halfway and directed it at the body and head of batsmen.

"Bill Woodfull had his principles and he stuck to them. By doing so I have no doubt that he added to his already great reputation as a sportsman. Had the same tactics been employed by Australia, the position could have grown infinitely worse than it was and it was far too bad already. By word and action England's top professionals could have forced a swift solution to all this. Both Hammond and Sutcliffe confessed to me they would not have played for five minutes against such bowling. But they declined to voice their views openly until much later."

Another to speak out against Bodyline was Jack Hobbs, *on his return to England,* as we shall see.

After lunch the moisture had left the wicket. Leyland and Wyatt, who captained the M.C.C. when Jardine was not playing but who was never officially named vice-captain, added 156 for the fifth wicket. Wyatt formed a happy friendship with attractive South Australian women's golf champion, Katherine Rymill, while in Australia. Maybe Kathie provided the inspiration for the three sixes he hit during his innings of 78. Wyatt's hooking and pulling of O'Reilly was savage, occasionally, and at one stage he and Leyland added 100 in 105 minutes.

Leyland fell to O'Reilly's desperation ball, that fastish straight one into the block hole. It took the middle stump with the score 186 and when Leyland needed 17 for his century. Dedicated contributions

133

from Eddie Paynter 77, and Verity 45, helped England on to 341 from their first day overnight score of seven for 237. Outstanding Australian bowler was Tim Wall who, on his home ground, took five for 72 from 34·1 overs without assistance from Bodyline.

The weather was warming up but Jardine banned sea bathing for all members of his Test side, although they were boarding at Glenelg's beach-front Pier Hotel. Swimming in sea water, declared Douglas, was apt to stiffen muscles. In this contention he is at odds with all of Australia's racehorse trainers, including that spectacularly successful trainer of Melbourne Cup winners, Bart Cummings.

It was on the afternoon of the second day, the Saturday, before that record Adelaide cricket ground crowd, that this Test match burst into flame.

Larwood began with the new ball to an orthodox field, with Allen as his partner. The pitch was fastish now and Fingleton left, caught Ames off Allen, with but one run on the board. It was the sixth and last ball of Larwood's second over that caused the first crisis.

Jardine, in his *In Quest of the Ashes* reported as follows, "With the last ball of his second over Larwood again brought the ball back from the off side and Woodfull, stepping *outside his off stump,* failed to connect with his bat and received a nasty crack on his left side. Pandemonium instantaneously broke out."

Larwood, in his *Bodyline ?,* wrote, "Woodfull, moving forward towards the off and *into the line* of the ball *which was a straight one,* missed it, and was hit over the heart."

George Hele was the umpire at Larwood's end. This is how he saw that ball: "I was at Larwood's end, the River end. Larwood pitched the ball just short of a length on the *leg* stump. It rose sharply and struck Woodfull over the heart. Woodfull jumped slightly in an attempt to get his straight bat over the top of the ball. He did not duck. After being hit he bent almost double in pain. He did not fall to the ground.

"As I was on my way down the pitch to ascertain Woodfull's condition, Jardine walked up to Larwood and said, 'Well bowled, Harold.' Larwood was standing at the finish of his follow through. He did not reply. Woodfull was in severe pain for at least three minutes. I asked, 'How are you, Bill?' He did not answer, but straightened up, then bent down to pick up his bat. Then, with an effort, he brought his body erect again.

134

"Two or three of the Englishmen showed concern at Woodfull's condition. Jardine was not among them. Don Bradman was at my end of the wicket. He said nothing to me. The crowd showed their displeasure by hooting, though Larwood's was quite a fair ball—one delivered to an orthodox new-ball field. When Woodfull said he would not retire but continue batting I called 'Over.' I should have called 'Over' earlier but forgot to do so in my concern at Woodfull's condition. On my way to square-leg I gave Larwood his cap. He made no comment to me. Allen delivered the next over to Bradman. During it the crowd kept hooting Jardine. Even then things looked dangerous and menacing. Woodfull quite clearly had not recovered from the blow to his heart before Larwood began his next over to him.

"The crowd had not seen Bodyline bowled before, but had read plenty about it. They thought the ball which hit Woodfull was a Bodyline ball."

To return to the Jardine version: "After sympathising with Woodfull and bidding him take his time, I walked down the pitch to Larwood, where I found Hammond encouraging him to take no notice of the signs and sounds of trouble that were brewing at the ringside. I added my words of encouragement and asked him if he was able to run the ball away at all, to which he replied that, far from making it go away, he was turning the ball back (from the off).

"I was, accordingly, not surprised when, at the start of his next over, Larwood made a sign to me that he wanted a leg-side field. Had either he or I realised the misrepresentation to which we were to be subjected, neither of us would have set that particular field for that particular over.

"Woodfull is an old hand and, had he been 'grey and groggy' as the majority of the Australian Press suggested, he knew perfectly well that he only had to ask me for leave to discontinue his innings for his request to be instantly and readily granted."

Now to Sir Robert Menzies: "I was sitting that day at Adelaide and it was before play commenced. I was chatting to the man next to me, whom I didn't know. He was quietly-spoken, cultured, and most interesting. We spoke of many things before the game started. That was the day Woodfull was struck by Larwood. I looked at that man again and he was a changed person. He was on his feet and his face was choleric. He shouted, he raved, and he flung imprecations at Larwood and Jardine because of what his eyes had seen."

135

In his *Afternoon Light,* published in 1967, Sir Robert has more to say about that ball from Larwood and its aftermath. "What happened thereafter is a part of cricket history; angry cables were exchanged; there was much bad feeling; all pleasure went out of the series. Jardine's action was a blunder of the first magnitude. He had in effect announced that Bodyline was designed as a physical attack; no more and no less. Many years afterwards, he conceded to me that he would like those five minutes over again."

Sir Robert also wrote, "Suddenly Jardine signalled to Larwood and swung the field to the Bodyline setting. It was almost as if he had said—'this man's a bit groggy; let's dispose of him!' A roar went up from 40,000 spectators. If it had been Sydney or Melbourne, I believe, and said so at the time to Plum Warner, who was next to me in the Committee Box, the crowd would have invaded the ground, and the Test match might have ended in tumult and disorder."

Sir Donald Bradman, the batsman at the bowler's end has nothing to report of this incident in his *Farewell to Cricket.* So back to George Hele, the man who was in the best position of all to see and whose integrity has never been questioned by players for whom he umpired.

"Before Larwood began this, his third, over, Jardine moved the field into the Bodyline setting, though Woodfull clearly had not recovered from the blow from the last ball of Larwood's previous over. The demonstration, as the Bodyline field was being set, was more angry than when Woodfull was hit. Woodfull looked as white as a piece of notepaper as he faced up to Larwood. Apart from an extra cover and the bowler, the entire field, including wicketkeeper Ames, were on the leg side.

"Larwood," continues Hele, "bowled at full pace well short of a length aiming at the leg stump but coming towards the upper body and head of the batsman. He delivered each ball from about the middle of the bowling crease, from halfway from the stumps to the return crease. The ball was still new but he was swinging in. Woodfull did just about everything to avoid another blow while the crowd kept hooting Jardine and Larwood, delivery by delivery. This was the angriest barracking of the series so far.

"Against Bradman, Larwood was firing the ball well short of a length on and just outside the leg stump. Bradman adopted the same tactics as he had used so successfully in the second innings in

Melbourne. Keeping as straight a bat as possible, he was using it as a shield in front of his chest and head. But this pitch was enabling Larwood to make the ball lift higher than it had at the M.C.G. Bradman was not tall enough to prevent a ball from cocking to Allen at forward short-leg from his uplifted bat. Australia two for 18 and McCabe the incoming batsman.

"Realising that Bradman's tactics could not succeed on this wicket, McCabe tried to attack Larwood with a horizontal bat but mistimed his hook and was caught by Jardine near midwicket. Three for 34.

"At 51 Woodfull played a ball from Allen on to his stumps. A doctor was summoned to examine him in the dressingroom. While he was lying on the massage table, waiting for the doctor, the two M.C.C. team managers, Warner and Lionel Palairet, called to see him. Woodfull had been batting for an hour and a half before his dismissal."

R. W. Wilmot, who played in the Melbourne Grammar School First XI and later gained his cricket blue at Melbourne University, reported what followed in his *Defending the Ashes*. He wrote, "Warner and Palairet expressed their sympathy to Woodfull. Woodfull replied, 'I don't want to discuss it.' 'Why, what is the matter?' Warner asked. Woodfull replied, 'Well, one side is playing cricket and the other is not. This sort of thing is ruining the game, which [using Mr Warner's own words] is too good to be spoiled, and it is time some men got out of it.' Messrs Warner and Palairet, who seemed astonished at Woodfull's reply, then left the room.

"Two days later," continued Wilmot, "Mr Warner handed to the Press, for publication in England and Australia, the following statement: 'Mr Warner states that Woodfull has expressed regret for Saturday's incident to Messrs Warner and Palairet. The incident is closed and we are now the best of friends.' Later in the day Mr W. H. Jeanes, the Secretary of the Board of Control, issued the following statement, one authorised by Woodfull: 'I did not apologise to Mr Warner for any statement I made. I merely told him there was not anything personal between himself and myself. I strongly repudiate any suggestion that I tendered any apology to Mr Warner for any statement I made.' "

Jack Fingleton wrote in his *Cricket Crisis*, "I was one of the Australians in the dressingroom when the Woodfull–Warner incident took place, and in his book Sir Pelham gives me the dubious

137

honour of making the story public. 'Unfortunately,' Sir Pelham writes, 'a member of the Australian Eleven, who was also a Pressman, was in the dressingroom at the time, and the story was blazoned all over the Australian papers on Sunday.' I had the chance that tour to write stories fit to make any editor's mouth water, but my newspaper employers never once embarrassed me by asking that I should trespass upon knowledge which the dressingroom gave me . . . I did not give the story out . . . I know, as do others, who gave the story out and, unlike Sir Pelham, I can give facts . . ."

Years later I tried to get Jack Fingleton to reveal to me just who did leak the story. "There was another Australian player who was writing for the Press," he replied. Jack refused to disclose his name.

Sir Pelham devotes very little space to the 1932–33 tour in his autobiography *Long Innings,* which was published in 1951. He says, "We returned, having won four of the five Test Matches, but 'Bodyline' as the Australians called it, cast a shadow over the tour. The Australians objected to it strenuously and not always tactfully— but thousands of words on the subject have already been written, some of them by myself and I do not propose to discuss it here. It would serve no good purpose . . ."

Jardine does not mention the incident in his book. Nor does Larwood. Neither cricketer, of course, was present.

Former Australian captain Warwick Armstrong had this to say of R. W. Wilmot: "He has become known all over Australia as a good judge of the game, a fearless writer, and a fair critic. I was a small boy at University College when he first wrote of me and my cricket and I have known him ever since. He is favourably known to all first-class cricketers in Australia and to members of English teams which have visited this country in the last thirty years. He writes of what he knows and in the columns of the *Argus* and the *Australasian* has worthily upheld the sporting traditions of those great papers."

Following Woodfull's dismissal for 22 at four for 51, Ponsford and Richardson carried on till stumps when Australia were four for 109. Ponsford adopted a unique method of answering Larwood and Voce's Bodyline. He turned his broad and fleshy back to the bumping ball and took the deliveries from waist to shoulder. When he returned to the dressingroom that Saturday evening he had six bruises on his back, bruises that had begun to go yellow. The Australian players were receiving thirty pounds a Test. Woodfull examined "Ponnie's" bruises and said, "A fiver per bruise 'Ponnie.' " Ponsford's reply is unprintable.

Turning from Ponsford, Woodfull noted a glum look on Stan McCabe's countenance. "What's the matter, Stan?" he asked. "There's no beer," replied "Napper." Woodfull then instructed the room steward to bring some. He came back to report that the Australian Cricket Board and S.A.C.A. secretary, Bill Jeanes, had told him to tell the Australian players that they had had their quota.

"Get Mr Jeanes to come here," said Woodfull.

The steward did. When Jeanes arrived, Woodfull said, "We want some beer for the boys." Jeanes replied, "You've had your quota." Woodfull, a teetotaller himself, then said, "No beer, no play on Monday and I mean that."

Says George Hele, who was present, "I've never seen a hand truck of beer move faster than the one which brought the beer from the bar to the dressingroom."

Attendance that day had been 50,962 and receipts $10,820, both Adelaide Oval records. After the dramatic events of the Saturday, the Monday seemed certain to produce a bumper crowd, and some bumpers.

George Borwick, his umpiring colleague, stayed with George Hele during the Test. On the Sunday morning they read their newspapers and held a discussion. Both again came to the conclusion that, except on appeal, there was nothing they could do about the bowling. They studied the Laws of Cricket again, but found nothing upon which they could have acted. However, George Hele crystallised his opinion of Bodyline bowling, that Saturday at Adelaide, in these words:

"I say without hesitation I'd rather do ten wash-ups than walk across the street to watch it. I believe the hostility of the crowd on the second day of that Test was warranted. I know that, had they invaded the ground, as I expected them to do, both umpires would have been in the firing line as well as the players. There is always the crank in a hostile crowd who lacks discrimination. Such was the crowd's hostility that one English player said to me, 'George, if they come over the fence, leave me a stump,' and I replied, 'Not on your life. I'll need all three myself.'

"Had they come over, it would have been the end of the match and tour and probably of all Anglo-Australian cricket. This is what

139

Jardine and those who backed him were risking on the altar of victory through the pinioning of Bradman. The pitch, too, would have been damaged beyond repair because most people wore leather-soled boots in 1933, not rubber soles and thongs. I saw one man with his foot on the top of the fence between the River end sightboard and where the Victor Richardson Gates now stand. Had the attendance on the Monday, when Oldfield was hit, been 51,000 as it was on the Saturday, I believe the crowd would have rushed the ground and attacked the English players.

"At the time of speaking I have been resident in Melbourne for forty years. I have watched cricket and football regularly during those years and I am certain that, as I know my Melbourne crowds, they would not have hesitated to leap the fence, had this kind of thing occurred in front of them. Had that blow to Woodfull and what followed it occurred before a large Victorian crowd, this would have been the last Test played between England and Australia. Yes, that is what Jardine was risking."

I asked Hele just who, he believes, were the architects of the Body-line plot against Bradman. He replied, "Larwood contended he got the idea at Kennington Oval when bowling to Bradman in 1930. But Archie Jackson came to Adelaide as a sick man in 1931 to try and restore his health in the drier climate there. While he was in hospital in Hutt Street I had several long talks with him. During them he told me that George Duckworth had admitted to him in England in September 1930 that he (Duckworth) was the instigator of the idea of using fast leg-theory after watching Bradman facing Larwood on that lifting pitch at the Oval.

"I am satisfied it was Duckworth who first thought of Bodyline. He had a very shrewd cricketing brain and he was very friendly with both Jardine and Larwood, on and off the field. Duckworth wanted to play in the 1932–33 Tests and was very disappointed that he didn't. His friendship with Jardine continued, however, despite his continual omission. He was one of the few professionals with whom Jardine spent time off the field. What Duckworth told Jackson in 1930 in England he confirmed to me when he came to Australia as M.C.C. baggageman and scorer after the second World War."

I also asked George Hele who had invented the word "Bodyline." " 'Bun' Wilmot, Chester Wilmot's father," he replied. "He invented it in 1932–33 and the rest of the Press grabbed at it."

140

If Duckworth originated the idea of Bodyline and Wilmot named it, as I believe we can accept, who implemented the idea, who took it through the drawingboard stages and packaged it ready for marketing?

It would be ridiculous to suppose that Duckworth did not discuss its potential with Larwood; and Larwood with Voce, his Nottinghamshire bowling partner.

Now let us read what Arthur Carr, Notts County captain at the time, has to say in his book *Cricket with the Lid Off*.

"We did not try it [fast leg-theory bowling] for Notts until 1931. It was 'invented' because we found that, when the shine was off the new ball, Larwood could not swing it. So the natural thing for him to do was to break it back and switch his field for catches on the leg side . . .

"Leg-theory was no good at all in the beginning with us. We started off with it in a match against Glamorgan at Cardiff and, if you please, M. J. Turnbull took a double century and Dai Davies a hundred off it.

"Next we experimented with it against Essex, but still without success. To be effective, leg-theory demands almost perfect direction and length and at first 'Lol' could not command these when he was bowling it. He gave a great many runs away on the leg side . . .

"Still there was obviously something in it and, although the newspaper cricket writers said little or nothing on the subject, some of those behind the scenes of big cricket began to hear whispers of the new bowling technique that we were trying out.

"My friend, Percy George (Bill) Fender (Jardine's County captain), who has a brilliant cricket brain and who is the finest captain who never skippered England, was one of the first to get to know about it. During the Surrey *v.* Notts match at the Oval in 1931, by which time both Larwood and Voce had been invited to go to Australia, he gave me the tip that Jardine wanted to learn more about my two bowlers, Larwood and Voce, and proposed to ask the two bowlers and myself out to dinner to discuss things. He did and we all went to the grill room at the Piccadilly Hotel and, although it took some time to persuade Larwood and Voce to talk in the company of their not exactly hail-fellow-well-met captain-to-be in Australia, they did eventually get going.

"What was discussed between us four that evening over dinner was

141

subsequently developed on the ship on the journey out by Jardine and Larwood, and by the time the team was in Australia they and the others of the team knew what the fast bowling plan of campaign was to be in the Tests."

Having dined with Carr, Larwood, and Voce, Jardine, according to Walter Hammond, "spent days painstakingly analysing all the scoring diagrams which Ferguson, the M.C.C. scorer, had made of the Australian batsmen's innings. Then he went to see F. R. Foster, the left-handed shock bowler of the 1911–12 tour of Australia."

Subsequently Foster disclosed to the Press that, "Before Jardine left for Australia in 1932, he came frequently to my flat in St James and secured from me my leg-theory placings. I had no hint that these would be used for Bodyline bowling. I would like all my friends in Australia to know that I am sorry my experience and advice were put to such an unworthy use."

So much for Jardine's statement at Launceston before the Second Test at Melbourne, "Leg-theory seems to have had its birth in Australian newspapers. We knew nothing about it, but have learned a bit about it since."

As we have seen, he used it in the south of England in 1932 in the match between his touring side and the Rest of England, that is, unless one of South Africa's finest batsmen of all time, H. W. (Herbie) Taylor, imagined his whole experience and dreamed of Frank Woolley facing it.

William Harold "Bill" Ponsford and his "Big Bertha" of a bat knew they were facing it on the Monday of the Third Test of 1932–33 at Adelaide. Ponsford's six bruises had progressed from yellow, through blue, to black over the weekend.

When the match resumed at noon Australia, four for 109, trailed England 341, by 232 runs. Bill Voce, who had left the field on the Saturday owing to the recurrence of an ankle injury, was fit to join forces with Larwood.

On this day Ponsford again showed he could take a hiding as well as anyone. He received many of Larwood's fastest deliveries on his ribs, shoulders, and back, took them there deliberately rather than use his bat and pop up a chance to the silly-leg squad surrounding him.

Says George Hele, "Ponsford took most of those blows on the meaty part of his back. I could hear the ball thudding against his flesh from the far end of the pitch. I believe Ponsford took the balls

142

on his back so he would not be struck in the face or lose his wicket in the way Bradman and McCabe had lost their wickets. I was fearful lest one of the bumpers would rise higher than he anticipated and strike him on the back of his head. Such a blow could have caused him permanent injury, if not worse.

"By the time he reached 85 he had received six more bruises, which made it now two pounds ten shillings per bruise. 'Ponnie' turned clockwise and covered his wicket with his body, most of the time. He adopted these tactics, however, only when the ball was short enough for him to know it would bump at least chest-high. At least seventy-five per cent of Larwood's did so during that first ninety minutes of the third day. He relied on bumpers to break this stand, probably, because the new ball was still so far away.

"I was distressed to see what Bodyline bowling was doing to one of the soundest batsmen and most competent stroke-players in Test cricket and dreaded the effect it was having on his technique. As Alan Kippax emphasised in his description of this match, Ponsford hardly made another run for the remainder of the season. Nor did Fingleton, who was almost equally blackened and blued in the previous Tests."

Despite the difficulties, Ponsford and Richardson added 80 for that fifth wicket before Richardson unluckily dragged a ball from Allen into his wicket.

Of Richardson's batting in this series Jack Hobbs wrote, "From the start of the tour Richardson had shaped as well as anyone against our leg-theory stuff. It was just sheer bad luck that he had not been more successful against it. In dealing with leg-theory he did not bring the bat right back, but used a shortened-arm swing with a lot of forearm and wrist-work in it. Everything the least bit short was hooked very hard."

Jardine had used Voce sparingly because of his ankle weakness. When Oldfield gave Ponsford plucky support and Australia was in the 190s with five wickets still standing, he brought Voce on. Ponsford walked too far across his stumps with his back turned. The ball from Voce did not rise as high as he had expected and he was bowled behind his back. Ponsford batted for 216 minutes and hit eight fours. From four for 109 overnight, Australia had gone to six for 194— Richardson 28 and Ponsford 85. Oldfield joined Grimmett, who began scoring most of his runs through slip and gully. The Englishmen did not bowl Bodyline at either Oldfield or Grimmett. Clarrie explained his almost miraculous direction of the ball through the gaps between the slips by saying that he had learnt the trick when giving slips catches to his students while he was coaching at St Peter's College.

The new ball was taken promptly on 200, when Grimmett and Oldfield were together. Back to Hele, "The ball was still new when Larwood delivered a ball in line with the stumps. It rose sharply from short of a length. Oldfield had been scoring most of his runs on the leg side. He stepped across to hook this ball and it came from the edge of his bat on to his temple. It was one of Larwood's faster balls.

"Oldfield's bat fell from his grasp, narrowly missing the off stump. With his cap still on and holding his gloved left hand to his temple, he reeled towards the slips and then fell to the ground. Larwood was at the end of his follow through. As Oldfield reeled away Larwood lifted his right arm and his face was covered with concern, which it had not been when he struck Woodfull that blow under (or over) the heart on the Saturday.

"Three or four of the Englishmen ran to Oldfield's assistance. When George Borwick and I reached Oldfield he was in no condition to speak. He was bleeding from the side of his temple, which was cut. Woodfull emerged from the pavilion and, helped by another player, he raised Oldfield from the turf and led him into the pavilion.

"The crowd was at boiling point now—even the sophisticated occupants of the Members' Enclosure. The demonstration was far worse than when Woodfull was hit on the Saturday. Oldfield had been batting for two hours for his 41 and had shown both talent and courage.

"I felt terrible," recalls Hele. "George Borwick and I were worried that the crowd would leap the fence and make an all-out assault on the Englishmen. I decided that, if the crowd did come, I would grab the stumps and use them to protect myself from attack. The Englishmen kept turning towards the eastern mound to watch the crowd there while Oldfield was on the ground.

"Loud booing persisted from most parts of the ring and Jardine was booed individually and heckled continuously for minutes."

Bill O'Reilly was the next batsman. He says, "When Oldfield was taken off it took me fifteen minutes to get to the pitch. Forty mounted troopers had been given orders to ride on to the field, if need be. I had to belt my way with my bat through the members standing on the steps and yelling from the bottom of the George Giffen Stand. I didn't care whether I got in or not, of course, to face Larwood in his present mood."

Jack Hobbs reported as follows: "A nasty mishap befell Oldfield, for he was hit on the head while trying to hook a short ball from Larwood. This looked an ugly crack—he dropped down near the wicket—and there was general relief when it was seen that things might have been worse. Oldfield left the field smiling, while Harold Larwood carried on amid a storm of hooting and concerted counting of his steps back for the run up to the wicket. It was unfortunate that Oldfield was not able to resume.

"When O'Reilly came in he made us smile. Six times in succession he tried without success to play Larwood, missing every ball; the seventh delivery wrecked his wicket. Wall played on. Australia were all out 222. Larwood having taken three for 55 and Allen four for 71."

Jardine's report of the incident is revealing. He wrote: "Oldfield, who had been playing very well, seemed on the point of opening out with the idea of getting runs as quickly as possible. In attempting an attacking, but rather cheeky, shot off one of Larwood's deliveries, *which by no stretch of the imagination could be described as having been pitched short,* Oldfield seemed to lose sight of the ball halfway through his shot and received the ball on the right side of the head.

"He is not a tall man, and he had stooped in an attempt to mow the ball round to mid-wicket. Whether he just touched the ball with his bat or not, I do not know, but the fact that he was hit on the right side of his head is evidence that he had gone right through with his shot.

"Needless to say, we were all extremely upset and even Oldfield's immediate assurance that it was his own fault for losing sight of the ball increased our regret for the accident to this splendid cricketer.

"Oldfield was prevailed upon not to continue his innings . . ."

Vic Richardson, who was to take the gloves in England's second innings, says, "Oldfield tried a species of hook at a bumper from Larwood. He deflected the ball from his bat to the temple and fell reeling to the turf. The blow slightly fractured his skull and caused concussion. The incident went as close as is possible to causing

145

a riot. Most spectators were not aware that Oldfield had deflected the ball on to his temple; they believed he had received a direct blow from the bumper. It was a toss-up for several minutes whether someone would jump the fence. If one man had, it is almost certain that thousands would have followed him. What could a few policemen have done had the field been invaded by angry spectators? Fortunately that question never had to be answered."

Jardine was standing near the wicket at leg-gully when the incident occurred. Later he went to deep fine-leg close to the scoreboard and took all the hooting and epithets that were hurled at him. One could only admire the air of contempt and defiance in the face of danger that he wore throughout all this.

Says Hele: "I saw the 1971 Snow incident at the Sydney Cricket Ground on television and Jardine's demeanour was much the same as Snow's on that occasion. I believe that, had the English authorities been present at the Adelaide Oval on that Saturday and Monday, they would have formed much the same opinion of Jardine's tactics as did almost all of the Australians present. I believe they would have felt that the text of the cable the Australian Cricket Board sent to the Marylebone Cricket Club *was* warranted—certainly not based on 'hysteria,' as was claimed.

"Unlike Vic Richardson and several others, I support the wording of the cables dispatched at the time by the Australian Board of Control and do not regard them as 'petulant' and 'hysterical.' I believe that, had the Australian Board accepted the M.C.C.'s offer to cancel the rest of the tour, the English authorities would have gone to water. I believe this because Jack Hobbs, Hammond, Allen, Sutcliffe, Maurice Tate, and Warner all supported the Australian outlook on Bodyline when they returned to England and would have done so while in Adelaide if the issue had reached an impasse."

The text of the five cables dispatched by the Australian Board to the M.C.C., and the circumstances of the sending of those cables, are as follows:

1. "Bodyline bowling has assumed such proportions as to menace the best interests of the game, making protection of the body by batsmen the main consideration, causing intensely bitter feeling between players as well as injury. In our opinion it is unsportsmanlike. Unless stopped at once it is likely to upset

friendly relations existing between Australia and England."

This cable was sent after those members of the Australian Board who were in Adelaide had interviewed Messrs Warner and Palairet, and asked them to put a stop to what was considered a dangerous and disastrous attack. The Australian Board were informed that the managers had no control over the captain in matters pertaining to actual play. The members of the Board in Adelaide then communicated with their Board chairman, Dr Allen Robertson, in Melbourne, and it was decided to make a formal protest to the Marylebone Cricket Club.

2. "We, the Marylebone club, deplore your cable," came the reply, "and deprecate the opinion that there has been unsportsmanlike play. We have the fullest confidence in the captain and team managers. We are convinced that they would do nothing that would infringe the laws of cricket or the spirit of the game, and we have no evidence that our confidence is misplaced. Much as we regret the accidents to Woodfull and Oldfield, we understand that in neither case was the bowler to blame. If the Board wishes to propose a new law, or rule, it shall receive our careful consideration in due course. We hope the situation is not now as serious as your cable appears to indicate, but if it is such as to jeopardise the good relations between English and Australian cricketers, and you consider it desirable to cancel the remainder of the programme, we would consent with great reluctance."

3. The members of the Australian Board felt the first cable and the spirit which prompted it had been misunderstood. A special meeting of the Board was held in Sydney and the whole question of Bodyline discussed. Delegates were not prepared to retreat from the position originally adopted, but they felt some explanation was necessary and sent the following cable to the M.C.C. on 30 January:

"We, the Australian Board of Control, appreciate your difficulty in dealing with the matter raised in our cable without having seen the actual play. We unanimously regard Bodyline bowling as adopted in some of the games of the present tour as being opposed to the spirit of cricket and as dangerous to players. We are deeply concerned that the ideals of the game shall be protected, and have therefore appointed a committee to report on the action necessary to eliminate such bowling from all cricket in Australia as from the beginning of the 1933–34 season. We will forward a copy of the committee's recommendations for your consideration and, it is hoped, co-operation as to their application in all cricket. We do not consider it necessary to cancel the remainder of the programme."

4. On 2 February the M.C.C. committee replied: "We note with pleasure you do not consider it necessary to cancel the remainder of the programme and that you are postponing the whole issue until the tour has been completed. May we accept this as a clear indication that the good sportsmanship of our team is not in question?

"We are sure that you appreciate how impossible it would be to play any Test in the spirit we all desire unless both sides are satisfied that there is no reflection on their sportsmanship. When your recommendation reaches us it shall receive our most careful consideration and will be submitted to the Imperial Cricket Conference."

5. On 8 February, two days before the Fourth Test was due to begin in Brisbane, the Board of Control cabled the M.C.C. as follows: "We do not regard the sportsmanship of your team as being in question. Our position was fully considered at a recent meeting in Sydney and is as indicated in our cable of 30 January. It is the particular class of bowling referred to therein which we consider is not in the best interests of cricket and in this view, we understand, we are supported by many eminent English cricketers. We join heartily with you in hoping that the remaining Tests will be played with the traditional good feeling."

Jardine's attitude was, in his own words, "Whether the team played another Test match or not did not rest with me, but after considering every point of view I was firmly determined that I should not lead them on to the field in another Test match, unless and until that charge [of unsportsmanship] had been withdrawn. I made no secret of this...I knew that many members of the Australian Board did not approve of the original telegram sent to the M.C.C., and I deemed it only fair they should not be in any doubt as to the position which I should take up with regard to that one particular word [unsportsmanlike]."

Jardine's ultimatum was also conveyed to the M.C.C., and there

148

is no doubt that this had a decisive influence on the reaction of that body.

But the response in England to the Australian Board's first cable was not calculated to assist what now might be called the "Australian cool."

In reputable English newspapers, even in English music halls, Australians were branded as a race of "moaners" and "squealers." The M.C.C. even sent a deputation to the Dominion Secretary, Mr J. H. Thomas, and it was suggested that, unless that word "unsportsmanlike" was withdrawn, the success of Australia's pending conversion loan might not be assured.

Mr J. C. Squire of London asked where was that tough Australian grin and ended his outburst with:

> "We won't believe the paradox,
> A whining Digger funking knocks."

A considerable section of the English press tried to justify the tactics of Jardine and his team. But on 25 January the Sydney *Referee* published the following article:

> "Australians Are NOT Squealing!
> They Want Cricket to Live.

"From England there has come a chorus of voices raised in approbation of the English cricketers' tactics in the present series of Test matches. That there are two camps was only to be expected. There is a lack of complete unanimity even in Australia, although public opinion was demonstrated a week ago at Adelaide. But the merits of the case must be decided upon the weight of evidence. That weight of evidence must be judged upon the standing of the persons giving expression to it and upon their experience and knowledge.

"Let us take Australian opinion first and then the views of leading Englishmen. Over a quarter of a century the outstanding Australian cricket brains have included M. A. Noble, Warwick Armstrong, and W. M. Woodfull. Their knowledge, experience, and standing in the community are unquestioned. What do they say? Every one of them has condemned the body theory as a new mode of attack that will cause grave injury to players—perhaps death—and incalculable and irreparable harm to cricket, both as a game and a spectacle to watch.

149

"And these men are supported by the opinions of practically all the greatest cricketers of the past fifty years who have so far spoken.

"Now let us take England. In the past twenty-five years, the outstanding cricket brains in the Old Country have included those of A. C. MacLaren, Ranjitsinhji, and none other than P. F. Warner. And every one of these has condemned body-bowling as an abhorrent thing that should never have been allowed to show its head. Read what they say:—

"A. C. MacLaren: 'In my time Australians never concentrated on attacking the body with the fast ball. Gregory and McDonald never packed the leg side field with five fieldsmen, nor got wickets on the on side. I utterly oppose it when less dangerous methods are equally successful. Tom Richardson and Ernest Jones never bowled at the body because it was too expensive. There's nothing to recommend this pounding of the body throughout an innings because eventually the batsmen will be seriously hurt. Other methods are more in keeping with the spirit of the game and will more readily obtain wickets without anyone complaining.'

"Ranjitsinhji: 'Though a batsman has a bat with which to defend himself, I disapprove strongly of leg side attack, if it is existent. I would rather lose the rubber than win over the bruised bodies of my opponents.'

"P. F. Warner: 'This is not bowling; indeed, it is not cricket, and if all the fast bowlers were to adopt these methods, the M.C.C. would be compelled to step in and penalise the bowler who bowled the ball at less than halfway up the pitch . . . These things lead to reprisals—and when they begin, goodness knows where they will end.'

"Can anything be more explicit," continued the *Referee,* "more emphatically condemnatory of the body attack than those declarations of these three eminent Englishmen? We don't need to quote Australians in the face of the utterly convincing views of such great cricket minds. One's only cause for regret is that P. F. Warner's opinion, alone of the three quoted, was written by him just before the Englishmen left the Homeland on their present tour, and that he has since maintained an indefensible silence while he sees our batsmen's bodies being battered and bruised and the game of cricket heading to its doom.

"In the light of the opinions expressed by these six highly qualified cricket minds in both countries, how, in the name of honesty and justice and fair play, can Englishmen—or sections of the London press—say that Australians are 'squealing'?

"Unfortunately, many of the vitriolic press attacks upon Australians and upon their well-founded objection to this body theory have been based upon sheer ignorance of the position and a lamentable distortion of the facts.

"For instance, the London *Times*, great newspaper as it undoubtedly is, says, 'There is nothing new in this kind of bowling.' To that I say without the slightest hesitation, IT IS NEW! It has never before been practised in a match between England and Australia. The *Times*, therefore, is palpably attempting to argue upon an entirely erroneous basis.

"Then the paper goes on to say, 'The English batsmen who suffered knocks from Gregory and McDonald have the right to recall their experiences. So long as a "shock" bowler is not deliberately bumping short-pitched balls or purposely aiming at the batsman, this type of bowling is perfectly fair.'

"Again there exists in this statement false premises that the *Times* would do well to realise. Gregory and McDonald NEVER bowled a body attack. They never bowled with a packed leg side field. And the last part of the view just quoted shows a further ignorance of a most unpardonable kind. The fact is that the present English 'shock' bowler IS deliberately bumping short-pitched balls and purposely aiming at the batsman. That is just what we Australians are complaining about. The *Times*, therefore, admits that this kind of bowling is unfair.

"The *Daily Mail*, like the *Times*, suggests that Gregory and McDonald, 'employed almost identical tactics' as Larwood and Voce . . .

"Surely Englishmen don't expect us to take all this lying down. When we see cricket and players of cricket suffering untold harm and personal injury . . . and when we see previous friendly relationships turning to bitter hostility, isn't it the duty of someone to call a halt? And because it is the victim who says, 'Play the game fairly or not at all,' we are accused of squealing. Was there ever such ludicrous reasoning?

"Australia has lost Test matches before now—and didn't squeal. And there is no reason to think that human nature and sporting instincts have undergone any change. Australia is not concerned only with the winning or losing of Tests. She is mostly concerned with the game and the sportsmanship of its players. Australia wants cricket to live—not die. The body theory will kill it; and therefore we must eradicate the noxious thing . . .

"The Board of Control's protest is emphatic and to the point. The only thing wrong with it is that it came too late in the day. The *Referee* warned our cricket legislators early in December of what would occur, and they did nothing. In the meantime Woodfull, Oldfield, Richardson, Fingleton, Ponsford, O'Brien, Kippax, McCabe, and Bradman have been pounded painfully by Larwood and Voce. Did all these men have to be injured in order that the Board might have proof of the danger behind this kind of bowling?"

Following the M.C.C.'s first cabled reply, the Melbourne *Truth,* on 28 January, had also supported the stand of the Australian Board. "If the cabled reply of that august body of English cricket, the Marylebone Club, to the justified protest of the Australian Board of Control against bowling at the man instead of the wicket, means that England sanctions this undoubted menace to human life and limb, then it is in the best interests of cricket that the remaining two Test matches should not be played," it wrote.

It continued, "The dignified members of the Marylebone Club Committee 'deplore' the cable sent them. They 'deplore' Australia's protest against the continued menace to the life and health of her batsmen. They 'deplore' our attitude in showing concern over balls so pitched as to cause concussion to a plucky and competent cricketer such as Oldfield and to seriously jeopardise the health of so sterling a player as Woodfull . . .

"Must we stand by and applaud while our men are battered and bruised and even more seriously injured, while they are knocked out of the game, while their future chances of successful careers are endangered? . . . Then, perhaps, we will earn the dignified patronage of the Marylebone Club Committee members . . .

"The Board of Control did what was very necessary—it pointed out to those whom it thought would be reasonably interested the dangers associated with England's method of attack. If that is 'squealing' then let us 'squeal' by all means . . .

"The only action that can be taken is the cancellation of the remaining Tests, if England persists in her attitude of continuing a policy that is against the ethics of decent sportsmanship. Let the Board of Control ask Mr Jardine what he intends to do. If it's more basher-bowling, then cancel the remaining Tests."

Back to Vic Richardson. "To sum up the question of Bodyline, it is my opinion that the tactics employed were quite in keeping with the laws of cricket, but entirely outside the ethics of the game . . . Bodyline tactics, in my opinion, were *the most serious blot that has ever fallen on the name and the game of cricket.* The passage of thirty-three years has only served to strengthen my opinion on this point."

Richardson claimed to have had many talks during that Test series of so long ago with Warner. " 'Plum' told me many times that summer," Vic says, "of his hope that the use of Bodyline would be reduced. He told me he had sent a report to the M.C.C. and was expecting a directive to reach him. He told me he had pleaded many times with Jardine to station fewer men on the leg side for the fast bumper attack, because the placement of so many fieldsmen there — eight and nine — made the tactics and intention so obvious. 'The skipper is adamant, however, I can do nothing with him on this subject,' Sir Pelham told me."

That, George Hele and I believe, just about seals the case, so let's return to the cricket, such as it was.

At the close of the Australian innings, the Englishmen left the field under a storm of hooting from all around the ground. Given his opportunity by Voce's ankle injury, "Gubby" Allen had taken four for 71 in this innings to Larwood's three for 55. In the second Australian innings he was to take four for 50 to Larwood's four for 71 — without bowling Bodyline. "But," says Hele, "it would be foolish to suggest that Allen would have achieved his success without the effect Larwood was creating in the minds of the Australian batsmen with his Bodyline at the other end. Between them Larwood and Allen took fifteen of the nineteen Australian wickets which fell."

England led by 119 on the first innings when Jardine and Sutcliffe came back on to the field to face what might aptly be called "The Anvil Chorus."

Vic Richardson, Australia's most versatile sportsman next to Reginald "Snowy" Baker, took Oldfield's gloves and received high praise for his performance from Jardine. During that England innings of 412 the unpractised Richardson allowed only 11 byes. Australian hopes, low at the time, were raised when Leo O'Brien,

153

the twelfth man, caught Sutcliffe brilliantly near long-leg from a hook off Wall.

That wicket at 7 was the only encouragement the still angry barrackers received that day. Jardine and Wyatt advanced the score to 85 before stumps—a lead of 204—one sufficiently promising for the England captain to decide to dine at a private home in North Adelaide that night.

The late Sidney Downer wrote of that dinner, at which he was present, in his book, *100 Not Out,* the history of the Adelaide Oval.

G. O. Allen and Ian Hayward, an old friend, met in the smoking room of the exclusive Adelaide Club after play. They were to dine with Hayward's father, Mr Dudley Hayward, later.

Before they left the Adelaide Club a call for Ian Hayward came from Jardine. Douglas reminded Hayward that his father had invited him to dinner at his home "any time I like." He asked if he could dine there that night. Knowing his father's reactions to the events of that afternoon at the Oval, Ian Hayward was horrified at what might happen at the dinner table but reluctantly agreed. He rang to warn his mother, suggesting that the subject of cricket be avoided at all costs.

On his arrival at the Hayward home Jardine said to Mr Dudley Hayward, "And did you go to the Test match this afternoon, sir?" "Yes, and if that sort of thing happens again, I'm never going to another one," was his host's reply.

Discussion over dinner ranged through fishing, hunting, shooting, the weather—anything but cricket—until a guest mentioned the death, that day, of the great Australian wicketkeeper J. M. Blackham, who used to stand up to the stumps to the "Demon" Spofforth years before Douglas Jardine was born on 23 October 1900.

Another guest mentioned the names of some of Australia's long line of great wicketkeepers—Jim Kelly, "Affie" Jarvis, Carkeek, and Carter. "And, of course," he added, "Oldfield."

"And now," thundered Dudley Hayward from the end of the table, "we have Vic Richardson."

On their way home on the night of that fateful Monday Jardine and Allen were confronted with the news poster:

"Premeditated Brutality—M. A. Noble."

During the closing stages of the afternoon's play, when drinks

154

were brought out, Woodfull took a glass of cordial to his opposing captain. "Don't give him a drink. Let the bastard die of thirst," a barracker called.

Jardine was a strange man. He considered this funny and said so in his book.

"Plum" Warner had been less amused that evening when an Adelaide cricket lover demanded why he didn't do something about Bodyline. "What can I do? What can I do?" he asked. "You could come down off the fence for a start, 'Plum,' " interjected Clem Hill.

Jack Hobbs came to Hele that night and said, "This is a bad business, George." Adhering to his policy throughout the tour, George did not answer.

Despite his "Black Monday," Jardine travelled on to 56 before being l.b.w. to Ironmonger at two for 91 the next day. "The highlight of the Tuesday's play," says Hele, "came with its last delivery. Hammond was 85 when Woodfull gave Bradman a bowl as a last desperate resort. The ball was a full toss. Hammond misjudged its flight and played back. He edged the ball on to his leg stump. His remark, as he passed me, cannot be published."

Ames 69, Leyland 42, Wyatt 49, and Verity 40 (following his first innings 45) took England to 412, a lead of 531. Between them, O'Reilly and Ironmonger delivered 107·3 overs in this innings, forty-two of them maidens, to take seven for 166. They squashed Jardine's announced plan for a batting onslaught by Hammond and Leyland.

Bodyline was used again in Australia's second innings, but the crowd did not react to it in the way they had on the Saturday and Monday. "The Australian Board's cable to the M.C.C. had been released to the Press," says Hele, "and maybe the 'unsporting' Australians regarded the case as *sub judice*.

"Woodfull batted through this innings, despite the effects of his injury—physical and psychological—for 73 not out in a total of 193. He was by no means fully recovered, but was spurred on, no doubt, by the wish to demonstrate that Australians are not 'squealers' and can take it.

"Bradman's 66 was one of the most spectacularly brilliant innings I have seen. It made many of us think back to Victor Trumper."

I was lucky enough to watch that innings at the admittedly

impressionable age of twenty. It was electrifying and inspiring—sheer magic to me. I can see almost every stroke of it now and I still play them over in my mind. Don cut through that English attack like Douglas Fairbanks Senior descending on his cutlass down the sail of a pirate ship in *Sea Hawk,* or was it *The Black Pirate*?

During the two overs Larwood bowled to him before setting the Bodyline field, this time as a form of protection, Don hooked and square-cut four deliveries which were almost identical in length and line. Two of them sped like bullets to the leg fence and two to the off boundary. They would have left the swiftest swallows wondering in their wake.

At the other end Don assaulted the left-handed and flighted accuracy of Hedley Verity, one of the four most disciplined spinners I have watched—Ironmonger, Grimmett, and O'Reilly being the others. Don kept dancing to the pitch of the ball and, abandoning principles developed over a decade, drove one delivery into the seats of the Members' Enclosure, where it landed on the superstructure of an ageing spinster who had believed excitement was a thing long past. As this elderly woman was being led away, Don danced down the pitch again, aiming for the Moreton Bay fig trees on the crest of the northern mound. Mistiming the stroke slightly, he was bravely caught and bowled.

He had entered at two for 12 and he left at three for 100, scoring 66 of the 88 runs of the third wicket stand with Woodfull. Another Australian batsman had found the bravery and brilliance to retaliate. Just how the Australians watching and wondering delighted at this derring-do is easily imagined even now. But this kind of batsmanship was too frenzied to endure—just a brief and brilliant flicker of the old Bradman flame.

"It was after this innings," says Hele, "that Woodfull said he would drop Bradman from the Australian side, if he had his way. 'Woody' had issued instructions to his recognised batsmen to stand in line of the fast leg-theory, and told Oldfield and his bowlers it was their task to make certain they were not hit. Don had defied his captain during his stirring defiance of Larwood."

This 66 from "The Don" certainly was a gambler's innings. But batting against Bodyline was itself a gamble. Don had tried to answer it with orthodox methods during his great century in Melbourne and in his first innings in the Adelaide Test. Doubtless he had decided, after that first innings failure on Saturday, that orthodox tactics had no hope of succeeding except on a pitch, like the one in Melbourne, which reduced the rise of the ball to reasonable levels.

One *had* to live dangerously or die. Don did both in this magnificent and spectacular seventy-three minutes. Of Bradman's performances in the last four Tests of this series, Sir Jack Hobbs, wrote: "When I left England for Australia I thought, 'I shall be satisfied if we get rid of Bradman for a century each time. It is the 200s and more that I fear. Why, that fellow can get a side's normal score off his own bat!' I certainly had, and still have, a great respect for Bradman.

"At the end of the tour Don's Test average was 56, which is about the same as that of Sutcliffe and Hammond, neither of whom had to face bowling as good as that which confronted Don. Neither had the Englishmen to face Larwood and his 'leg-theory-cum-Bodyline.' Yet Bradman is written down as a failure, simply because he did not soar into double centuries. This goes to show how difficult it is for a batsman to please those supporters who expect continuous super-human performances. What really happened to Bradman was that he was only subdued. For that the credit goes to Larwood . . .

"In a line, Bradman was brought down to the level of the ordinary batsman and his colleagues were some way behind that level . . . It looked to me as if Bradman had had a little inquest in his mind and returned this verdict: 'If I am hit by a ball travelling as fast as Larwood can make it travel my career may be finished. That isn't going to happen.'

"The outcome was that Don played gamblers' innings, hitting hard, if he could, at any height or in any direction, without that fine regard for keeping the ball low which used to be his strong point. He took not the faintest risk of injury and, in view of his slight physique, I do not blame him. But there were times when he need not have surrendered quite so wholeheartedly as he did. Don made magnificent shots with his feet placed quite wrongly, while other shots were just crude tennis strokes that lofted the ball in the air. How that young man changed his game!

"I cannot throw Bradman to the wolves in this way without further comment. I want to pay a tribute to him because he had the courage to follow his convictions. It could not have been easy for Don to give in to Harold Larwood, especially as he had such a big reputation. But having made up his mind not to get injured, he

157

stuck to and followed out his view, a procedure requiring great moral courage, especially as his own supporters, those who had made him a national idol, called him very hard names . . .

"My candid opinion of Bradman? Well, it is this: He is the best batsman in the world on dry wickets and probably on all wickets, if given the opportunity to get used to the wet ones . . .

"It was not ordinary fast bowling, even of the Larwood or super type, that reduced Bradman and Australia. That was done by Bodyline bowling—leg-theory, with short balls interspersed, plus Larwood's great pace and accuracy, together with exceptionally clever field setting. More than enough, I think you will agree, to make any batsman think. Shortly, I considered it bowling the purpose of which was to intimidate the batsmen.

"In my cabled accounts of the play in Australia, which appeared in the *Star,* I made no mention of my views on 'leg-theory-cum-Bodyline' bowling. I purposely avoided this, because I did not wish to embarrass Jardine or his men by giving the Australians another peg on which to hang their fierce attacks."

Woodfull was a different man from Bradman, as different a man as he was a batsman. His whole character also came out in his cricket and especially his batsmanship. Later he was to make a superb headmaster of Melbourne High School. On this fifth and sixth day at Adelaide in 1933 he batted for four hours, right through the second Australian innings, for 73 not out. His motives were obvious. He was determined, as we have said, and as we do not apologise for repeating, to show Englishmen that Australians were not "squealers," that they could take and survive everything Jardine, Larwood, and Voce could fling at them. And this he bravely did.

Only Vic Richardson gave him any determined support, during a fifth wicket stand of 55 which ended when Vic was again unluckily caught, this time from his thumb while attempting to hook Larwood to the boundary for the second ball in succession.

McCabe 7, was the fourth highest Australian scorer and England's margin was 338 runs.

Whether or not the series would continue was still in doubt and remained so until 8 February, twenty days later.

Had George Hele been Woodfull, this is what he would have done:

"Woodfull had two opportunities as captain," he says. "One was to declare Australia's first innings closed after Oldfield was hit, stating

158

for publication that he had done so to avoid the possibility of injury to his bowlers, O'Reilly, Wall, and Ironmonger. The other was to retaliate with Bodyline from Wall in England's second innings."

Had Woodfull adopted the first of these courses, he would have added strength to the Board's first cable. He could hardly have adopted the second course once that cable was sent.

Woodfull, it must be remembered, was physically groggy and mentally upset after being hit himself and inflamed with resentment and a sense of injustice after the injury to Oldfield.

"He wasn't in a condition," says Hele, "to think coolly and his players did not want to upset him further by renewing their advocacy of retaliation."

Hele does not believe the M.C.C.'s offer to cancel the tour on 23 January, four days after a Test that had them leading 2–1 in the series, would have been proceeded with under pressure. Had the series been cancelled, England would have forfeited her excellent chance of regaining the Ashes. "The entire purpose of the Bodyline plot," George contends, "would have been cast to the winds.

"The Australian Board's prime reason for wishing to continue the rubber, in my opinion, was its anxiety to reap the rich financial harvest the matches were providing. This factor also would have profoundly affected the English attitude, had matters come to a deadlock."

It was the nearest that international cricket ever came to total war, but the series continued and Bodyline was not used as recklessly and ruthlessly again.

The "Iron Duke" Wills Through

DURING THE TWENTY-ONE DAYS WHICH SEPARATED THE ADELAIDE and Brisbane Tests the cabling equipment of the Overseas Telecommunications Commission, Australian Associated Press, and Reuter ran red hot. While the English cricketers relaxed near Ballarat's Eureka Stockade and admired the oleanders of Toowoomba, words—waterfalls of words—flipped dot-dash-dot across the equator between Australia and England.

Very few of them emanated from cool, unprejudiced minds.

At one stage it seemed Australia would cease to be a Dominion and constitute itself a Republic in the cause of cricket.

Says Bill O'Reilly, "It was a verbal battle between the distraught and the uninformed." Eventually the "distraught" were defeated. Australia lost the first battles, on the field and off it; England, uncharacteristically, was to lose the war. General Jardine, the "Iron Duke" as he came to be called, and his cavalry leader, Harold Larwood, went gradually to their cricketing doom during 1933 and 1934. The Marylebone Cricket Club, better informed now about Bodyline bowling, turned its august back upon both of them, with what dignity it could.

While this turn-about was deciding his destiny, Jardine defiantly and disdainfully struck his first and only century in Test cricket—127

160

at Manchester against the Bodyline bowling of West Indians Constantine and Martindale. He demonstrated, it was written, that "a cricketer untroubled by nerves could not only defend himself and his wicket with his bat against this brand of bowling, but also score runs with considerable freedom." More sensible Englishmen realised that Constantine and Martindale at Manchester were a faint imitation of Larwood's all-out fury in Australia.

During those twenty-one days of January and February 1933 Australia's selectors did less than distinguish themselves. Consequent upon their frantic deliberations, they sent Woodfull and Australia into the vital and decisive Fourth Test with but three recognised bowlers—Wall, O'Reilly, and Ironmonger. Between them O'Reilly and Ironmonger had to bowl 175·4 overs.

In late January Jardine's men promulgated their loyalty to him in the following resolution:

"The members of the M.C.C. England team have no desire to enter into public controversy, for they deplore the introduction of any personal feeling into the records of a great game. In view, however, of certain published statements to the effect that there is, or has been, dissension or disloyalty in their team, they desire to deny this definitely and absolutely, while assuring the public of England and Australia that they are and always have been, utterly loyal to their captain, under whose leadership they hope to achieve an honourable victory."

Owing to anxiety regarding the condition of Voce's ankle, Larwood was rested from the games against a Combined Country XIII of Victoria at Ballarat, the return match against New South Wales at Sydney, and given only 11·6 overs, from which he took eight for 28, against a Queensland Country XII up at Toowoomba on the Darling Downs. Against Queensland he bowled seventeen overs taking, in the two innings, eight for 62.

Between that third and fourth Test, I made my first Eastern States tour with the South Australian Sheffield Shield side. Vic Richardson was our captain and Clarrie Grimmett the bowler we should least have liked to be without. We were all very fond of "Grum." We well knew his worth and he was like a cricketing father to many of us.

Clarrie shared train cabins and hotel rooms with me on the way from Adelaide to Brisbane. During the journey he insisted there *was* a way by which Australia's batsmen could defeat Bodyline. This, he said, was by moving inside the line of the bumpers pitched on the leg stump and outside it and ignoring them. If all Australia's batsmen adopted this policy, "Grum" claimed, the game would come to a halt so far as scoring was concerned, the English bowlers would exhaust themselves to no avail and the crowd eventually would have the final say.

Grimmett, as I know, preached this gospel to Woodfull, Ponsford, Bradman, McCabe, and Richardson. None of them paid any heed. It surely *was* worth trying, albeit easier said than done.

Grimmett was to play no further part in the Bodyline series. The Australian selectors dropped him. Admittedly he had taken only five wickets for 326 runs at Sydney, Melbourne, and Adelaide, but he had conceded only just more than two runs from each of his 147 overs, and had, as we have seen, easy chances missed from his bowling. His accuracy in partnership with O'Reilly and Ironmonger had proved valuable.

It was on the Saturday night of the South Australia–Queensland game, 29 January, that news of Grimmett's omission was released. The news came out over the radio about 9 p.m. Clarrie had taken me to watch his favourite film actress and entertainer, Gracie Fields, at a Brisbane cinema. Not sharing Clarrie's fervour for Gracie Fields, I excused myself halfway through the main feature film and returned to the Carlton Hotel to find several members of the South Australian team in a state of considerable consternation.

"Where's Clarrie?" they asked. "Why?" I enquired. "Because they've dropped him from the fourth Test team and included Bert Tobin in his place."

"He's at the pictures watching Gracie Fields," I said. "He was as happy as Larry when I left him. We hadn't heard the news."

My teammates decided they didn't want to break that news to "Grum" that night. He was a very proud little man as well as a most lovable one. They knew just how much bowling for Australia meant to Clarrie and they decided to go to bed before he returned.

It was as they were leaving the hotel lounge that Jack Hutcheon, President of the Queensland Cricket Association and a senior member of the Australian Board of Control, came in the main door of the hotel and said he wanted to congratulate Bert Tobin.

We were intrigued at Tobin's selection. He was a fastish bowler, who could deliver a bumper. We wondered whether Australia had

Top: Victor Trumper demonstrating perfect balance in completing a straight drive. *Bottom:* George Hele is not alone in regarding Constantine (shown diving for the ball) as one of the most agile slips fieldsmen the game has seen

at last decided upon retaliation. We also knew where Tobin was spending his Saturday night. Bert was a reasonably handsome bachelor with an eye for the opposite sex. To our knowledge, he was downstairs in the Carlton Hotel cabaret, dancing with what might, with some understatement, be described as a devastating Brisbane brunette.

Mr Hutcheon was a formidable character. He was also the nearest approach Australia had owned until that time to an administrative cricketing dictator. He was the kind of man Oliver Cromwell would have welcomed as his right-hand man among his Puritans and Roundheads, and a great believer in curfews for first-class cricketers during matches, a modern Covenanter, shall we say.

We tried our utmost to deter Mr Hutcheon from completing his mission, all to no avail. Eventually we led him down the stairs to that cabaret, our hearts in our mouths, all our fingers crossed.

Here we found Australia's "counterpart to Larwood and Voce" embracing that brunette at the end of a dance. The cabaret was deserted except for the two of them and the three members of a band playing without enthusiasm.

Bert had his back to us as we entered. We steered Mr Hutcheon over to him and announced to Bert his presence and mission. Tobin took one arm from the brunette, without even turning his head, and held out his bowling hand towards Hutcheon. The President of the Q.C.A. and senior Board member grasped it in silence, turned, and stalked out.

There was still a chance, we thought and hoped, that Clarrie would be restored to the Test side. For Mr Hutcheon was one of the Australian selectors.

Down in Sydney the following Friday Vic Richardson posted the South Australian team to play New South Wales on the back of our dressingroom door. Vic was a beautiful calligraphist and there was no mistaking the fact that B. J. Tobin had been named twelfth man—*for South Australia!*

It was the role he was to fill the following week for Australia.

Tobin, when a schoolboy cricketer at Rostrevor College, had given promise of becoming one of the most talented all-round cricketers Australia had produced. Many times Vic Richardson would declaim during a Sheffield Shield game that Bert had more natural ability, as a bowler, batsman, and fieldsman, than any other

Top: Jack Hobbs sets out on the hundredth run of his hundredth century, scored in Adelaide in 1923. *Bottom:* Bradman put great effort into his shots, and this stroke is no exception

member of his State side. But nature had nothing left to bestow upon Bert when it lavished this sporting talent upon him.

Shortly afterwards he gave up cricket in Australia and took a contract with a Lancashire League Club. In Manchester, thanks to his charm and good looks, he married exceptionally well—unknown to his old friends in Adelaide.

During the mid 1930s, Ross Sawers, an outstanding South Australian amateur golfer, was in Manchester. He ascertained Tobin's address, hired a limousine, and set out to call upon him. The address he was given near Oldham proved to be that of a stately mansion standing back from the road along a drive, bordered by poplar trees of some resplendence.

Assuming he had received the wrong address, Sawers had his chauffeur drive him to the imposing main door of the mansion. It was opened by a butler who would have put Wodehouse's Jeeves on his mettle.

"Could you direct me to the home of Mr B. J. Tobin?" Sawers asked.

"The master, Sir," replied the butler, "is away grouse shooting in Scotland."

Bert Tobin's own comment regarding his one and only representation of his country at cricket was, "The team said I made the best drink waiter they ever had."

Other changes in the Australian team were the replacement of batsmen Fingleton, after his 1, 0, and 0, by Len Darling, and of O'Brien by that other left-hander, Ernie Bromley. Love came in for the unrecovered Oldfield. There were no Queenslanders in the side for this Brisbane Test. None of that State's batting candidates for selection were ever heard to complain. They had learned enough about the 1932–33 Larwood.

England brought in leg-spinner T. B. Mitchell in place of Voce, whose ankle was still weak.

Adelaide's Dr Charles Dolling was an Australian as well as a South Australian selector that summer. On the morning of the Fourth Test Vic Richardson met him at Woolloongabba.

"What's the matter with you, Doc?" he asked.

"Why, Vic?"

"Well, you've chosen Tobin for the Test and we dropped him from the South Australian team, the one *you* helped to choose."

"We've taken your tip. He's twelfth man here, too," said Dolling. On this morning of the Test "Plum" Warner came to George Hele in front of the players' stand and said, "I'm extremely sorry for what occurred in Adelaide. It was very painful and upsetting, not only for me but for the team as well."

George stuck to his code. He did not reply, and walked away. "I think 'Plum' wanted to air his feelings to someone," George says. "They must have been weighing heavily on his mind. But I didn't want to commit myself, not before I discovered what tactics the Englishmen would adopt in *this* Test. To this stage and indeed throughout most of the series, the English players were quite affable towards me and George Borwick. I don't believe we had given them cause to be anything except affable. They did not seem to regard the two of us as part of the common enemy, though we were Australians. They appeared to regard us purely as umpires and, therefore, as neutrals, which we were, with the proviso that we had formed and held our own opinions regarding Bodyline. These views we had kept to ourselves.

"Both of us, as I have said, dearly wished Sir Frederick Toone has been managing the M.C.C. team. He had shown his calibre with Gilligan's and Chapman's sides in 1924–25 and 1928–29. Under his strong management I believe the Bodyline bogy would have been killed behind the scenes after it was revealed for what it was in the M.C.C.–Australian XI game at Melbourne.

"Jardine had a strong mind and a determined manner during his two tours of Australia. But Sir Frederick was an even stronger personality and character. Toone loved Australia and Australians. He understood Australians and got on well with them. I believe he would have insisted on placing Anglo-Australian cricket, and Anglo-Australian relations generally, paramount and done all he could to ensure they were not jeopardised on the altar of subduing Bradman and in order to achieve ultimate English victory.

"I don't believe Bodyline would even have got off the ground had Toone been the 1932–33 manager."

Vic Richardson became Woodfull's partner after Bill won the toss for the third time in four Tests. "Will you go in first with me?" Woodfull asked. "Anywhere you like," Vic replied. When they reached the pitch Richardson said to his captain, "I think we can get on top of this fellow. I'll try to give him a belting. If Allen bowls any outside the off stump, as I think he will, I'll give *him* a bashing, too."

"I'll stick around, then," Woodfull said.

"When Vic *did* give Allen a belting to balls outside the off stump," says George Hele, "Gubby was not at all pleased with his own bowling; Richardson just smiled, and patted the pitch. He had no fear of Larwood's Bodyline at all and I believe he should have been called upon to open the Australian innings earlier in the series. He had a superb hook stroke, which Fingleton lacked. Vic *could* hit back. He had hooked Larwood into the top seats of the George Giffen Stand at Adelaide in 1928–29, while scoring his 231 against the M.C.C., and had scored 134 against Larwood for South Australia earlier this 1932–33 summer. Only three Australian batsmen ever struck Larwood for six in Australia. Vic Richardson was one of them.

"Vic played a few streaky strokes at the start of his innings, as was to be expected. But he soon settled in and honoured his promise. The partnership developed into the highest opening stand of the summer by Australia, one of 133, and Vic contributed 83. Nearly all his strokes were made in front of the wicket—drives, squarish-cuts, and hooks."

"Everyone," wrote Jack Hobbs, "has to admire Victor Richardson: he is always prepared to take a fifty-fifty chance with the bowlers. No sitting on the splice for Victor! He treated all the bowlers alike and was upset by none. He lost his wicket when trying to glide a ball from Hammond to leg, left his crease, and missed the ball. Though he lost no time in getting back, Leslie Ames was too quick for him. This was a very fine piece of stumping. I doubt if even George Duckworth could have done better."

During Vic's innings a bumper from Larwood went very close to his head.

"Sorry Vic, I thought it was going to hit you," Larwood called.

"If it happens again I'll knock your bloody block off," replied Vic.

Woodfull was bowled by Mitchell when 67 with the score at 200. Australia had reached the double century without losing a wicket to Bodyline, though Larwood was producing it unrestrainedly. He was having to go it alone, however, without Voce and Bowes to help him. The pitch was a good one, not as fast as Sydney or Adelaide but faster than Melbourne. Larwood's shorter balls rose chest and head high.

166

Richardson had scored 49 and 0, 34 and 32, 28 and 21, and now this 83. He had scored 246 against Bodyline, at 35·1 an innings, by playing his natural game. At one for 133 and two for 200 the stage was set for a big Australian score. The heat was affecting Larwood and Allen and there were no other pace bowlers on hand. Bradman had come in at the fall of Richardson's wicket and, though he took an unusually long time to begin scoring, he then cut Larwood fiercely to the third-man fence and hooked Allen for four.

Here now, as at Adelaide when England were four for 30, Australia had her chance. Four recognised batsmen—McCabe, Ponsford, Darling, and Bromley—besides Bradman, had to be disposed of before England could get at the "tail."

Vic Richardson believed at the time, and told George Hele later, that if Don Bradman reverted to his natural game he would consolidate the opening stand and Australia should level the series at two-all. Vic also suggested this to Bradman.

"Don, like Vic," says George, "was a law unto himself, however. Don *did* try to crack Larwood hard and often, though, when he settled in. But his batting for the rest of that afternoon did not approach the standard of his 103 not out in the Melbourne Test or of his 66 at Adelaide. Don seemed to have lost faith in the prospects of an orthodox answer to Bodyline, despite Richardson's demonstration that it would, and *did* work. Don had become determined to attack the fast bowling with a horizontal or diagonal blade in an all-out effort to force it, unnaturally, to the untenanted off side field."

Alan Kippax wrote on this subject: "I believe Australia opened the 1932–33 season with the greatest run-getting strength she ever possessed. With the exception of Archie Jackson, practically all the batsmen who contributed the mammoth scores of 1930 in England, were still available. Bradman was obviously a better player than ever before; he had more strokes and better ones, as Jack Hobbs said. McCabe had developed out of all recognition and his Sheffield Shield performances of 1931–32 had even surpassed those of Bradman. Ponsford and Woodfull had shown their finest form in the earlier Sheffield Shield matches, while Richardson and Fingleton each made a century in his first appearance against Jardine's team.

"It is almost incredible that such a batting side could be shattered, but shattered it was. Its only consolation is that its disruption was effected by methods hitherto unknown to cricket."

Hele continues: "It was noticeable that in this series, McCabe, Bradman, Ponsford, and Fingleton each played one great innings but could not bring themselves to repeat it against the Bodyline attack. Woodfull and Richardson were the ones who kept soldiering on, refusing to lose their sense of balance and alter their methods of batting.

"McCabe, admittedly, was out at 20 to a miraculous left-handed catch by Jardine at gully off Allen, one which would have done for Percy Chapman. At the close Australia were three for 251 — Bradman 71 not out and Ponsford 8 not out.

"Listening to the radio that night I heard the weather forecaster predict a heavy overnight downpour. Wickets were not covered then and Ironmonger was in the Australian ranks. But that forecast of rain proved to be wrong.

Douglas Jardine, in his book, *In Quest of the Ashes 1932–33,* claimed that the second day of the Fourth Test at Brisbane was "the greatest day which English cricket had known for twenty years. In spite of the boiling heat and the gruelling and disheartening experience we had had on the previous day," he wrote, "to get the seven outstanding Australian wickets for a paltry 89 runs and to reply with just short of 100 without the loss of a wicket was, I maintain, a wonderful example of the indomitable fighting spirit with which our team was imbued."

No fair-minded Australian would deny that Jardine had justification for those words. It was a novel suggestion by assistant manager R. C. N. Palairet that helped the Englishmen through. When they were unable to force any solid lunch down he suggested that each of the English bowlers be given half a dozen sips of champagne. Jardine agreed to the idea and, between them, Larwood, Allen, Hammond, and Verity downed three-quarters of a bottle of the beverage which, we are led to believe, helped Dr William Gilbert Grace to many a hundred.

"Larwood," says Hele, "made a supreme effort on the second morning, helped by a sound sleep and a cool breeze behind him. Bradman stepped well back from the wicket when he was 76 to try and cut a ball that was directed at his leg stump, and was bowled. In the same over, Larwood bowled Ponsford behind his back. Three for 250 had become five for 267."

Wrote Hobbs, "If a schoolboy tried to cut a ball on the leg stick, you would smack his head, yet here was Bradman doing it. It proved what I had always thought—that leg-theory forces you into making strokes you would never dream of trying in the ordinary way. I was not surprised to see Ponsford go because, like Bradman, he refused to play at many deliveries that only just missed his stumps."

Says Hele, "The two untried left-handers Darling and Bromley were left to face the music. Darling had faced Larwood's bowling only in the M.C.C.–Australian XI game in Melbourne, when he was bowled by Bowes for 4. Bromley had not faced Larwood. Larwood let his fastest ball go at Bromley. It rose sharply and touched the peak of his cap. The next ball was equally fast and, with all due respect to Bromley, I've never seen a batsman take a sitting position on a cricket pitch faster than Ernie did. When that first ball flicked Bromley's cap, 'Lol' gave a wry look in my direction but the narrow escape for the batsman did not deter the bowler from repeating the dose.

"Allen got Darling for 17 at 292 and Larwood had Bromley caught for 26 at 315. Though 'Dainty' Ironmonger compiled his highest Test score to date, a score of 8, Australia were all out for 340, having been two for 233."

Larwood, four for 101 from thirty-one overs, was man of the hour, the man who probably prevented Australia from amassing about 600. Allen, Hammond, and Mitchell shared the other wickets. But it was Hedley Verity 27/12/39/0 who won special praise from his captain. "I would stress the fact that the four wickets which Larwood took for 31 runs on this day were due in some measure to Verity's extraordinarily accurate bowling at the other end," wrote Jardine.

Jardine and the sleek, raven-haired Sutcliffe reached 99 without separation in the 150 minutes before stumps on the second day. It was during this display that a Brisbane barracker called to the England captain, "Leave *our* flies alone." At stumps O'Reilly showered and walked out on to the players' pavilion balcony. He says, "Jardine was standing there watching curator Jack Farquhar lay the covers. Facetiously, I said, 'Well played, Douglas.' He replied, 'Really, Bill O'Reilly, I thought I was like an old maid defending her virginity.' "

O'Reilly had taken the new ball for Australia. This use of a spinner as an opening bowler was not new. In the 1926 series in England both Grimmett and Charles Macartney opened with Jack Gregory, Macartney and Warwick Armstrong partnered "Tibby" Cotter in

1909, and Hordern did so in 1911–12. Off-spinner Hugh Trumble took the new ball regularly for Australia in the early 1900s.

On the morning of the third day Jardine came to Hele and Borwick and asked permission to have the wicket rolled in two five-minute sessions, instead of the normal, single, ten-minute spell.

Hele replied, "You may, but play resumes at noon." The first rolling began at 11.45. Hele assumed Jardine wanted the break between rolling to allow what moisture had been raised to the surface by the first rolling to dry before the roller was again applied. Jardine did not disclose his reasons. The roller was put back on the wicket at 11.58 a.m. At noon Hele told curator Farquhar to remove it from the ground.

The first of several subsequent arguments between Jardine and Hele followed. Jardine said, "Mind your own business." Hele ignored him and repeated his order to Farquhar, who obeyed it. By this time Woodfull had led the Australians on to the field. Jardine turned to Hele and said, "You've umpired your last Test." His face was livid, but Hele again ignored him. Woodfull came to Hele and asked, "What's going on?" Hele told him of Jardine's request and why he had ordered the roller from the ground—because play was due to begin.

"Don't worry, George," said Woodfull. "I had my watch on him, too."

And so another Test day began in acrimony.

Nothing more was said until lunch when Jardine sent a messenger to Hele, asking him to call at the English dressingroom. Hele said to the messenger, "Tell Mr Jardine that if he wants to see me he knows where I am." Jardine came to the umpires' room. "George," he said, "I'm sorry about that misunderstanding. I've had a look at the rule book and you umpires were right." Hele replied, "You knew that at the time." Jardine said, "Forget it," and walked away.

Says Hele of Jardine, "Douglas was a pleasant enough personality in 1928–29. He was also a splendid batsman who played more like the traditional English amateur than he did in 1932–33. He scored three centuries in his first three matches in 1928–29. His personality, like his batting, had greyed in 1932–33. I enjoyed the talks I had with him in 1928–29. Few such talks took place in 1932–33."

Maybe Jardine was upset by his altercation with Hele that third morning of the Brisbane Test. He left, caught Love bowled O'Reilly,

170

for 46 at one for 114. The snick came from the back of his bat when he tried to hook. O'Reilly, against normal custom, began against the wind. It was when he transferred to the other end that he got Jardine. According to Hele, O'Reilly used his zipping leg-break as his stock ball in 1932–33.

"Later he was to use the wrong-un as his stock ball and his leg-break as a surprise. After the total reached one for 157 five more English wickets fell cheaply, those of Sutcliffe, Hammond, Wyatt, Leyland, and Allen. Chasing 340, England trailed by 134 with only Ames, Paynter, Larwood, Verity, and Mitchell left.

Hele recalls, "Paynter was in hospital over the weekend, suffering from tonsillitis. He had been in bed since Friday and was very weak. He did not tell Jardine of his condition before the match. He went from his hotel bed into hospital on the Saturday night. On the Sunday Jardine called to see him there. During their discussion Paynter and his captain agreed that, if he had to break bounds and bat on crutches, Paynter would do so without a care for the consequences.

Hobbs wrote, "Paynter walked very, very slowly to the wicket when he came out to bat. He looked smaller than ever under a big Panama hat, cheered by the entire crowd . . . Woodfull's offer of a runner was refused, but was appreciated as a really sporting gesture."

At stumps Paynter was 24 not out and the total eight for 271.

Woodfull went all the way to the English dressingroom to offer him that runner. Significantly, Jardine does not record this gesture, or the cheering of the crowd, in his account of the tour, *In Quest of the Ashes 1932–33*. Paynter's temperature was above 100 degrees when he came in to bat. He went back into hospital that night before resuming his epic innings on the fourth day.

On the third day England had lost eight wickets for 172 in 300 minutes. Australia had yet a third chance to keep the series and Ashes issue open for decision in the Fifth Test at Sydney. But for the patriotism and pluck of Paynter, it most probably would have done so.

Paynter and Verity took England on to nine for 356—batting right through the morning session together. Even Bill O'Reilly's most deadly deliveries were met with the centre of the bat. Paynter was finally caught by Richardson off Ironmonger at cover for 83, and the Australians applauded him all the way to the fence. He left the field amid a storm of cheers.

During this innings of 356, which gave England a lead of 16, O'Reilly bowled 67·4 overs, twenty-seven of them maidens, to take four for 120; and Ironmonger forty-three overs, nineteen maidens, to take three for 69. Together they bowled 110·4 overs for 189 runs on a batsman's wicket. At times the two of them must have wished some inventive Australian would find a spin bowling equivalent to Bodyline.

Given sound authoritative batsmanship from its three world champion batsmen, Bradman, McCabe, and Ponsford, Australia would have had this Test match under control. But batting is a lonely business and none of these cricketers was in a settled, let alone confident, state of mind.

Richardson again began by attacking Larwood and Allen. Technically, he was not in the same class as Bradman, McCabe, and Ponsford, as a batsman, however. He was to them even less than his grandson Ian Chappell is to his other grandson Greg. Vic's stout heart was not enough. When he was 32, Jardine caught him brilliantly at mid-off, off Verity. Again he had hit his way through Larwood's first ferocious burst.

When Bradman entered, Woodfull did his utmost to keep him away from Larwood. For a time Don seemed only too happy to co-operate in this conspiracy. As Jack Hobbs has written, he took singles when twos were possible for strokes against Larwood. In earlier and later times it was his wont to take threes when only twos seemed possible.

Suddenly Don, without a word to Woodfull, decided to change his tactics and meet violence with violence. In one over he played two beautiful square-cuts past point from the Bodyline bowling.

"I was standing at point because of the stacked leg field," says Hele, "and lucky not to be hit. Bradman took ten from that over of Larwood's but, in the next, tried another square-cut from a ball in line with his wicket and spooned an easy chance to Mitchell who was standing a few yards behind me.

"When Ponsford, promoted above McCabe, came in at two for 79, I moved to an umpire's normal position at square-leg. I did so because he never hooked at Larwood in the way Richardson and Bradman occasionally did. Larwood was standing alongside me as Allen bowled to 'Ponnie.' I don't think I've seen Ponsford play a better stroke than the first and only one he executed in this vital

172

innings. He turned the ball off his ankles and it hardly left the ground as it travelled to the left of 'Lol.'

"Larwood laconically lowered his left hand and the ball was travelling so fast that it stuck. Harold laughed and said to me, 'I didn't think I had a hope in hell of holding it. It was a fluke.' Ponsford passed us on his way to the pavilion. 'Bad luck, Bill,' Larwood called to him. 'Go to blazes,' growled Ponsford. Larwood just shrugged his shoulders. I turned my back.

"It was proof enough for me, though, despite all I had read to the contrary, that Ponsford was *not* happy to leave his wicket, even when Larwood was bowling Bodyline to him."

Ponsford had now scored 32, 2, 85, 3, 19, and 0 in this series—a total of 141 at 23·5. This from the only batsman in the history of first-class cricket who twice passed the 400 mark in single innings. Following his 187 not out at Sydney, Stan McCabe had managed 32, 32, 0, 8, 7, and 20—a total of 99 at 16·5.

Hobbs declares he cannot remember a shot Woodfull made that day, but he was still there at four for 81 when McCabe came out on the last limb of Australian hope.

After struggling to 19 in ninety minutes, Woodfull was caught by Hammond off Mitchell. This made it four for 91. Bodyline and the effect it had on batsmen's minds, even when they were batting at the other end, had brought the flower of Australian batsmanship down like ninepins.

On the fifth day McCabe and Len Darling proceeded comfortably. Larwood failed to make the early strikes expected of him and, when he left the field, Hobbs confessed that his fears of defeat increased.

Voce was not playing and Larwood was off the field, but the deep psychological impression their bowling had made upon Australian batsmen still stalked like a phantom on the pitch.

Full concentration was lacking. McCabe was bowled by a low-bouncing ball from Verity for 22 at 136, Bromley left for 7 at 163 and Love and Darling became involved in a mix-up which brought Darling down, run out 39, to the last ball before lunch.

The score of seven for 169 (thirteen thirteens) looked ominous for Australia.

Says Hele, "Never once during this series did Woodfull, Richardson, Fingleton, McCabe, O'Brien, or Darling desert the line of flight of the full length or short of a length delivery. They only

173

demonstrated, however, that the orthodox reaction against Bodyline was ineffective. Neither right- nor left-handed batsmen could score consistently or tellingly against it while using orthodox methods. In his book Jardine asserted that the right-handed batsman was in no danger from Bodyline. From my position behind the stumps at the bowler's end I decided that the right-handed batsman was in far more physical danger than the left-hander. This is because Larwood's prevailing movement of the ball was from the off to leg, as also was the left-handed Voce's.

"Bradman was hit only once during the series, a glancing blow on the left forearm from Larwood in the Fifth Test. This was because his reflexes and footwork were so fast. Bradman's most prolific scoring arc, before and after Bodyline, was between square-leg and mid-on. Because of the length and height of the bowling he could not use this area for runs against Larwood or Voce. Had he adopted his normal style he must have been hit more blows, but I doubt very much whether he would have scored more runs. Had he batted normally I believe his Test average would have been in the thirties, not in the fifties. Don was not tall enough to get above the bumping ball as the more-than-six-foot-tall Jardine did against 'Bull' Alexander in the Fifth Test and against Constantine and Martindale in 1934 at Manchester."

It was while Larwood was bumping his Bodyline at McCabe on this fifth day that a barracker called, "Eh, Harold, that would have been a yorker if you'd been bowling from the other end." Years later Cowdrey was to explain why he never played forward to that dragon among "draggers," Australia's Rorke, by saying, "If I had, he'd have trodden on my toes." When it comes to cricket, humour can never be entirely squashed.

George Hele, who watched Bodyline from start to finish, is adamant that neither Hobbs nor Hammond, the two greatest English batsmen he saw, would have averaged 30 an innings against it. "I don't think Hammond would have averaged 20," he says, "Wally either could not, or would not, hook and his leg side play, generally, was remarkably restricted. The English batsmen who might have fared best were Sutcliffe and Leyland but, in my opinion, neither of them could have mastered it."

Len Darling, who has much of the make-up of his more famous uncle, Joe Darling, deserved great credit for top-scoring with 39.

174

But Australia's last four batsmen added 16 between them and England required only 160 to win.

Losing his partner Sutcliffe for 2 at one for 5, Jardine hardly progressed for eighty-five minutes—defending that "virginity" again. Because Hammond had bowled thirty-three overs for the match, Jardine promoted Leyland, who scored 86 of the next 133 runs in a masterful manner. Australia's one pace bowler, Wall, had a badly bruised heel. O'Reilly and Ironmonger delivered sixty-five overs for 112 runs. With rain threatening, Ames struck O'Reilly over the long-off fence and Paynter pulled a deliberately bowled full toss from McCabe over long-leg for another six to bring England handsomely home by six wickets.

George Hele declares he did not see that second six. He was too busy grabbing the stumps.

After the match, Woodfull went to the English dressingroom and congratulated Jardine and his team on their victory. Later Sir Leslie Wilson, Governor of Queensland, spoke to the assembled teams in the main pavilion. Hele, who was present, describes the scene.

"The English and Australian players stood on opposite sides of the room, George Borwick and I by the door between them. We wanted to be able to get out quickly. Neither Woodfull nor Jardine spoke, but Sir Leslie said a few kind words. The general atmosphere could have been much more cordial than it was. Jardine's face was a study in sternness and Woodfull's much the same."

It was on 16 February 1933, the final day of that fourth Test, the day on which Australia lost the Ashes, that Archie Jackson died, aged twenty-three. Archie lived only four years and eight days after he scored that magnificent 164 in his first Test innings at Adelaide. His body was brought to Sydney for burial. The English and Australian teams attended his funeral and Woodfull, Victor Richardson, Ponsford, and Bradman led the pall-bearers.

Amazingly, those who now compile *Wisden's Cricketers' Almanack* have deleted Jackson from its list of *Births and Deaths of Famous Cricketers,* though he qualified to remain there by representing Australia on a tour of England.

Attendance at the Brisbane Test was 93,143.

175

Sir Pelham Loses a Pennant

ENGLAND SUFFERED TWO LOSSES, RARITIES FOR HER ON THIS TOUR, early in the Fifth Test at Sydney. One was the toss—for the fourth time in five Tests; the other was "Plum" Warner's tattered but precious Marylebone Cricket Club flag.

This almost medieval piece of bunting, Warner claimed, had never flown over an English defeat. In the odd match?—Yes. Above an entire series?—No. It was his banner when he led England triumphant over Australia in 1903–04. It flew above all Australian grounds when England, under his non-playing captaincy, recovered the Ashes in 1911–12. It flew on the ivied keep of Lord's pavilion in 1926. Warner was one of England's selectors that summer.

That flag, in the words of Jack Fingleton, had become for "Plum" "a symbol of English supremacy in every clash with Australia with which he was personally associated." He hoisted it to the masthead of the S.C.G.'s old Showboat pavilion on Friday 23 February 1933, to celebrate the recapture of the Ashes at Brisbane. On that Friday and on the Saturday English fieldsmen dropped many chances. "Twelve at a moderate estimate," claimed Jardine.

On the Monday Leslie Ames was ruled run out, very questionably in the opinion of the Englishmen, by a brilliant throw by Bradman from the boundary. Ames returned to the dressingroom to find it in a state of pandemonium—not over the manner of his dismissal, however. "Plum" had just discovered that his precious flag was missing—*had* been missing for days. He immediately attributed those dropped chances, that "butter-fingers burlesque," as it was called, and the run out, to the disappearance of the flag which had "flown over victorious English cricketing campaigns for thirty years and never been hauled down over the loss of a rubber."

Attendants were questioned, search parties sent hunting in all directions. At one stage during the next twenty-four hours Arthur Mailey suggested summoning Sherlock Holmes. Quite clearly, somebody had stolen the pennant from the flagpole. On the fourth morning of the Test it was found outside the English dressingroom. The fact that it had been mistakenly used for most of the Monday by a N.S.W.C.A. barman to mop up the beer slops from the Show-boat pavilion main bar was mercifully concealed from the M.C.C. manager and, later, cricketing knight.

Douglas Jardine was downcast, indeed, at the loss of his fourth toss out of five. After all, Woodfull was utterly innocent. He had merely spun the coins. Jardine had done all the calling. Douglas, George Hele feels, might have been more philosophical had he remembered what had happened to his predecessor, Sir Stanley Jackson.

Jackson, who topped the batting and bowling averages for the 1905 series in England with 492 runs at 70·28 and thirteen wickets at 15·46, also won all five tosses from Joe Darling. Before the Fifth Test at the Oval he came into the Australian dressingroom intent on making it five out of five, an all-time record.

Joe Darling had a chest like one of Spain's fighting bulls. It was also almost as hairy. When Sir Stanley, as elegantly and immaculately attired as ever, entered the dressingroom, he found Darling bare-chested and in shorts.

"What about the toss, Joe?" he asked. "We're not going to toss, we're going to wrestle for choice of innings," replied Darling, without a glimmer of a grin. "Hurry up, Joe, there's not much time," said Jackson. "I told you we're going to wrestle for it." Jackson studied that expanse of chest, patted Darling on the shoulder and smiled.

"Not this time, Joe, I want to win all five," said Sir Stanley. And this he did. That other famous English athlete, treble Oxford

Blue, and long-jump world-record holder, Charles Burgess Fry, whom Sir Stanley had considered summoning to wrestle Darling, then proceeded to score 144, part of it during a third-wicket stand of 151 with Jackson.

How Jardine and Woodfull would have fared in a wrestle at this stage of such an acrimonious series, is perhaps best left to the imagination. "Simply not done, old chap."

Jardine had brought his men down from Brisbane by ship. On the way they dropped in to Newcastle, where Hobbs and Warner were conscripted from retirement, to fill the tiring ranks of the M.C.C. team. Opening the M.C.C. innings, Hobbs scored 44 against an attack which included that excellent opening bowler, Hal Hooker, and Arthur Chipperfield, who later was to bowl his leg-breaks for Australia. Warner, then sixty years old, was bowled for one.

Chipperfield scored 152 in Northern Districts of N.S.W.'s first innings against an attack which contained Voce, Bowes, Maurice Tate, Freddie Brown, and Mitchell. The Newcastle side 322, led the M.C.C. 254, on the first innings and followed with a second innings total of 236 before time ran out.

Voce returned to the England team for the Test. Australia dropped Ponsford, Bromley, Wall, and Love, bringing in O'Brien, South Australian off-spinner P. K. Lee, Oldfield, and "Bull" Alexander. Alexander was faster than Wall and Australians, by and large, hoped he would live up to his nickname.

The Englishmen, having won the series and recovered the Ashes lost so decisively in 1930, were hardly looking forward to five or six days barracking from the spectators on the Hill. The words "barrackers" and "barracking" were coined in Australia.

When cricket matches were first staged by Sydney's Military Club outside the Victoria Barracks in Paddington, those confined to barracks were permitted to watch them from the uncomfortable broken-glass-topped barrack walls. They were a particularly vociferous coterie and they came to be known as "barrackers."

On 12 June 1933, the Marylebone Cricket Club, in a dispatch to the Australian Cricket Board of Control, was to have this to say:

"With regard to the reports of the captain and managers of our recent tour of Australia, while deeply appreciative of the private and public hospitality shown to the English team, we are much

Voce's inner leg field placings when bowling to Ponsford at Adelaide in the Third Test of the 1932–33 series

concerned with regard to barracking, which is referred to in all the reports, and against which there is unanimous deprecation.

"Barracking has, unfortunately, always been indulged in by spectators in Australia to a degree quite unknown in this country. During the late tour, however, it would appear to have exceeded all previous experience, and on occasions to have become thoroughly objectionable. There appears to have been little or no effort on the part of those responsible for the administration of the game in Australia to interfere, or to control this exhibition. This was naturally regarded by members of the team as a serious lack of consideration for them. The Committee are of the opinion that cricket played under such conditions is robbed of much of its value as a game and that unless barracking is stopped, or is greatly moderated in Australia, it is difficult to see how the continuance of representative matches can serve the best interest of the game."

Previous to this dispatch an Irishman, who lived for some years in Australia and learned to love the country and its people, had written:

"I believe few things would do Australia more good in the eyes of all the Empire, than the knowledge that she had resolutely tackled and put down barracking. It seems to me a great pity that a country, which most certainly loves and appreciates fair play and sportsman-like conduct, should deliberately 'blacken its face,' as the Indians say, with all the world by sticking to a custom which, in its least objectionable form, is childish, and can easily degenerate into a definite assault on the nerves of a player.

"If there is any excuse for it in cricket there is equal excuse in any other game. Can you imagine the scene, and the newspaper comments, if a French or American champion playing in the Davis Cup at Wimbledon was hooted and yelled at by the spectators every time he served a ball? It would take the persuasive oratory of a Demosthenes himself to persuade France, or America, that 'English fair play' was anything but a myth.

"Would it not be possible to work up public opinion on this matter? I am sure there are many in Australia who would follow if they got the lead. I know that, as a rule, Australians resent any criticism of this custom and say that it is all done in good humour, and that only a 'touchy ass' would resent it. That may be and, of course, Australian players are used to it and take it for what it is worth.

Top: The Englishmen come to the assistance of McCabe after he had been struck in the First Test. Such gestures of concern became less frequent as the tour progressed. Bottom: Jardine caught at slip by Richardson off Ironmonger in the Fifth Test

But I doubt if the average Australian realises what a bad name the custom has given Australia.

"The London *Observer*'s comment in a special article on 22 January 1933 that 'courtesy and good sportsmanship, to which visiting teams over here in England persistently bear record, are not to be expected "down under," ' is a mild way of putting what I have heard said frequently and forcibly, not only at home, but in India and Africa for forty-odd years."

George Hele, as an Australian umpire for some twenty-five years, and I, as a player in first-class matches for fifteen, agree with much of what that Irishman wrote forty years ago. We regret that it has had so little effect. We do feel, however, that the unsporting comment from an Australian barracker is very much the exception and that more humour emanates from Australian outer grounds than from those of anywhere except Yorkshire. Unsporting comment *was* far more rife during the Bodyline series and for this Jardine must accept much of the blame.

One despairs, however, of any improvement in the conduct of Australian crowds, especially from near the scoring-board bar at Adelaide, behind the Richmond end sightboard at Melbourne, the heart of Sydney's Hill, or under those Malayan fig trees on the mounds of Woolloongabba, unless those responsible for the administration at these venues take concerted and continuing action. And they cannot even keep kids off a wicket.

Australian barracking can have reached no lower ebb than when a section of the S.C.G. crowd cheered when Jardine was hit a painful blow while batting in the Test we are about to describe. In contrast, however, it should be remembered how Larwood was cheered all the way back to the pavilion by the *entire* crowd after being caught for 98. "It was a really wonderful ovation," wrote Jack Hobbs, "all the members standing up to cheer."

Play in the Test began on a hot day and on a typically fast Sydney wicket. The crowd, wanting to see its fielding hero of the 1928 Test, Vic Richardson, tilt with Larwood as he had done in both innings at Brisbane, was disappointed. He was caught at gully in the first over of the game, by Jardine, the fieldsman he liked least, from Larwood, the bowler he liked least.

At the end of Larwood's over, Jardine threw the ball to Allen. Sutcliffe walked up to Allen, took the ball from him and threw it to

Voce. "Jardine," says Hele, "looked surprised but did not interfere. Led by Hammond and Sutcliffe, the field moved to the leg side and adopted the Bodyline setting as Bradman took strike. Jardine, having won the series, probably intended to put a pleasant front on things by the delivery of a few orthodox overs while the ball was new. Not so Sutcliffe and Hammond. Maybe they had seen all they wanted to see of Don in 1930. Bodyline from Larwood and Voce, they believed, would have him back in the pavilion far sooner than Allen's outswingers."

In view of Sutcliffe and Hammond's action, however, it is intriguing to recall Vic Richardson's written statement, "Both Hammond and Sutcliffe confessed to me that they would not have played for five minutes against Bodyline bowling." The sauce for the Australian goose was *not* good for the English gander, it would seem. What other conclusion can be reached?

For Bradman the die had been cast. In the words of Jardine, "On his home pitch . . . he started right away to give a display of fireworks, edging away from his wicket in order to puncture the off side when leg-theory was being bowled and when off-theory was in force, stepping across and hooking the ball to the vacated on-side.

"Here, again, the pace seemed a little too hot to last. In his second spell, Larwood once again proved Bradman's master, clean bowling him when he was attempting an unorthodox shot which, when successful, is dazzling to a degree, but when, as in this case, it results in a broken wicket, looks unworthy of a great batsman."

Bradman, 48, left at two for 59.

"When the score was 64," recalls Hele, "Larwood delivered what Jardine and I consider to have been the fastest ball we have ever seen. It soared from a length over Woodfull's off stump. The next ball was almost as fast and Woodfull, though he appeared to play it in the centre of his bat, found it proceeding on to his stumps.

"Australia lost three wickets before lunch, when Larwood had three for 14. All this on what was described as a 'batting paradise' by commentators who had never faced Larwood at his fastest from twenty-two yards. Confronting this kind of Larwood on any surface can scarcely be regarded as 'paradise.' "

Australia's position was, however, soon to be retrieved when McCabe and O'Brien added 99 for the fourth wicket. O'Brien, for whom Larwood stationed five off side slips, was dropped three times while scoring 61. He was missed twice by Voce and once by Ames, each time off Larwood. Before the Australian innings ended Darling was to be dropped by Sutcliffe off Hammond and by Allen off his own bowling, Oldfield was to be missed by Verity and by Allen off Larwood, O'Reilly by Ames and Verity off Larwood, and by Voce and Jardine off Allen.

While these mistakes were being made Jardine's stern countenance was a study. When Jardine himself missed O'Reilly, high and one-handed at gully, all the members of the team turned their backs to conceal their mirth. Jardine found himself with the ball at his feet and nobody to throw it to.

To quote the words of Dr William Gilbert Grace on a far earlier occasion, "This was an epidemic, but it wasn't catching."

Back in front of the crowd which had watched his superlative 187 not out three months before, McCabe, though severe upon Voce, played mostly restrained though beautiful cricket while scoring 73. Darling 85 and Oldfield 52 played pluckily and with some luck, and the heavily built Keith Lee batted lustily for 42 which included five boundaries and was compiled in thirty-five minutes.

At the end of the first day Australia was five for 296. In the dressing-room Jardine could not manage a laugh, even when George Duckworth tried to cheer the team by reminding them that Lancashire once dropped fourteen chances *before lunch* off the former Australian fast bowler Ted McDonald.

Jardine must have felt happier when, after Australia were out for 435, he was missed twice himself in the first two overs of the English innings. He became his normal brand of "Il Penseroso," however, when he snicked O'Reilly to Oldfield after scoring 18 of 31.

Hardly had the English innings begun than Jardine got into holts with Woodfull. Alexander, short but sturdy of build, used to jump into the air as he delivered the ball. He had an erect arm action and early in this innings made a few balls fly.

Jardine complained to Woodfull that his new fast bowler was following through unfairly along the pitch. Following this altercation and while Jardine was prodding the pitch in an effort to strengthen his case, Alexander walked back along the wicket after delivering a ball and picked up a blade of grass from almost under Jardine's rather Roman nose. "You missed this, Douglas," the "Bull" said, but Jardine ignored him.

182

Woodfull then asked Alexander to bowl around the wicket. At the end of the fourth day's play Jack Hobbs inspected the pitch. He wrote, "I found the wicket in quite good condition, the only marks being those made by the feet of bowlers. The edge of one of the marks *was* just outside the leg stump, creating a very nasty patch for our batsmen."

It was just before Jardine's innings ended that Alexander made a shortish ball lift and strike Jardine. It was then that a section of the crowd cheered—in Vic Richardson's words, "to their everlasting shame."

"Jardine," says Hele, "took the blow and the cheers like a statue, but was caught by Oldfield off O'Reilly soon afterward, possibly because of loss of concentration.

"Hammond then batted beautifully for his second century of the series, but his 440 at 55·00 in this rubber did not measure against his 905 at 113·12 in 1928–29. I believe Hammond's decline as a run-maker came from two causes. These were that Woodfull's bowlers aimed predominantly at his leg stump, not at his strong point—the off stump—as Ryder's had done, and because the entire atmosphere in which the series was contested affected his concentration."

Sutcliffe was caught by Richardson at short-leg off O'Reilly for 56 at two for 153. Larwood came in as a night watchman. Years later he was to become another kind of night watchman at the Pepsi-Cola factory in this same city, when he made his home in Australia. Larwood said he took this occupation because it shielded him from communication with the outside world. He had grown to be a recluse. In contrast, his five daughters accepted jobs on the switchboards of Sydney firms.

England was two for 159, chasing 435, at the close of the second day. Larwood, it was said, "was very unlucky to be caught by 'Dainty' Ironmonger after a hard-hitting and crowd-pleasing 98." Ironmonger made only three catches in his fourteen Tests. According to Jardine, "he made a lot of ground to hold a good catch at mid-on."

According to his son, "Dainty" never missed a chance in those fourteen Tests. His catching record was 100 per cent. Maybe opposing batsmen were afraid to lift the ball in his direction.

However this may be, Larwood received that wonderful ovation from all round the S.C.G. as he went off. According to Hele, "Bradman's reception at Melbourne after his 103 not out in the

183

Second Test was no warmer than this one of Larwood. It was shown quite clearly that Sydney cricketlovers blamed Jardine, not Larwood, for the Bodyline tactics."

Encouraged by his catching of Larwood, Ironmonger went on to even finer things as a fieldsman. He could be excused for believing he was Alice in Wonderland when he held a shot from Bob Wyatt, beside his shoelaces, at mid-on off the bowling of O'Reilly to make it seven for 374. Ironmonger had caught two out of two in a Test during which England already had missed twelve chances and Australia six. Where those fine fieldsmen McCabe, Bradman, and O'Brien had been found lacking, "Dainty" had proved impeccable—though handicapped by the loss of two and a half fingers from his more important left hand.

Prior to Wyatt's dismissal, from an O'Reilly full toss, "The Tiger" had been fuming at his own misfortune. Almost throughout his innings of 51 Wyatt had been snicking and edging balls from O'Reilly. In the previous over Bill had beaten him badly three times. After being caught by Ironmonger, Wyatt walked passed O'Reilly. "The Tiger" turned to him and muttered, "And I thought *I* was unlucky."

This verbal Irish artillery left Wyatt, known as "Deadpan," utterly unmoved.

In the outcome England, 454, led by 19. "Gubby" Allen got 48. As in its first innings, Australia lost one for 0. Vic Richardson had been caught from a late lifter from Larwood in his first innings. This time he tried to hook Larwood. Allen at short-leg threw up his left arm to try and grasp the ball, which had come from Richardson's thumb. He checked the flight of the ball and, just as it seemed certain to escape him, he made a frantic grab at it with his right hand. This time he was successful. "I felt sorry for Richardson, game fighter that he is," wrote Hobbs, "for a 'pair' in a Test is a nasty blow."

Victor York Richardson, like Keith Ross Miller after him, was never a lucky batsman. I cannot remember seeing Miller missed during his eighty-eight innings in Tests. Yet he still scored 2,958 runs. Richardson scored 706 in thirty knocks.

Though Larwood was stirred to his greatest pace and hostility by Allen's catch and Bodyline was again given free rein, Woodfull and Bradman added 115 for the second wicket. Bradman began in much the same manner as he had in the first innings—stepping away from Larwood's bumpers and slashing them with horizontal

184

and diagonal bat to the off side. He made some truly savage cuts and strokes in front of the wicket, twice hooking Voce for four. He would not attempt to hit Larwood to the on side, however. He was caught at gully from a no-ball from Allen when 37, then hooked the next three deliveries to the boundary, the last of these strokes flying like a flash to the long-on fence as Bradman fell away from his wicket.

He reached his 50 with a beautiful cover drive off Verity and sent up the 100 with a great stroke to the leg boundary off Hammond. Larwood, who had hit Bradman on the forearm earlier when, according to Jardine, "he was six inches outside the leg stump endeavouring to play in the direction of point," was now becoming lame. His foot was causing him great pain. He had lost the skin from two of his toes and he left the field. An X-ray revealed that he had also splintered a bone. Before he left the field Larwood made one final all out blast at Bradman. During this Verity deceived "The Don" with a fast yorker, which bowled him for 71 at two for 115. Of this innings Hobbs wrote, "It was from first to last that of a gambler, but it was beautiful to watch, some of the strokes being similar to those described in schoolboys' tales."

Woodfull had been hit a severe blow, low down on his back, by Larwood early in his innings and then on his shoulder by Voce. According to Hele, however, "he settled down so soundly and began to play strokes that suggested he would again bat through an Australian innings. Woodfull was a schoolmaster by profession and he had shown that he could learn. He stayed bravely until he was 67, when he played a ball from Allen on to his stumps again. His partners, O'Brien, McCabe (suffering from a severe throat infection), Darling, and Oldfield scored 5, 4, 7, and 5, respectively and Australia, having been one for 115 at one stage, was all out for 182, despite Larwood's disappearance shortly before tea. Verity, five for 33 from nineteen overs, had stepped into the breach.

Ironmonger again distinguished himself by preventing a hat-trick and remaining 0 not out.

England scored the 168 she needed for the loss of Jardine 24 and Leyland 0 (both of them to Ironmonger), despite the presence of the mark on the pitch, just wide of the leg stump.

Ironmonger delivered twenty-six overs, twelve of them maidens, for 34 runs before Hammond struck a six, as had Paynter at Brisbane,

185

to end the proceedings and be 75 unconquered following his first innings of 101.

It was during this England innings according to George Hele, that O'Reilly and Oldfield had a disagreement. O'Reilly appealed for l.b.w. and Hele refused it. At the end of the over Oldfield came to O'Reilly and said, "I thought George was wrong." "So did I," replied "The Tiger." "It's about the first time you've ever supported me, by the way."

"Yes," said Oldfield, "I thought he was wrong because he should have pulled out a stump and banged you over the head with it for appealing."

Hele and Borwick were greatly relieved when the series ended.

Says Hele, "All through we had feared serious injury to players and we had not enjoyed the reaction of the crowds. In addition we had had to endure the unpleasantness existing between the players. Jardine, particularly, made us feel continually on edge by his demeanour and almost constant moodiness.

"In return for all this I received a total of seventy pounds—ten pounds for the Test in Adelaide and fifteen pounds for each of the Tests away from there. George Borwick, who umpired two Tests in his home city, Sydney, received only sixty-five pounds.

"Over twenty-six playing days this works out at less than three pounds a day. Nowadays Test umpires get the same payment as the players—250 dollars."

Infallibility can rarely have been expected for so miserable a reward in any field of sport, as it was forty-odd years ago.

186

Australia Wins the Bodyline War

THE COMMITTEE APPOINTED BY THE AUSTRALIAN CRICKET BOARD OF Control, to "report on the action necessary to eliminate such [Bodyline] bowling," comprised Mr Roger Hartigan (Queensland) who represented the Board, Mr M. A. Noble (New South Wales), Mr W. M. Woodfull (Victoria), and Mr V. Y. Richardson (South Australia).

All members of the committee had represented Australia at cricket. Noble and Woodfull had captained Australia and Richardson was to do so in 1935–36 in South Africa.

All Australian Sheffield Shield States had announced support for the Board's belief that an alteration of the Laws of Cricket was necessary to ensure that Bodyline bowling would not be repeated.

For a considerable time the English authorities failed to share this belief. They were in a difficult position. Few of them had seen the 1932–33 Tests. To admit the necessity for a change in the Laws to eliminate Bodyline predicated an official admission that the Ashes had been recovered through improper, though legal, practices, that Jardine *had* been unsportsmanlike.

Many Australians thought the Australian Board should have supported its original cable with documentary evidence and a selection of responsible opinion. It had not done so.

Victor Richardson, the Australian vice-captain, had opposed the dispatch of the first cable during the Adelaide Test for four reasons:

1. He felt that people so far away in England could have no conception of what Bodyline was really like;
2. He believed the M.C.C. would support its team in the absence of first-hand knowledge of what was occurring;
3. He knew that the word "unsportsmanlike" would be, to Englishmen, like a red rag to a bull;
4. He felt the cable was ill-timed, as Englishmen would think Australians were squealing about being beaten.

Richardson advocated the completion of the series and *then* the sending of a secret report, including suggestions for the elimination of Bodyline bowling and stressing that its continuance involved grave danger to the whole spirit and atmosphere of the game at all levels.

Richardson was overruled. So, often, was the young Winston Churchill.

During and after the 1932–33 series, a number of responsible and respected Australians expressed their opinions of Bodyline bowling. These opinions included:

M. A. Noble (Australia's captain 1903–04, 1907–08, and 1909): "We have seen sufficient Bodyline bowling this season to realise that it does more to kill cricket than any other force ever brought into play;"

Clem Hill (Australia's 1911–12 captain): "We call it Bodyline bowling but it is really bowling at the man. If the members of the· Marylebone Cricket Club had seen this attack in operation in Australia there would be no doubt about their attitude;"

Dr Reg Bettington (N.S.W. captain and a former Oxford University captain): "The determination to win at any price was deplorable. Many cool critics in Australia believe that there was an intention to injure the batsmen. My own opposition to leg-theory is entirely confined to this question of injury;"

W. J. O'Reilly: "To a good batsman short-pitched bumpers are chicken feed. But when allied with the Bodyline field placing they are murder;"

Jack Fingleton: "Nobody can point a finger at a fast bowler who happens to hit a batsman with a legitimate bumper but the Bodyline

188

case differed because the thick English placing of the leg side field on the batsman's 'blind spot' tied down and cramped the batsman and did not give him a cricketing chance to deal with the bumper . . . The Bodyline field was concentrated to tie the batsman down while the ball played about his ribs and ears. He was cribbed, cabined, confined, and battered."

On the final afternoon of the fifth Test of 1932–33 at Sydney, the Australian team returned to the Coogee Bay Hotel. With them went George Hele. That evening Woodfull asked Hele and the Melbourne *Age* cricket correspondent, Frank Maugher, to join him on Coogee Beach. Together there on the sand they discussed ways and means by which Bodyline bowling could be legally eliminated from cricket. Their discussions lasted three hours. During that time they evolved a new law which in November 1934 was incorporated, almost identically, into the Laws of Cricket.

Says Hele, "During our talk Woodfull, Maugher, and I discarded the idea of limiting the number of leg side fieldsmen. We did so because, if bumpers were not delivered persistently, there was no threat to life and limb from a packing of the leg field.

"The law we arrived at did cast a great responsibility on the umpires, who would have to decide what was 'intimidatory' and what was not. If the bumper was prevented from being delivered persistently, the batsman would know he had to face only one or at most two an over. He could ignore these if he wanted to, in the knowledge that he could score runs from the other balls by orthodox methods."

Experimental Law 46, Note 4(vi) today reads: "The persistent bowling of fast short-pitched balls at the batsman is unfair if, in the opinion of the umpire at the bowler's end, it constitutes a systematic attempt at intimidation. In such event he must adopt the following procedure:

(a) When he decides that such bowling is becoming persistent he forthwith 'cautions' the bowler.

(b) If this 'caution' is ineffective, he informs the captain of the fielding side and the other umpire of what has occurred.

(c) Should the above prove ineffective, the umpire at the bowler's end must:

(i) At the first repetition call 'Dead ball,' when the over is regarded as completed.

189

(ii) Direct the captain of the fielding side to take the bowler off forthwith. The captain shall take the bowler off as directed.

(iii) Report the occurrence to the captain of the batting side as soon as the interval of play takes place.

A bowler who has been 'taken off' as above may not bowl again during the same innings."

When the members of the committee appointed by the Australian Board held their deliberations *they* also discarded the idea of limiting the leg side field. Their ultimate recommendation that umpires be given power to prevent bowlers from using deliveries designed to intimidate or injure batsmen was adopted by the Australian Board, referred to the Marylebone Cricket Club, and late in 1934 was adopted in principle by the Imperial Cicket Conference.

In June 1933 the Marylebone Cricket Club cabled the Australian Board: "The new law recommended by the Australian Board of Control does not appear to the M.C.C. Committee to be practicable. Firstly it would place an impossible task on the umpire and secondly it would place in the hands of the umpire a power over the game which would be more than dangerous, and which any umpire might well fear to exercise.

"The Committee have had no reason to give special attention to leg-theory as practised by fast bowlers. They will, however, watch carefully during the present season for anything which might be regarded as unfair or prejudicial to the best interests of the game. They propose to invite opinions and suggestions from County Clubs and Captains at the end of the season with a view to enabling them to express an opinion on this matter at a Special Meeting of the Imperial Cricket Conference."

In the same cable the M.C.C. stated, "The term 'Bodyline' would appear to imply a direct attack by the bowler on the batsman. The Committee consider that such an implication applied to any English bowling in Australia is improper and incorrect. Such an action on the part of any bowler would be an offence against the spirit of the game and would be immediately condemned . . ."

The whole issue was becoming one of fact and England was beginning to learn the facts, to realise what *had* happened.

On his return home, Jack Hobbs wrote: "I am distinctly not in favour of leg-theory or Bodyline, or whatever you care to call Larwood's methods. I think such tactics are not in the best interests

190

of the game. To me they seem contrary to the spirit of cricket, and I consider it absolutely wrong that they should be used by anyone at any time . . . A batsman facing a fast bowler who sends down fast leg-theory has to play strokes more in protection of his body than with the idea of defending his wicket or scoring runs. And he knows all the time that with three or four, and sometimes five, men standing close in on the leg side, he is almost certain to lose his wicket off a stroke he has made merely to protect himself. If the ball happens to be pitched so short that it can be hit hard to deep leg, there are two men waiting for a catch . . . Oh, it seems to me leg-theory is a most venomous thing."

The opinions of few people in England were more respected at the time than those of Jack Hobbs.

The editor of England's "cricketing bible," *Wisden's Cricketers' Almanack*, wrote in a special article in the 1934 edition:

"D. R. Jardine, on his return to England, stated definitely in his book that the bowling against which the Australians demurred was not a direct attack by the bowler on the batsman and Larwood, the chief exponent of it, said with equal directness that he had never intentionally bowled at a man. On the other hand there are numerous statements by responsible Australians to the effect that the type of bowling *was* calculated to intimidate batsmen, pitched as the ball was so short as to cause it to fly shoulder and head high and make a batsman, with the leg side studded with fieldsmen, use the bat as a protection for his body, or his head, rather than in defence of his wicket or to make a scoring stroke.

"Victor Richardson, the South Australian batsman, has said that, when he took his ordinary stance at the wicket, he found the ball coming on to his body; when he took guard slightly more to the leg side, he still had the ball coming on to him; and with a still wider guard the ball continued to follow him. I hold no brief either for Jardine or Larwood or for Richardson, Woodfull, or Bradman; but, while some of the Australians may have exaggerated the supposed danger of this type of bowling, I cling to the opinion that they cannot *all* be wrong.

"Ordinary leg-theory is very different from the kind sent down at top speed with the ball flying past the shoulders or head of the batsman who has only a split second to decide whether he will duck,

191

move away, or attempt to play it with the bat high in the air. Against ordinary leg-theory a perfectly legitimate and reasonable stroke could be played without any apprehension of physical damage; against the other it seems to me that by touching the ball in defence of the upper part of his body or his head a batsman would almost be bound to be out.

"One would not accuse Hammond or Hendren of being slow on their feet, yet Hendren, at Lord's on one occasion this summer, was not quick enough to get out of the way and received a crashing blow on his head, while last season at Manchester Hammond, in the Test against the West Indies, had his chin laid open and, on resuming his innings, was caught from a similar kind of ball.

"We saw in that particular match at Old Trafford what I should conceive to be a somewhat pale—but no less disturbing—imitation of Larwood in Australia, when Martindale and Constantine on the one hand and Clark of Northamptonshire on the other were giving a demonstration of fast leg-theory bowling. Not one of the three had the pace, accuracy of pitch, or deadliness of Larwood, but what they did was sufficient to convince many people with open minds on the subject that it was a noxious form of attack not to be encouraged in any way . . .

"For myself I hope that we shall never see fast leg-theory bowling as used during that last tour of Australia exploited in this country. I think that (1) it is definitely dangerous; (2) it creates ill-feeling between the rival teams; (3) it invites reprisals; (4) it has a bad influence on our great game of cricket; and (5) it eliminates practically all the best strokes in batting. Mainly because it makes cricket a battle instead of a game, I deplore its introduction and pray for its abolition . . ."

The truth had crossed the world and taken root. But the English are a proud people. Nobody finds it easy to admit to having been embarrassingly wrong.

When the Australians played England under Woodfull in England in 1934 no legislation banning Bodyline bowling had been introduced. But the English selectors had their problems on this score largely solved for them by the retirement of the still intractable Jardine and by Larwood's highly publicised refusal to take the field against Australia. Voce, whose methods had upset some of the Counties, was not considered for selection.

192

Legislation designed to outlaw Bodyline bowling was passed in November of 1934. Larwood, though top of the 1936 English first-class bowling averages, stated his unavailability for the 1936–37 M.C.C. tour of Australia. Voce placed himself unreservedly at the disposal of the selectors and, without bowling Bodyline, topped the Test averages with the superb figures: 162·1/20/560/26/21·53.

The England captain, G. O. Allen, did a great deal to dim Australian memories of four years before, though no adult Australian of the early 1930s will forget Jardine to his dying day—particularly that long-term English migrant to Australia, Harold Larwood.

Noble Was the Noblest of Them All

HIGH WYCOMBE'S CRICKET GROUND SLOPES GREEN FROM ITS PIGMY white pavilion towards a fold in the beautiful Chiltern Hills. The curator of the ground, "Laddie" Page, reminded me rather of the image I'd rightly or wrongly formed of the ploughman in Gray's *Elegy*. "Laddie," be it emphasised, rarely looked weary, even at cricketing curfew times—just old and gnarled and sturdy as the oaks he loved and lived among in Buckinghamshire. Perhaps it was the way he plodded with bent shoulders towards me up the rise from long-leg.

As he plodded, taking care to keep beyond the white-washed boundary line, 1,000 Lancaster bombers were flying on their way to bomb Cologne, or Köln as the Germans spell it. It was spring of 1945; those oaks and the elms and horse-chestnuts were coming to rich leaf on either side of the ancient stone pepper and salt mill.

"Never thought to see a sight like that over the old ground, sir, and I've been 'ere for sixty years," "Laddie" said as he reached square-leg. "Village green cricket and a 1,000-bomber raid all on one Chiltern evening. Makes you think, sir, it does, think what's 'appened to us 'umans. You've picked a good spot to field though, sir. Ball rarely mounts this 'ill."

"You've been curator here for sixty years, 'Laddie'?"

"Yes, sir. 'Alf a lifetime, sir. Since I was seventeen. Saw 'W. G.,' sir. That I did. And Lohmann and Ulyett, too. They all played 'ere in the Eighties on my pitch."

Sixty years watching English cricket and most of it Minor County. It bespoke a deep love for the game. Well, George Hele has spent even longer than that watching Australia's cricket champions—its greatest captains, batsmen, bowlers, and fieldsmen. He began watching them—Trumper and Hill, Noble, and Syd Gregory, and England's "Ranji" and Archie MacLaren, too—in the early 1900s at the Adelaide Oval.

Seventy-three years later he's still watching their successors from the V.C.A. Delegates' sanctum at the M.C.G.

No wonder George took so long to name the greatest of his champions in the order he believed they deserved to rank.

We decided to talk of the great captains first, for they *were* the leaders and should, we agreed, come first.

Slowly and ever so fondly, George reduced them, firstly in chronological order, to Joe Darling, Monty Noble, Herbert "Lucky" Collins, Vic Richardson, Don Bradman, and Richie Benaud—before he remembered England's Johnny Douglas, that is, and discarded Douglas Jardine.

He had not seen enough, did not know enough, of Pelham Warner and Archie MacLaren as captains to assess their leadership "accurately and with justice" and, despite his tremendous qualities as a captain, Douglas Jardine's resort to Bodyline bowling disqualified him in George's eyes.

On the score of merit as captains, George ranks Monty Noble first, Don Bradman second, and brackets Joe Darling, Herbie Collins, Johnny Douglas, Vic Richardson, and Richie Benaud in a photo finish for third. I would place Benaud first.

"I had many a long chat with Monty Noble. He loved to chat about cricket," George said. "It's the little things that count when you come to consider captaincy. As C. B. Fry said, 'Detail *is* important.' That's where Monty Noble was so great.

"Monty told me once of a day he was leading Paddington in a Grade game in Sydney. 'I was bowling to a Test batsman, Syd Gregory, and I had a particularly safe catcher in my Paddington side. I had a talk to him before one of my overs to Syd Gregory, before I positioned him at point. "You are only going to get one ball

195

to field all day," I told the chap. "When it comes, catch it." I fed Syd Gregory three half-volleys just outside his off stump, did so on purpose, and he hit them all for four.

"'Then I bowled him a ball a fraction shorter than the other three. Syd went for his fourth four in succession, but he didn't quite get to the ball. It flew from the outside edge of his bat straight to that fellow I'd put at point. Despite my warning, he wasn't ready for it. It hit him fair between the eyes and laid him cold. I was about the only one who didn't go to his help. Later in the day he came to me in the dressingroom, before we went out to bat. The chap had recovered from that blow from Gregory, but he had two beautiful black eyes. The best shiners, they were, I've ever seen. All I said to him was, "Next time do what you are told."'

"Monty Noble was a martinet," continued Hele, "he didn't seek popularity, only respect and complete obedience, from his men. That's one of the reasons I put him first among all the captains I've watched and known. He was as shrewd a tactician as ever took the field and he used unorthodox schemes to achieve dismissals. Nobody answered him back. He stood six feet four inches in his socks.

"He is the only man who packed the Adelaide Town Hall for a lecture on cricket. He commanded his audience that night as he used to command his teams. He won the loyalty of his men to a degree I've not seen equalled, except by Herbie Collins. Herbie had his players at his fingertips, literally on a string.

"It was Monty Noble who invented the inner and outer ring of fieldsmen and changed the whole character of cricket. I've always wondered just how fast Don Bradman would have scored against the old, nineteenth-century placings.

"Noble was never a boisterous or excitable character. He was quiet and reserved. He came on to the field as if he'd been fitted out in Savile Row and he expected all his players to pay attention to their clothing and appearance. If they didn't, they were sent from the field. Monty was a General Montgomery as a disciplinarian and he never had an iota of trouble on the score of insubordination. When he placed a fieldsman in a certain position, woe betide him if he wandered from the exact spot he'd been given. He demanded that every one of his players keep a constant eye upon him before each ball was bowled, so that they could be moved secretly when required. Nowadays, even in Test matches, this habit is honoured more in the breach than the observance. Ian Chappell, possibly because of what his grandfather, Vic Richardson, told him, is gradually putting it right.

"Noble had great sides to lead but it was he who lifted them from individual greatness into team greatness. He was far more than worth his own place as a player. He took 121 wickets at 25·01 and scored 1,997 runs at 30·25 in forty-two Test matches, when thirty was an exceptionally good Test batting average. He also held twenty-six catches and missed precious few. If he hadn't been a reliable fieldsman himself, he couldn't have reprimanded that character at point. Monty led his men from the front by his own superb, often superlative, example.

"Formidable though he was in appearance and character, he was a man you could talk to. He would listen to you, then point out the good points of your argument before getting to the weaker ones. If you have read his tribute to Victor Trumper [in *Captains Outrageous?*] you will appreciate the depth of his insight into ability and character.

"His knowledge of the technicalities of cricket was equally deep. Probably that is why he was the first bowler to perfect the late out-*swinger*, as distinct from the *swerving* ball. Charles Fry always considered Noble to be a more difficult bowler to face than the great Sydney Barnes.

"Noble led Australia in fifteen Tests, all against England. Australia won eight of those Tests, and lost five, at a time when England was particularly strong in talent—in the days when she had Ranjitsinhji, Stanley Jackson, J. T. Tyldesley, C. B. Fry, Gilbert Jessop, Archie MacLaren, and the young Jack Hobbs to bat for her and Barnes, Rhodes, Blythe, Braund, Hirst, and Bosanquet to bowl.

"He first played for Australia in 1897 and retired in 1909.

"His astuteness and meticulousness as a leader is well revealed by what happened in the game between New South Wales and South Australia at the S.C.G. in January 1900. Fred Hack, one of the South Australian opening batsmen, was injured and called for a runner. The South Australian captain and great left-handed Test batsman, Clem Hill, came out to perform this function. Hill had been dismissed a little earlier.

" 'What are you doing back here, Clem?' Noble demanded.

" 'I've come to run for Fred.'

" 'Listen, Clem. Go and get someone his own pace between wickets or he won't have a runner at all.'

197

"Hill left the ground and sent another batsman to run for Hack. Hack was slow between wickets, owing to his huge feet. The new runner was faster than Hill, about Bradman's pace. Noble sent him back to Hill in the pavilion while the crowd waited for play to resume. 'Tell him to send out someone who is Hack's own pace,' Noble told the second runner. Hill came back on to the field, crossed to Noble and said, 'I haven't got a runner who's as slow as Fred. Do you want me to put one in hobbles?'

" 'If you can't find the right kind of runner, I will,' said Noble. Eventually Hill found a batsman particularly slow between wickets and the game went on. Imagine this kind of thing happening today while TV and radio commentators guessed what was going on. But Noble was absolutely within his rights.

"If Noble's players indulged in the antics modern ones do when a wicket falls, he would have sent them all home to their girlfriends to do their hugging in private."

Hele places Don Bradman second to Noble as a captain. "Don," he said, "was perhaps the most astute cricketer I ever watched, or umpired for. I umpired his first Sheffield Shield and his first Test match. He was as shrewd as they come, even as a youngster. His anticipation was psychic. He seemed to know just what was about to happen by second nature and he was ready for it when it did. I have told how he answered Test veteran Sutcliffe when accused of aiming a ball at Herbert's head in his second Test match. 'If I was aiming at you, I would have hit you,' Don said. Well, in the Adelaide Test of 1931–32, Jock Cameron, the Springbok captain, snicked a ball from O'Reilly to Oldfield. On appeal I would have given Cameron out, but no appeal came. At the end of the over drinks were taken. Oldfield didn't have a drink. Instead he walked along to me and asked, 'George, did he hit that ball?' 'You can always appeal, Bert,' I replied.

"Bradman was fielding at deep mid-off for the ball in question. He came up to us and asked, 'Don't you fellers appeal when a man's out?' When Cameron returned to his crease Oldfield asked, 'Did you nick that one, Jock?' 'Yes,' said Cameron. At the end of the over Oldfield told O'Reilly that Cameron had touched the ball. 'Why in the hell didn't you appeal then?' demanded Tiger. 'That's the last batsman who'll ever get away with it while I'm bowling.' Not many did.

"Bradman was three years younger than O'Reilly and eleven years younger than Oldfield, but he'd made both of them look like boys.

"It was Don who planned Wally Hammond's dismissal at a crucial stage of the Adelaide Test of 1936–37. Not only the result of the Test but the fate of the series and destination of the Ashes hung on Hammond's innings. In the dressingroom, before the session in which Hammond was dismissed for 39, Bradman told Fleetwood Smith the kind of ball he wanted him to deliver to Wally. 'Chuck' produced it and down went Hammond's middle stump.

"Nobody I have known has devoted as much thought to cricket as Don did, and still does. He lives the game from dawn till dark and on into the night. He has at least as keen a brain as any cricketer who ever lived and was like lightning in detecting a weakness among his opponents, *and* an opportunity.

"I have placed Noble ahead of him as a captain simply because Monty was a great bowler and knew how to help his bowlers better than a specialist batsman could possibly do. Noble, by the way, never patted divots on the pitch. Asked why, he replied, 'I have to bowl as well as bat.' Noble led Australia against English teams that were stronger than the ones Bradman opposed in 1936–37 and 1948 and ones that were better led than England was by G. O. Allen in 1936–37, by Hammond in 1938 and 1946–47, and by Yardley in 1948. 'Plum' Warner, in 1903–04, and Archie MacLaren, in 1909, were finer captains than those three.

"Don gained the respect of his men, I feel, rather from his greatness as a cricketer than from his personality. He did not have Noble's commanding figure, nor did he attempt to discipline his teams to the same degree. He lived and captained in a different age, of course. Certainly Noble was the more successful tosser. He won eleven tosses in fifteen Tests to Don's six in twenty-four. Don had the advantage of his own ability as a batsman to swing the course of Test matches and it is probably due to this factor, more than any other, that he led Australia to eleven victories in 19 Tests as against Noble's 8 in 15."

As we have seen, Hele brackets together Joe Darling, Herbie Collins, Vic Richardson, Johnny Douglas, and Richie Benaud after Noble and Bradman. Collins, he contends, was the canniest captain of them all. "If he could not see an opening, he would create one,"

Hele says. "He had a sense of humour and an understanding of human nature, as distinct from character, well above that of Noble and Bradman. To all appearances he was a laconic character, himself, but his outward blandness concealed the kind of wisdom that has won for Sydneysiders their reputation as the outstanding confidence tricksters in the world. Arthur Mailey always insisted that Collins was the brains behind Warwick Armstrong's leadership and Armstrong *was* the most successful captain Australia ever had.

"In his first Test match at Sydney in 1920–21, Collins scored seventy run out and 104. Thus early did he demonstrate his temperament. In his first Test as Australia's captain Collins scored 114 and 60. His partner Bill Ponsford was playing in *his* first Test. He experienced great difficulty in playing Maurice Tate early in his first knock. Collins sized up the situation, spoke to Ponsford, and took the strike against Tate for the next six overs. Largely as a result, Ponsford scored a century.

"Every member of Collins' sides loved him. He had deep consideration for every member of his side and was a master diplomat. He demonstrated this to me when he said, 'George, you retired twenty-five years too soon.'

"When Australia had lost six for 119 in the opening innings of the Adelaide Test of 1924–25 Collins took advantage of an interval in play to have a long talk with Jack Ryder and Tommy Andrews, who were not out. Ryder and Andrews did just what he told them and added 134 for the seventh wicket. Ryder, batting completely against his natural bent, went on to 201 not out, by which time the last four Australian wickets had produced 360 runs. Ryder and Andrews were naturally attacking batsmen but they subdued themselves at the behest of a captain they respected.

"My mother, Elizabeth Hele, was at this match. When Australia were six for 119, she said to me, 'George, if they could only get 150.' When they were 150, she said, 'George, if only they could get 200.' When they were all out 489, she said, 'What a pity, George, they didn't get 500.'

"Collins faced one of his many dilemmas as a captain on the last morning of that Test. The gates were thrown open to the public because England, with two wickets standing, needed only 27 to win. The English captain Arthur Gilligan was one of the batsmen. Freeman was with him and Strudwick yet to bat. Collins had Jack Gregory,

Charles Kelleway, Arthur Mailey, Arthur Richardson, and Ryder as bowlers. All of them, except Mailey, could be relied upon for accuracy. Collins began with his trump card, Gregory, whose first ball went for four byes—23 needed. I thought Collins would play it safe by bowling Kelleway with Gregory. But he didn't, he brought Mailey on, with Vic Richardson close in at silly-point.

"Gilligan decided to get rid of Richardson but Vic took a magnificent catch by his chest from a full-blooded drive at mid-off, off Gregory. England only needed 17 now and again I thought Collins would play it safe. Instead he continued with Mailey, believing that extreme pace and sharp wrist spin were his best bets. He was always a gambler and finished life as a bookmaker. When England were 11 short of their goal, Freeman was caught by Oldfield off Mailey. Collins had given Gregory and Mailey his confidence and they justified it.

"Collins' knowledge of cricket and cricketers was revealed as early as 1919 when he took over the leadership of the First A.I.F. team from Kelleway in England. It was he who discovered Jack Gregory and Oldfield, picking them out of a ruck of some 100 rookie candidates.

"He was always a droll personality. When he had scored 99 against South Africa at Johannesburg in 1921–22, he asked the Springbok Jim Blanckenberg to bowl him a leg side full toss. Blanckenberg obliged and Collins hit it for four. When he had reached 199, Collins repeated the request. This time Blanckenberg just laughed in his face. When Springbok captain Zulch asked Collins, on the night of that Test, whether Ted McDonald was fast, Herbie replied, 'Quite quick—*after he's warmed up.*' Next morning Collins ordered McDonald to warm up behind the pavilion and then bowl full-out from the word 'go.' His second delivery broke Zulch's bat in two. One piece fell on his wicket. 'Yes, he is quite quick—*after he's warmed up,*' said the Springbok, as he walked out past the Australian captain.

"No other Australian quite typified the 'Australian Digger' to me as much as did Herbie Collins. Herbie, of course, *was* a 'Digger' in the true sense of the word. He was a corporal in the Sixth Australian Light Horse in Palestine and a member of the Fifth Division Artillery in France. He went through most of the stints in France, including the worst year on the Somme. His promotion to Warrant Officer failed to dampen his appetite for 'two-up.' The rank of Generalissimo would have failed in this respect."

Of Collins, Sir Pelham Warner said at Kennington Oval in 1926, "I do not believe cricket history records a better loser." He had more than his share of Test victories, too.

Joe Darling, like those other Australian captains, Clem Hill and Ian Chappell, attended Prince Alfred College, Adelaide. Darling twice retired from Test cricket and, after the second retirement, became a much respected Member of Parliament in Tasmania. As Vic Richardson was later to do, Darling captained Sturt and South Australia before gaining the national captaincy. It was he who led this nation to victory through the most excruciatingly close struggles England and Australia have ever fought—those of the 1902 series in England, when the issue was decided by 3 runs in Australia's favour at Old Trafford in the fourth Test and by one wicket at the Oval in England's in the fifth. Darling first led his country in the 1899 series in England. In that rubber Australia won the only decided Test. In his first Test as captain Darling had to counter the leadership of Dr William Gilbert Grace.

"When Joe Darling took his first team to England," says Hele, "he was warned to watch himself and his team's interests closely. Australians had got to know a bit about Dr Grace and his tricks, back in 1882. When Prince Ranjitsinhji came to Joe on the eve of a Test match and asked if he could borrow Australia's fast bowler, Ernie Jones, to attend one of his famous banquets, Darling smelt a rat. Why had 'Ranji' invited only Jones of all the Australian team? 'Jonah' enjoyed his drink.

"'Ranji' assured him that 'Jonah' would be well cared for, and would be fit for the morrow, fit enough even to bowl another bumper through W. G. Grace's beard. Jones had a barrel of a chest and hands strong from the blacksmith's trade at which he had originally worked.

"'The problem,' said 'Ranji,' 'is that I have a guest who makes a habit of gripping everyone by the hand when he's introduced, of holding on and forcing them to their knees. I fancy "Jonah" is just the fellow I need to put an end to his antics.'

"'Ranji' warned Jones of what was expected of him. When the guest was introduced, 'Jonah' stuck his giant chest out and his shoulders back and took a firm grip of the outstretched hand. Within minutes he had the character kneeling like a monk on the carpet. Next day at Lord's he caught and bowled his host for 8. He also dismissed C. B. Fry, Archie MacLaren, and the Hon. Stanley Jackson on his way to seven for 88 from 36·1 overs to prove to his captain he could handle the English cricketing Establishment.

"It was Ernie Jones, of course, when asked by King Edward VII whether he had attended Adelaide St Peter's School Collegiate, who replied, 'Yes, Sir. I drive the dirt cart there every Monday morning.'

"Joe Darling was bandy-legged, hairy-chested, and strong as an ox, himself," Hele said. "He was also the kindliest of men. He opposed the selection of the young Victor Trumper for that 1899 tour of England on the ground that he was 'brilliant but still too unreliable.' When Vic scored 300 not out in a day against Sussex, Monty Noble went to Darling and asked, 'What do you think of the youngster now?' 'Think of *him*,' replied Darling. 'I thought *I* could bat.'

"Joe Darling was a tremendous fighter as a captain when his team faced a crisis. He compiled his greatest innings at times like this. He topped the Australian batting averages in 1897–98 with 537 runs at 67·12, hitting 101 at Sydney, 178 at Adelaide, and 160 back at Sydney as an opening batsman. Vic Richardson always claimed Joe Darling taught him most of what he knew.

"Probably the finest tribute paid to Darling as a leader was his reinstatement as Australia's captain for the 1905 tour of England following his retirement from cricket at the end of 1902. Noble led Australia exceedingly well at home against Warner in the 1903–04 series, scored 417 runs at 59·57, and took sixteen wickets at 20·50."

England's captain on the 1911–12 and 1920–21 tours of Australia, Johnny Douglas, and Victor Richardson had much in common, according to George Hele. Both of them were first-class boxers. Douglas defeated Australia's Reginald "Snowy" Baker in the middleweight division final of the 1908 London Olympics. Richardson boxed professionals in "Red" Mitchell's gymnasium in Adelaide. Douglas was drowned after a ship collision in the North Sea when he was 48. Up on the main deck, as the lifeboats were being lowered, he could not find his father. All passengers had been ordered on deck, but Douglas went below in search of his father and was not seen again.

Douglas and Richardson were at their best against fast rising bowling, standing right over the line of the ball. Neither of them knew the meaning of the word "retreat." Both of them were outstandingly brave men, physically and mentally, in a generation that placed great emphasis on physical and moral courage.

When South Australia had to begin an innings in a bad light near the end of the day you could bank on it that Richardson would take strike. On just such an evening at Lord's Douglas was taking most of Maurice Tate and Bill Howell's bowling on the splice of the bat and his gloves. His partner, Number 11, appealed successfully against the light. Douglas came down the pitch and cursed the appealer. "Just fancy," he muttered, "a bloody Number 11 appealing against the light!"

Johnny Douglas' philosophy, according to Raymond Robertson-Glasgow, was simply "fight on." Richardson's was the same. They set this example to the men they led.

"At his best," says Hele, "Victor Richardson, like Keith Miller whom he so much resembled in so many ways, was at least the equal of any other cricket captain. But Vic led South Australia, usually against tremendous odds, for fifteen years before he was chosen to captain Australia on the 1935–36 tour of South Africa. Even then, at the age of forty-one, he showed just what he might have done had he been taken to England in 1926 and had he been named captain of his country when Herbie Collins retired.

"Vic was a man amongst men and those who played under him recognised this. When he was angry he went white with rage, but I never saw him do an unsporting thing. No Australian cricketer or sportsman, in my opinion, has been more deeply admired or loved than was Vic during the evening of his life. I've not known a more unselfish cricketer or a more compassionate man.

"Vic knew his cricket laws as word perfect as did Bradman and, like Don, he always treated umpires with respect. He studied the characteristics and qualities of the men he captained and knew how to bring the best out of them when it was required. Clarrie Grimmett and Bill O'Reilly will vouch for this. It's partly why they took forty-four wickets at 14·59 and twenty-seven at 17·03, respectively, on that tour of South Africa in 1935–36.

"Vic was as great an Australian Rules Football leader as he was a cricket captain. In the 1924 S.A.N.F.L. premiership final he was captain of Sturt. He was a centreman and had been playing in that position until three-quarter time. At this stage Sturt were trailing my club, West Torrens, by six goals. In the last quarter Vic went on the ball and such was the inspiration he gave his team that they kicked five goals without reply until Vic blew out and we went on to win."

Hele regards Richie Benaud as the finest of those he classes as "modern" cricketing captains, but his admiration for Ian Chappell is mounting year by year.

"I would class Richie as the most impressive leader Australia has had since Don Bradman retired," he says. "Like Noble, Richie was an all-rounder and knew the inner secrets of every department of the game. His finest moments as a captain came probably on the last day of that fourth Test at Old Trafford in 1961 and at Brisbane during the Meckiff incident in the Test against South Africa in 1963.

"On that last afternoon at Old Trafford, England needed 256 at 67 runs an hour to win. A magnificent 76 in eighty-four minutes by Ted Dexter brought the game to a gripping climax. Though he was suffering pain from a fibrositic shoulder, Benaud went round the wicket to aim at a patch just outside the leg stump to both left and right-handers after he had dismissed Dexter. He bowled Peter May for 0, and then Subba Row. Three more quick wickets to the Australian captain had England seven for 171 after being one for 150. From thirty-two overs Richie took six for 70.

"Benaud, though he was captain, did not know why Australia's selectors chose the 'suspect' Ian Meckiff for the first Test against South Africa at Brisbane in 1963. Nor did he enquire until after the South African innings. It was on the second afternoon that the 'Meckiff Execution,' as Vic Richardson called it, began. Benaud gave the ball to Meckiff after Graham McKenzie had bowled the first over of the Springbok innings. During Meckiff's first and only over Colin Egar no-balled him four times from square-leg for throwing. At the end of the over Egar told the Springbok captain and opening batsman Trevor Goddard that, if he or Eddie Barlow had been dismissed by any of Meckiff's twelve deliveries, he would have called 'no-ball' after the event.

"The crowd of more than 10,000 yelled for Egar's blood, and for the blood of Sir Donald Bradman, the Chairman of Selectors. When Richie replaced Meckiff after that single over they called for *his* blood as well. They wanted him to bowl Meckiff from McKenzie's end so Umpire Lou Rowan would also have to decide whether his action was legitimate or not. Though Goddard scored 52 and Barlow 114, Benaud refused. He was determined to get on with the game.

"'We want Meckiff. We want Meckiff,' came the continuous cry. When Benaud was bowling the crowd jeered at him so angrily that Barlow had to stand away from his wicket. Meckiff, on his own admission, had become a man in a trance—psychologically unfit to bowl, as his captain knew. During the worst of the demonstration Benaud dismissed Goddard, Peter Carlstein, and Dennis Lindsay for fifteen runs, went on to get Barlow and Peter Pollock, and to finish with five for 68 from thirty-three overs in South Africa's 346. If he had bowled Meckiff again, and Rowan had passed his action, anything could have occurred.

"After the innings he went to Bradman to ask why Meckiff had been chosen and was given, as was Meckiff, a satisfactory answer. One of the great things about Richie was, and still is, his willingness to learn. In this respect he supplies a distinct and sensible contrast to the majority of the players since the second World War, so many of whom seem to find it so difficult to talk, let alone to listen, to the champions of former days.

"Perhaps that is why he (with Frank Tyson and Colin McDonald) is one of the few Australian TV commentators that I, as an Australian, can feel proud of in the company of John Arlott, Trevor Bailey, and Brian Johnston. Like Bradman and Vic Richardson, he was also exemplary in his reaction to umpiring decisions. When Greg Chappell was given out l.b.w. in the Oval Test of 1972 Trevor Bailey said, 'Richie I haven't heard your opinion of that l.b.w. decision;' and Richie replied, 'I haven't given an opinion, and I won't.'

"What a pleasant contrast to so many modern cricket commentators and writers, who seem to be umpiring the umpire rather than reporting the match."

"The Don" Was the Greatest

WHILE DON BRADMAN WAS ON HIS WAY TO YET ANOTHER CENTURY in first-class cricket, his 103rd of an eventual 117 from 338 innings in which he averaged 95·14 for 28,067 runs, an Indian fieldsman threw a ball from near the boundary of Adelaide Oval, on the full towards Peter Sen, the tiny wicketkeeper.

Sen was yards from the flight of the throw. It would have gone for overthrows had not Don caught it *on the blade of his bat* as Rod Laver and John Newcombe catch tennis balls thrown to them by ball boys on their racquets.

Don was on his way to 201 at the time. He not only "caught" the ball on his bat, he then juggled it on the bat until he had it under control then batted it on the full to the bowler.

When this incredible piece of conjury was reported on the radio and in the Press nobody would believe it had occurred. "Don't give me that rubbish," one listener rang in to say. Learning of this, Don repeated the feat later in his innings.

Such was his control of the ball. Don was to batting almost what Walter Lindrum was to billiards. Applying the precision Lindrum employed, he used to score threes from the last balls of overs, not singles, to retain the strike.

"I have watched all the great batsmen of the twentieth century,"

207

says George Hele. "I watched Victor Trumper's perhaps most brilliant and beautiful innings, his 214 not out against South Africa in Adelaide in 1910–11. I saw Jack Hobbs bat in Australia in 1907–08, 1911–12, 1920–21, and 1924–25, I umpired for him throughout the 1928–29 series, and I fully appreciate his mastery of the art of batsmanship. I umpired for Walter Hammond during his greatest Test season, when he scored 905 runs at 113·12 against Australia in 1928–29. I saw Stan McCabe at his greatest against Bodyline at Sydney in 1932–33 and I have watched Clem Hill, Len Hutton, Denis Compton, Neil Harvey, George Headley, Herbie Taylor, and the 'Governor-General,' Charlie Macartney. In more recent years I have seen Gary Sobers and Barry Richards, Frank Worrell, and Everton Weekes.

"Trumper, Worrell, and McCabe, not forgetting Alan Kippax, Paul Sheahan, Greg Chappell, Ian Redpath, and Archie Jackson, were more graceful and beautiful batsmen than Bradman; Hobbs was more copybook. But, in my opinion, and into it enters not a shadow of a doubt, Sir Donald Bradman was the greatest of all the batsmen I have watched—the most valuable and devastating batsman any Test team of any country ever owned.

"Vic Richardson has said, 'As captain of a team opposing Don I would willingly offer him 100 every time he batted, if he would give his wicket away for that score.' No other batsman that I know of has ever been paid so telling a tribute by a cricket captain.

"Just look at the record books," George said. And we did. They revealed many facts, including the following:

1. Bradman's Test average for eighty innings was 99·94 for 6,996 runs over a career which lasted from 1928 to 1948. He averaged about 40 runs an innings more than Graeme Pollock 60·97, George Headley 60·83, Herbert Sutcliffe 60·73, Gary Sobers 59·94, Walter Hammond 58·45, Jack Hobbs 56·94, Len Hutton 56·67, and Dudley Nourse 53·81. He averaged nearly 50 more an innings than Denis Compton 50·06 and his closest Australian rival, Neil Harvey, 48·41.

   His margin over them constitutes a Test match average which such great players as Peter May, Maurice Leyland, Charles Macartney, Stan McCabe, and Bill Ponsford were, or are, proud to own.

2. Bradman scored the three fastest double centuries in the history

of Anglo-Australian Tests, the Tests which provide the criteria of greatness. These are his 200 in 214 minutes on the way to 334 at Headingley in 1930, as well as his 200 in 234 minutes on the way to 254 at Lord's in 1930, and his 200 in 283 minutes on his way to 244 at the Oval in 1934.

3. His 300 in 336 minutes at Headingley in 1930, at 53·7 runs an hour, is the fastest triple century in Anglo-Australian cricket, indeed in any Test cricket. The one Englishman who scored 300 against Australia, Len Hutton, took 662 minutes, nearly double Don's time, to get there.

4. Only Gilbert Jessop seventy-five minutes, Joe Darling ninety-one minutes, Victor Trumper ninety-four minutes, and J. T. Brown ninety-five minutes have scored faster single centuries in Anglo-Australian matches than Bradman's 100 in ninety-nine minutes at Headingley. Bradman and Trumper are the only batsmen who have reached 100 in under two hours twice in Anglo-Australian Tests. Bradman did so in successive innings.

5. Bradman holds the three top places for the most boundaries hit in one day of an Anglo-Australian Test match—42 fours at Headingley in 1930, 39 fours and 2 sixes at Headingley in 1934, and 32 fours and 1 six at the Oval in 1934.

6. Bradman also holds the three top places for the most runs in an Anglo-Australian Test day—309 at Headingley in 1930, 271 at Headingley in 1934, and 244 at the Oval in 1934.

7. Bradman averaged 90 or more in four successive Anglo-Australian Test series—a performance not approached by any other player. On five occasions he scored a century in one session of these Tests.

"How can you go past all that?" asked Hele. There is, of course, only one answer to his question. You can't. Who but the prejudiced would want to?

The 1930 Test matches in England were limited to four days of play. In those Tests, on his first tour of England, on wickets utterly unfamiliar to him, Bradman scored 974 runs at 139·14.

"Records, they say, are made to be broken," continued Hele. "But I don't believe Don's overall record will *ever* be broken." England captain G. O. Allen always claimed bowlers win Test matches, but he made one exception and that exception was Don Bradman."

When Bradman retired in England in 1948, needing four runs to average 100 in all his fifty-two Test matches, Sir Neville Cardus' only rival as a cricket writer, R. C. Robertson-Glasgow, wrote: "So must Rome have felt on hearing of the death of Hannibal."

"What about the other batsmen, George?" I asked.

"The most technically correct of all the batsmen I watched was Jack Hobbs. His footwork was like that of the finest boxers. That is why he was able to give the finest exhibition of batting I have ever seen on a sticky wicket, his 49 at Melbourne in 1928–29. Robertson-Glasgow wrote of Hobbs: 'He was perfectly equipped by art and temperament for any style of innings, on any sort of wicket against any quality of opposition.'

"Victor Trumper played the most beautiful and exciting innings I have watched, namely his 214 not out against South Africa at Adelaide in 1910–11. He, Alan Kippax, Stan McCabe, Archie Jackson, and 'Ranji' were the most aesthetically pleasing batsmen I've seen, but Bradman was the greatest. If you watched Don's bat, not his body, he was just as attractive as the others."

Bradman, in my own opinion, always did *all* the work when executing his strokes, other batsmen allowed the ball to do some of the work for them. Perhaps that is why they were more elegant, certainly why they were more effortless. It is also, I submit, why Bradman was more consistent.

For greatness, irrespective of charm, George ranks Walter Hammond, charming enough, George Headley, Bill Ponsford, Charles Macartney, Herbert Sutcliffe, and Clem Hill after Bradman and Hobbs.

"Hammond's greatness was limited, by ability or design, to the arc from mid-on to third man. Sutcliffe was the most imperturbable batsman I've known and he played later at the ball than anyone, so late at times that even an umpire thought the ball had beaten him. Herbert held the face of his bat towards cover-point. There were times when he gave slips fieldsmen nightmares. He would withdraw his bat from the ball more often than any other player.

"His imperturbability was never more clearly illustrated than when he played that ball from O'Reilly on to his stumps in the Sydney Test of 1932–33 without dislodging a bail. In the photograph of the incident McCabe, Richardson, and Oldfield are standing aghast. Sutcliffe remained utterly unruffled. All he said was, 'What about proceeding with the game?' Sutcliffe is the one English batsman whom I believe might have succeeded against Larwood's Bodyline. He had the temperament to remain cool and collected against it, to decide calmly which ball to ignore. He was also a magnificent hooker. Herbert is the one player who might have taken Clarrie Grimmett's advice and, by ignoring it, reduced Bodyline to a farce.

"I have a tremendous admiration for Bill Ponsford, both for his technique and his courage. When the English Pressmen came to the M.C.G. nets in 1954–55, a fifty-four-year-old was having a knock, just for the fun of it. 'That fellow can bat,' one of the cricket writers said. 'Take a good look at him,' I replied, 'can't you recognise him?' 'No.' 'That's Bill Ponsford,' I said. 'Hm. No wonder,' he answered."

"And who was the greatest left-hander, George?" I asked.

"Clem Hill," he replied without hesitation. "And that's no reflection on Neil Harvey, Gary Sobers, Arthur Morris, Maurice Leyland, or Graeme Pollock. Clem confirmed his greatness when he returned to first-class cricket at the age of forty-five. He'd played in only one first-class match, one in 1919, since he scored 105 and 60 against Victoria in 1914, yet he made 66 and 39 in that George Giffen testimonial of February 1923 against Victoria.

"He proved that day that the batsmen of the Golden Age could hold up their heads in any company—except Don Bradman's."

It's Harder With Bowlers

ONE OF THE FIRST QUESTIONS THAT NORMAN BANKS, GERALD LYONS, John Laws, Lou Richards, and, yes, Gwen Plumb, fire at you on their Melbourne and Sydney radio and television programmes is, "Who is the greatest bowler you've seen or batted against?" Another is, "Who was the fastest?"

With thousands, many of them, you are told, mothers of school-boys hanging on your opinion and preparing to quote it as gospel to their young, you *do* feel a strong sense of responsibility in offering your views.

But, even when given time to reflect at length, and in depth, about the respective merit and value of Harold Larwood and Bill O'Reilly, of that "Typhoon" Frank Tyson and that gentle and deceptive zephyr Arthur Mailey, of that whirlwind Wesley Hall and the utterly undainty "Dainty" Ironmonger, how can one decide with conviction?

Even when the great bowlers of cricket history are compared in their respective categories there are so many pros and cons to weigh.

George Hele is just as adamant that Harold Larwood was the greatest fast bowler cricket has ever known, and Bill O'Reilly the greatest wrist-spinner, as he is that Bradman was the greatest batsman. And I agree with these opinions, having batted against both Larwood

212

and O'Reilly, and many of their great contemporaries and immediate successors.

But George believes that Ernie McCormick, for two overs, was even faster than Larwood and with this, even though Ernie has been gracious enough to contribute the foreword to this book, I cannot concur. Fortunately, I faced Larwood for only one, for me, memorable over at the Adelaide Oval in 1932. I batted against McCormick many times and on several occasions against Ray Lindwall, Keith Miller, the Aboriginal Eddie Gilbert, Ken Farnes, Bill Voce, and "Gubby" Allen.

I managed to play forward at times to Lindwall, Miller, Farnes, Voce, and Allen, even to drive them past cover. Against those balls from Larwood I stood like a petrified sapling. Those six almost explosive deliveries of his either flew past my bat before I had assessed their speed and direction or sent a shivery shock up the bat handle before I had time to tighten my grip to withstand their unnerving force.

Ernie McCormick *was* fast, faster than Lindwall or Miller. He was also the funniest fast bowler I've ever known, cricket's incomparable and incurable comedian, but in my experience he wasn't quite as fast as Larwood.

That so short a man as Larwood, a man of only five feet eight inches, could bowl at such a terrific and bewildering pace has been a source of wonderment to both George and me for more than forty years. The speed, we think, came from his powerful chest, those long, strong arms, and the most perfect and economical action any bowler has owned. The rhythm of his run-up, delivery stride, and follow-through was beautiful to watch, except from twenty-two yards along the line of his aim and ambition. And, for a bowler of his extreme speed, his accuracy was phenomenal. It came from his uplifted long left arm, which guided the ball on its journey, and from the fierce intensity and concentration with which he aimed each ball.

Larwood's run to the wicket was made over twenty-six yards; he delivered from his fourteenth step and followed through for another five. To deliver his 210 overs in the Tests of 1932–33 he calculated that he ran and walked 35·79 miles. In terms of concentration of strength and effort he wasted not one yard of them. Every ball he bowled was geometrically directed.

"Larwood," says George, "was one of the most dedicated cricketers

213

I have known. His only fault, if it can be called a fault, was complete obedience to his captain. My admiration for him as a bowler is equalled by my respect for him as a man. His demeanour on a cricket field was consistently impeccable. He never caused me, as an umpire, one iota of trouble.

"I have never believed that either he or Voce had any intent or desire to injure batsmen during the Bodyline series, but merely to drive them into a state of mind that prevented them from playing their natural game with confidence and from exercising their normal judgement. In this Larwood succeeded, even in the case of Bradman. He ruined Bill Ponsford's magnificent technique and twice bowled the 'unbowlable' Bill Woodfull.

"I spent several hours with Larwood during the fourth Test of the 1970–71 Anglo-Australian series. That fine English actor, Trevor Howard, was with us. He seemed surprised to learn we were such good friends and said so. 'My friendship for Harold has never altered,' I replied, 'and it's weathered some torrid times.' 'I would have loved to have been in your position out there umpiring for him in the middle in 1932–33, in the box seat at so much drama,' Howard said. 'For your fee or mine?' I asked."

Next to Larwood in greatness as a fast bowler, George Hele ranks Ted McDonald, whom Victor Richardson, that superb opponent of pace during the 1920s and 1930s, placed first.

"I fancy you will think I had stars in my young eyes," he said, "when I name Ernie Jones and 'Tibby' Cotter, drooping shoulder and all, after Larwood and McDonald. But no modern fast bowler could sustain the speed and hostility they did so long into a day. Both had tremendous strength of chest and shoulder, and arms like the limbs of trees. Only then do I come to Jack Gregory, Lindwall and Miller, Tyson, and Wesley Hall, though Miller's fastest ball was up with Larwood's and McCormick's."

"And what about Dennis Lillee?" I asked.

"The wickets on which he has had to bowl are not as fast as were those from 1900 to the early 1960s. Lillee improved his pace and control tremendously in England in 1972.

"Recovery from injury and continuation of this improvement, and the use of more solid boots, could cause him to take a place in cricket history as one of the few greatest of his class. Much depends on his captain, Ian Chappell, for whom Dennis would bowl his heart out, as Larwood did for Douglas Jardine—even when the skin had gone from his toes. Lillee was certainly faster by yards than any other bowler of his time. He would have been appreciably faster on that old black Bulli soil. Intikhab Alam, don't forget, contends that Wesley Hall was significantly faster than Lillee, and Hall, in my opinion, never approached Larwood's pace.

"Larwood had the hate of a hungry coalminer in his make-up. Of the bowlers I have named, only Ernie Jones, who began life as a blacksmith, shared this state of mind and, because he shared it, mustered that extra yard or two of speed that made batsmen fear him so."

Among the great fast-medium bowlers, Hele places Maurice Tate above Sydney Barnes, whom Englishmen regard as the game's greatest bowler of all time. He does so because Tate had the tenacity which the temperamental Staffordshire and Lancashire champion lacked.

Next to Tate and Barnes he ranks J. N. Crawford, Charles Kelleway, Tim Wall, Alec Bedser, Johnny Douglas, and John Snow, in that order. Tim Wall would have been higher on his list had he not been so friendly a cricketer, if he had developed the approach to bowling and batsmen that was so great a help to Snow.

"Tim, like Ernie McCormick, had an irrepressible sense of humour, which is incongruous in, and unhelpful to, a fast bowler. After Clarrie Grimmett took ten for 37 against Yorkshire in 1930 he grinned at Wall and said, 'When you get figures like these, Tim, you can call yourself a champion.' Two years later at the S.C.G., Wall took ten for 36 against New South Wales, including the wicket of Bradman. Clarrie failed to take a wicket that day and when he congratulated Wall, Tim just smiled and said, 'You gave me the idea, "Grum," remember, at Sheffield.' Then he added, 'I've bowled better than I did today many times and taken none for 100.'"

The South African, Neville Quinn, who kept having Don Bradman missed in slips and bowling Bill Ponsford behind his legs in 1931–32, was the finest left-handed fast-medium swing bowler Hele remembers. Next to Quinn he ranks Bill Johnston, Bill Whitty, and Alan Davidson. Bill Whitty's bowling action, he says, was the finest of any bowler of any type whom he has watched. It was Bill Whitty who got his own back on George's profession after he had been refused an appeal for a catch at the wicket. Whitty delivered a ball well wide

215

of the off stump soon afterward. Though the batsman did not even offer a stroke at the ball, Whitty appealed again. When the umpire rebuked him for so doing, he replied, "Just thought you could make two mistakes, Ump, in one day."

Hele places Bill O'Reilly in the category of medium-pace bowlers, though he was a wrist-spinner, not a front-of-the-hand spinner or cutter of the ball. If George was asked to name *the* greatest bowler he has umpired for, or watched from beyond the boundary, "The Tiger" would be the one. "O'Reilly had all the cunning of Clarrie Grimmett, and equal, if not greater, endurance and courage. In addition he had a competitiveness I've not seen equalled by any bowler."

Keith Stackpole, who called Bill a "straight-breaker," please note.

"As I have said earlier," George continued, "I formed my opinion of Bill during that Melbourne Test of 1932–33 when he took ten for 129, collecting the wickets of Sutcliffe, Hammond, Leyland, Wyatt, Pataudi, and Ames along the way, and I've never had reason to change it. O'Reilly provided a rather lonely counter to Larwood, Voce, Bowes, and their Bodyline over those four days and with Fingleton and Bradman's help, gave Australia her only victory over a team led by Douglas Jardine. Never have I seen a great bowler fight quite so hard as he did while delivering 58·5 overs for 129 runs against some of the greatest batsmen England ever owned.

"Monty Noble, because of his late swing from the leg, extreme accuracy, and late-kicking off-break, and Hughie Trumble, who used his tremendous height and had the largest hands and the longest fingers any bowler was blessed with, came next among the mediums but neither of them had a leg-break, let alone a wrong–un."

Among the wrist-spinners who bowled at classic slow pace, Hele places Dr Herbert "Ranji" Hordern measurably first, followed by Grimmett, Mailey, and Richie Benaud. Hordern was a dentist by profession and the first of Australia's five great googly bowlers. He was a man of his own mind and would not accept hot returns from the field, even during crucial times in Test matches, if he felt he might harm his hands.

"Though Hordern played in only eighteen first-class games, including seven Tests, he took 122 wickets, almost seven a match," George stressed. "In his seven Tests, two against South Africa and five against the powerful 1911–12 England side, which won the series 4–1, he

216

captured forty-six wickets at 23·36, five times taking five or more wickets in an innings.

"He was far superior to any member of that Springbok googly squad of Reggie Schwarz, Bert Vogler, Aubrey Faulkner, and Gordon White, in 1910–11. He out-bowled them on his own. Bosanquet, who invented the googly ten years previously with the help of Schwarz in England, was not in Hordern's class. Hordern had to bowl against Hobbs in his brilliant pre-war prime, and against Wilfred Rhodes, Frank Woolley (whom Mailey could rarely handle), George Gunn, Phil Mead (another great left-hander), Jack Hearne, and Johnny Douglas in that 1911–12 series. Yet he equalled Monty Noble's achievement of thirty-two wickets in a series against England, and took only two less wickets than George Giffen did in 1894–95. For Australia only Arthur Mailey, thirty-six in 1920–21 against a war-weakened England, and Grimmett, forty-four at 14·59 against South Africa, have surpassed these three bowlers since. For England Jim Laker took forty-six for 442 at 9·6 against Australia in 1956, thanks to that 'Dust Heap.'

"Though the googly was a novelty in 1910 and 1911, Hordern had sufficient control of it to open the bowling for Australia with Cotter."

George finds it very difficult to choose between Arthur Mailey and Clarrie Grimmett. Arthur, as Sir Neville Cardus wrote, "bowled like a millionaire" and Clarrie "like a miser."

"Mailey had by far the sharper leg-break and his wrong-un was the more difficult to detect. Mailey bowled to a short- and Grimmett to a long-range plan. Mailey derived more fun from cricket; Grimmett more satisfaction. During his playing career Mailey was the kindlier character, though I've met few kindlier *old* men than Clarrie. When I was umpiring in a Sheffield Shield game in the early 1920s Arthur was bowling from the other end. The umpire was a newcomer to big cricket and Mailey asked me his name. I told him. 'Is he an experienced umpire?' Arthur asked. 'No, this is only his first or second Shield match.' 'I won't appeal then, not unless I'm certain the batsman's out.'

"On another occasion, in 1925, Arthur appealed for l.b.w. and I refused to give the batsman out. It was the last ball of the over. As he walked past me Arthur muttered, 'Bloody cheat.' 'Who's a cheat?' I demanded—very hot under the collar. 'I am,' grinned Mailey, 'for appealing.' With Arthur you never knew what to expect. He was brought up in extreme poverty in Zetland, Sydney. His family was so poor, he once told me, that he, his three brothers, his sister, and mother took it in daily turns to breakfast on the tops of his father's hard-boiled eggs.

"Grimmett was the more difficult of the two on English wickets, Arthur on Australian—mainly because of his sharper spin and higher trajectory. So thorough was Grimmett about his bowling that he delivered only one no-ball in his entire career. Not bad for a bowler who delivered 14,573 balls in Test cricket and 28,064 in Sheffield Shield. In Test matches Grimmett took 216 wickets at 24·21 to Mailey's ninety-nine at 33·91. In Shield cricket Clarrie took 513 wickets at 25·29 to Arthur's 180 at 32·59 so I guess I should place him first.

"Benaud was a mixture of Mailey and Grimmett. He took 248 wickets at 27·03 in Test matches and 266 at 27·11 in Shield, but the batsmen of his era rarely used their feet to spin bowling as they did in the 1920s and 1930s. They didn't go way out along the wicket in the way that Bradman, Macartney, Tommy Andrews, and Bill Ponsford did.

"Doug Wright was by far the best of the British wrist-spinners I have watched, but I gave up trying to tell the Englishmen this. They all seemed to think I was kidding."

We are left with what are called the orthodox, or front-of-the-hand, spinners. Of the right-handers Hele, rather surprisingly, places Springbok Hugh Tayfield first, above even the slow-medium Hughie Trumble, who took 141 wickets, all against England, at 21·78 in thirty-two Tests, and Jim Laker, who took nineteen for 90 against Australia in one at Old Trafford.

"Tayfield was as clever as they come," said George, "and had pinpoint control of the ball. Just imagine how he would have fared under the present l.b.w. law. As it is, he took 170 wickets at 25·91 in thirty-seven Tests, mostly for the losing side.

"Choosing the finest orthodox left-handed spin bowler occasions me no doubt whatsoever, though I've watched Rhodes, Alf Valentine, Hedley Verity, and 'Farmer' White. Had Bert Ironmonger been taken on a tour of England he would have been recognised everywhere as the greatest bowler of his type ever. Woodfull and Vic Richardson cabled the Australian Board while on their way to England in 1930, seeking his inclusion, but I believe this was because

218

'Patsy' Hendren had circulated the story on his return home in 1929 that Ironmonger threw the ball. Hendren explained later, 'Had "Dainty" been chosen, England would have lost all five Tests and I couldn't have that happening, could I?' He'd have been useful on that Headingley fungus fusorium in 1971, by the way. He'd have made Derek Underwood look third-class. Underwood, when I watched him in Australia, lacked appreciation of the value of variation of pace and flight, the two most important tricks in his type of trade. Laker made the same mistake out here."

So there you have it: Larwood, Tate, Quinn, O'Reilly, Hordern, Tayfield, and Ironmonger—the nucleus of a reasonable attack. With these bowlers, and Don Tallon behind wicket, three batsmen—say Jack Hobbs, George Headley, and Don Bradman—would probably suffice.

Cricket Quiz

GEORGE HELE, HAVING APPEARED WITH CLEM HILL, VIC RICHARDSON, Ian Johnson, Norman Banks, Peter McAllister, Jack O'Hagen, and others, on many radio programmes during Test matches, is no stranger to cricketing quiz sessions. His memory for cricket incident and anecdote is more amazing even than was Vic Richardson's. There were a number of questions I still wanted to ask him and he agreed to my playing the role of a quizmaster.

Question—"What team of twelve would you choose from the world to play Mars, assuming those unpiloted space ships are wrong and they *do* have people up there?"

Answer—"Hobbs, Trumper, Bradman, Hammond, Sobers, Clem Hill, Macartney, Oldfield, Larwood, Hordern, O'Reilly, and McDonald. What would yours be?"

"Hobbs, Grace, Hammond, Bradman, Trumper, Sobers, Hill, Miller, Tallon, O'Reilly, Barnes, and Larwood," I told him.

Question—"Who are the greatest all-rounders you have watched, naming them in order of preference?"

Answer—"Sobers, Hammond, J. N. Crawford, Miller, Rhodes, Constantine, Noble, Giffen, Jack Gregory, Armstrong, Macartney, and Worrell. I never saw Sir Stanley Jackson, but he topped the

220

England batting and bowling in 1905, captained her in all five Tests, and won all five tosses. That makes him quite an all-rounder."

Question—"Who are the greatest wicketkeepers you have watched and in what order?"

Answer—"Oldfield, Strudwick, Tallon, and Evans. But the three Springboks, Percy Sherwell, Jock Cameron, and Johnny Waite ran them close. Waite was the best wicketkeeper-batsman. He scored 2,335 runs at 30·32 in Tests with four centuries and dismissed 136 batsmen. Sherwell 36, Cameron 51, and Waite 136 dismissed 223 Test batsmen between them."

Question—"Which was the finest team Australia ever sent to England?"

Answer—"Neil Harvey, who should know something about selecting teams, said on the radio during the Trent Bridge Test in 1972, 'I think the 1948 side was superior to Armstrong's 1921 team.' Well, Armstrong said the 1902 team, in which he played for the first time in England, 'would have beaten the 1921 side by an innings.' Bradman's 1948 side played five five-day Tests and won four of them. The 1902 Darling side won two Tests to take the rubber, in three days, and the 1921 side won the first three Tests all inside three days. The 1921 side relaxed after that. When Armstrong was asked why he was reading a newspaper along the boundary, he replied, 'I just wanted to make certain who we were playing.'

"How many Tests would Bradman's side have won inside three days? I believe the 1921 side was stronger than the 1948 side and, if Armstrong wasn't starry-eyed about his first tour, that makes the 1902 side the best. Don't you agree?"

"I was minus 8 in 1902," I replied. "Even so, I can't see the 1902 side beating Bradman's 1948 side by an innings inside three days. To do so Trumble, Saunders, Noble, and Armstrong would have had to dismiss Sid Barnes, Arthur Morris, Don Bradman, Lindsay Hassett, Keith Miller, Bill Brown, Ian Johnson, Don Tallon, and Ray Lindwall (who scored a Test century), twice in about a day and a half."

Question—"What are the funniest cricket stories you know?"

Answer—"The time Jack Fingleton was short of beds in Canberra and had to put Ernie McCormick under his grand-piano on a mattress for the night. 'Fingo' brought Ernie a cup of tea in the morning and asked him how he'd slept. 'Fine,' replied Ernie, 'I'll never sleep under an upright model again.'"

"That's a cricketers', not a cricket story," I interjected.

"Well, the time South Australia played a country bowler, who'd won the South Australian Country Bowling Competition the previous week. His name was Carragher and he didn't turn up on the second day, much to Bill Ponsford's annoyance. 'Ponnie' had hit him all over the field on the first day and was still batting.

"After play had resumed for about an hour, 'Ponnie' crossed to Clem Hill, who was captaining South Australia. 'There's that bowler of yours, Clem, up on the middle of the mound,' he said. 'You'd better send for him.' Clem did. When Carragher came on to the field, Clem asked him where in the hell he'd been. 'Sorry, Mr Hill. I've never played in a two-day match before.' 'This one's four days,' said Hill, 'get down on the fence by the scoreboard.' 'The scoreboard, Mr Hill?' 'Yes, that structure halfway up the mound. You'll see your bowling figures on it—two for 102.'"

Question—"Who are the greatest fieldsmen you've seen?"

Answer—"Bradman was the finest outfieldsman. I put him first because of his throw. It was so fast you could *hear* it coming. It was also the most consistently straight. Don used to hit the stumps from the boundary more often than any other player I've known. Vic Richardson was the safest catch. He only missed three during a first-class career of sixteen years. Constantine was the most electrifying and dynamic fieldsman. Next to him I'd rank Jack Gregory, Neil Harvey, the Springbok Colin Bland, and Paul Sheahan. Sheahan covers more ground at cover than anyone I've known. Hammond was magnificently safe at slip, but he rarely fielded anywhere else. Percy Chapman was the most phenomenal gully catcher."

Question—"Who was the most immaculately attired and best-behaved player?"

Answer—"You're making it hard aren't you? If I *have* to answer, I'd say Alan Kippax. He was the 'Jack Crawford' of cricket; flannels perfectly pressed, sleeves buttoned to the wrist, cap peak always straight. As a man, he never had an enemy on earth. Twice in my experience he walked out when I would not have given him out. I've told of his behaviour during that famous incident in the Sydney Test of 1928. The character who wrote the lines:

'When the great scorer comes to write against your name,
He writes not of how you won or lost,
But how you played the game '

222

must have had 'Kippie,' or 'Kelly,' as his great friend, Vic Richardson, called him, in mind.

"And his batting was as graceful as himself."

Question—"What is your most rewarding memory of cricket?"

Answer—"The knowledge that I am occasionally mentioned in the same breath as those great Australian umpires, Bob Crockett, George Borwick, Dave Elder, Mel McInnes, Joe Travers, Alf Jones, Jim Phillips, Charles Bannerman, Tom Brooks, Colin Egar, and Lou Rowan.

"Of these, Crockett, of course, stood supreme. He was my idol as a boy and still is. He umpired in thirty-three Tests from 1901 to 1925 and was a tremendously sincere and kindly man. As honest as the day. When Harold Gilligan, brother of Arthur, brought an M.C.C. team to Australia and New Zealand in 1929 he made a special request that Crockett umpire one of the matches. When told Crockett was a very old man, he replied, 'None of my men will appeal unless we are certain a batsman is out. We would dearly like to have the honour of playing under Mr Crockett.' They did.

"George Borwick, who umpired in twenty-five Tests, ranks second to Crockett, in my opinion. I regarded it as a very sad day when Mel McInnes retired. I watched a lot of his umpiring and it was of the highest quality. Dave Elder was the same lovable kind of man that Crockett was."

Question—"What are the most vital qualities required for umpiring?"

Answer—"A thorough knowledge of the laws of cricket, the confidence to give a decision when called upon, without fear or favour, and plain commonsense. I believe commonsense will invariably lead an umpire to the right decision, almost invariably. You have to have good eyesight, of course, and tremendous powers of concentration."

Question—"Do you believe the contribution umpires make to sport is properly appreciated?"

Answer—"No, certainly not. Good umpires are vital to the success of any sport, and especially in the case of cricket. One decision in cricket can decide the result of a Test match. In football and tennis an umpire can make several mistakes which may not alter the outcome. Their mistakes very often even out. During my life I have read many comments about umpires and listened to quite a number from players. One day I watched a match at the M.C.G. On the opening day thirteen wickets fell and three chances were dropped. The players, therefore, made sixteen mistakes, at least, that day. One of the umpires made *one* mistake, it was thought. And did he get a roasting!"

Question—"Does an umpire need to have played first-class cricket to be a top-class umpire?"

Answer—"That doyen, as he was called, of English umpires, Frank Chester, said so. His was an incredible statement. If he was right, Australia only had, from memory, three top-class umpires—Charlie Bannerman, Joe Travers, and Tom Brooks."

Question—"Have you any advice for cricketers in relation to umpires and umpiring?"

Answer—"Yes, I suggest they all read Sir Donald Bradman's brilliant passage on this subject on pages 281 to 284 of his book *Farewell to Cricket*. Don took the trouble to present himself before the N.S.W.C.A. Umpires' Board and passed his examination on the laws. When he took the field as a player and, later, as a captain, he knew exactly what the laws were. Never in my life have I seen, or heard of, him disputing an umpire's decision. And he didn't do so badly overall."

Question—"Any regrets?"

Answer—"Only one—that my son Ray Hele, who umpired in nearly fifty first-class games, was never appointed to officiate in a Test match."

Question—"Any particular expressions of gratitude?"

Answer—"I should like to thank all the Australian State cricket associations for the kindness they have shown me over the years and, particularly, the Victorian Cricket Association—the late Bill Dowling Jack Ledward, Ray Steele, Jack Ryder, Brian Cosgrave, and all—for always making me feel so welcome when I visit the M.C.G. and the V.C.A. Delegates' suite each summer. The friendships I have made at the M.C.G. over the past half a century form one of the most important and enjoyable things that remain to me in my now very old age.

"Those who are caring for the M.C.G., including Ian Johnson, Hans Ebeling, John Leichhardt, and Bill Watt, have the right to be tremendously proud of their work. For the M.C.G., I have been told by Englishmen, can hold up its head with Lord's.

"It is the 'cathedral,' as Sir Robert Menzies would say, *and* the 'treasury' of Australian cricket."

Question—"What is the finest definition you have read of a sportsman?"

Answer—" 'To brag little, to show well, to crow gently if in luck. To own up and shut up if beaten are the true virtues of a sporting man.' "